D1518444

Biofeedback Frontiers

STRESS IN MODERN SOCIETY: NO. 15

ISSN: 0884-870X

Series Editor

JAMES H. HUMPHREY

Other titles in this series:

Lilian Rosenbaum, Ph.D. established and directed one of the country's first biofeedback programs at the Georgetown Family Center from 1975 to 1988. She is Clinical Associate Professor, Georgetown University School of Medicine, Washington, D.C. (1970 to the present), past Treasurer of the Biofeedback Certification Institute of America (BCIA), past President of the Biofeedback Society of Washington, D.C./ Maryland, served on committees of the Biofeedback Society of America, and a charter member of the American Family Therapy Association. She supervised or consulted in the training of over 3,000 people including medical students, fellows, interns, and a variety of professionals. She has been in private practice in psychotherapy and biofeedback in Washington, D.C. and Maryland for 20 years. Listed in *Who's Who of American Women,* she pioneered biofeedback for diabetes and the synthesis of biofeedback and family systems theory.

STRESS IN MODERN SOCIETY
Number 15

Biofeedback Frontiers

Self-Regulation of Stress Reactivity

Lilian Rosenbaum, Ph.D.

AMS Press
New York

Library of Congress Cataloging-in-Publication Data

Rosenbaum, Lilian.
    Biofeedback frontiers: self regulation of stress reactivity /
Lilian Rosenbaum.
        p. cm. – (Stress in modern society; no. 15)
    Bibliography: p.
    Includes index.
    ISBN 0-404-63266-1
    1. Biofeedback training. 2. Stress management. I. Title.
II. Series.
RC489.B53R67 1989
615.8'51 – dc19   86-82030
                                                              CIP

All AMS books are printed on acid-free paper that meets the guidelines for performance and durability of the Committee on Production Guidelines for Book Longevity of the Council on Library
Resources.

AMS Press, Inc.
56 East 13th Street
New York, N.Y. 10003

MANUFACTURED IN THE UNITED STATES OF AMERICA

To

the memory of my parents
Rosita Widawer de Rosenbaum and Guillermo Rosenbaum
who influenced my
eagerness to learn, do, and grow;

to
Marleen & Edward
and
Clarence David of the new generation;

to
Russell
Denise
Valerie

Brenda & Fredy
Sonia & George

and
Bernie

with love for all, who each in their own way contributed to
this work and enrich my life.

With respect for
the many people, professionals and consumers, who made
biofeedback real and who continue to challenge frontiers.

CONTENTS

Contents ix

Contents   xi

Contents xiii

FOREWORD:
Quick Questions
And Answers

Q. What is Biofeedback?
A. Biofeedback is the process which provides immediate and continuous information (through auditory or visual signals) of physiological responses of which we are ordinarily unaware. Biofeedback instruments provide information and verify the processes being learned. This information facilitates physiological, emotional, social and cognitive self-regulation and more control over own life. Biofeedback "therapy" or "intervention" often includes training with a variety of self-regulation techniques such as breathing exercises, cognitive behavior modification, and imagery. Successful self-regulation in one area of life often leads to improved nutrition, exercise, relationships, and life style. Increased self-confidence in the ability to control one's own physiology voluntarily increases self-confidence in other aspects of life.

Biofeedback applications are based on years of research. The first national society was formed in 1969 and was called the Biofeedback Research Society. In 1975 it was renamed the Biofeedback Society of America. The early title reflects the focus on research and careful clinical work. In 1988 the new name "Association for Applied Psychophysiology and Biofeedback" will indicate the current emphasis. Research began in the 1960s and biofeedback treatment for medical and behavioral disorders has been provided since the early 1970s.

New applications are continually developed by investigators in universities, medical schools, private and government institutions.

Q. Who can benefit from using Biofeedback?

A. Biofeedback for individuals of all ages can improve some aspect of life – family, work, social, leisure, education and health. It can be used by students, homemakers, workers (physical laborers, executives, professionals), retired, sedentary or athletic, healthy or sick people. Applications for a variety of conditions include:

allergies
anxiety
  panic attacks
  phobias
asthma
cardiovascular disorders
  arrhythmias
  hypertension
  tachycardia
diabetes
depression
eating disorders
  anorexia
  bulimia
  obesity
education
  learning disabilities
  enhancing performance
  testing anxiety
enhancement of functioning
  cognitive
  emotional
  physical
  social
gastrointestinal disorders
  colitis
  Crohn's disease
  diarrhea/constipation

irritable bowel syndrome
  ulcers
headaches
  migraine
  muscle contraction
hearing impaired,
adaptations for management
  of chronic illness
  cancer
  epilepsy
  home care special needs
  multiple sclerosis
  recovery, surgeries
marital conflict
muscular disorders
  neck & shoulder pain
  lower back pain
oral disorders
  TMJ
  bruxism
pain management
pelvic & rectal pain
Raynaud's disease
relationship problems
sexual & reproductive
  functioning
  anorgasmic experience
  childbirth preparation

dysmenorrhea
infertility
menstrual cramps
pain during intercourse
PMS
uterine prolapse
sleep disorders
sports applications
stress management

substance abuse management
alcohol
drugs
prescriptions
smoking cessation
tinnitus
urinary & fecal incontinence
vision disorders

Certified, responsible biofeedback professionals require that a physician, vision care specialist, or dentist collaborate in the referral and follow-up process. Ask your physician how much your symptoms are affected by your response to stressors.

Q. Why use Biofeedback?
A. The now frequently computerized electronic biofeedback instrumentation provides information (feedback) which helps learn more quickly how to relax and gain control of the body's performance – physical, emotional, intellectual and social. (Like a skier watching himself on videotape, or a dancer watching herself in the mirror, it is easier to learn if one can see what one is doing.) Biofeedback instrumentation amplifies biological signals and converts them to visual or auditory signals which the individual sees or hears and learns to regulate. It lets the consumer "see," "hear," or "feel" (for hearing impaired) the responses of one's own body such as muscle activity, temperature, skin moisture and brain waves. Usually the sensors which pick up and amplify the signals are non-invasive (meaning the sensors are applied on the skin, on the surface of the body). Biofeedback makes it easier, more accurate and much more interesting to learn voluntary control of one's body, thoughts, feelings or behavior. Most motivated people find it interesting and challenging.

Q. Where to obtain Biofeedback?

A. Most major cities and many small ones have biofeedback practitioners who have been certified by the Biofeedback Certification Institute of America (BCIA). Write to BCIA, 10200 West 44th Ave., Suite 304, Wheat Ridge, CO 80033, (303) 420-2902 (enclose a stamped self-addressed envelope) for names of clinicians in a specific geographical area. The BCIA Register lists over 2,000 practitioners (their training, experience, and specialization) in the U.S.A. and some foreign countries. Many universities provide biofeedback. If the consumer is too sick or injured to go to an office, a few clinicians (for instance Georgetown staff) provide biofeedback in the home. Many hospitals provide biofeedback as an inpatient service, especially for pain management.

Q. Cost?

A. Cost varies depending on the provider's training and geographical site, often comparable to psychotherapy. Some centers have a sliding fee scale based on income. Some insurance companies cover a portion of the fee if the service is rendered by appropriately credentialed providers. At a time of spiraling health care costs, biofeedback is cost-effective and encourages self-reliance.

Q. When to do Biofeedback?

A. Biofeedback is usually done once a week for an hour in the laboratory for several weeks. Length of training, treatment or follow-up varies depending on the problem, the theory and style of intervention, and especially on motivation of the person seeking change. Many practitioners require home practice of relaxation skills and some loan or rent home instrumentation. The practice is recommended on a regular schedule, often with audio cassettes. Consumers are asked to keep a record of important daily events, feelings, and thoughts to help integrate the biofeedback-learned skills into daily life.

Q. How is Biofeedback provided?

A. Normally some orientation or demonstration is provided first, then intake session, biofeedback baseline, and biofeedback training. It is important to know the theoretical orientation of provider and the provider's specialty and training. For example, is the provider BCIA certified and professionally licensed? It is also important to have a clear understanding of the treatment itself, and how it would be coordinated with other treatments, interventions or educational activities. Is the disorder one of the few which requires special precautions with biofeedback training? What is the individual's responsibility to make the intervention successful?

Q. How can professionals become certified to provide Biofeedback to Consumers?

A. Health care providers (including mental health, general or family physicians, physical and occupational therapists, dentists, nurses, social workers) teachers, musicians, athletic coaches, corporate executives or other professionals who are licensed in their own fields can request from BCIA (address in Question #4 above) the Guidelines for Certification including the areas of knowledge "blueprint" and locations where training is offered. Contact the Biofeedback Society of America (BSA) (same address) for information on membership and benefits including meetings, workshops and courses. Please send stamped self-addressed envelope. Some universities and centers accept volunteers or have internships which may help decide if that work is interesting and relevant. Arrangements for training for certification are flexible: universities, private centers and practitioners, and workshops sponsored by the BSA, its state societies and other professional organizations can make the training personally meaningful and advance professional goals.

ACKNOWLEDGEMENTS
Photographs

(A) BIOFEEDBACK WAS PROVIDED BY INVESTIGA-
TORS OR CLINICIANS IN THE FOLLOWING SITUA-
TIONS (photographs courtesy of):

1. G. Lawrence Fisher, Ph.D., Director, Allied Health Services, Rockville, MD. Seminar for executives on stress management and biofeedback in the organization.

2. Loretta Engelhardt, EDD., Director, Healthwork, Spearfish, S.D. Coaching children to do biofeedback in a public
school.

3. Victoria Harrison, M.A., Biofeedback Program, Georgetown University Family Center. Biofeedback childbirth training is in addition to the childbirth preparation classes couples
attend elsewhere.

4. Susan Middaugh, Ph.D., Dept. of Physical Medicine and
Rehabilitation, Medical University of South Carolina,
Charleston, S.C. Young man with cerebral palsy is working
on active wrist extension to improve hand function.

5a. National Aeronautics and Space Administration (NASA),
Washington, D.C. 51B/Spacelab 3 crewmembers. Onboard
scene in the science module for Spacelab 3 in the cargo bay of
the Earth-orbiting Space Shuttle Challenger. Some people in

Spacelab 3 participated in Dr. Cowings' AFT biofeedback research.

5b. Space Shuttle Discovery (biofeedback not used in this situation).

6. Lilian Rosenbaum, LCSW, Ph.D., Director Biofeedback Program, Georgetown University Family Center, Washington, D.C.

7. Lilian Rosenbaum, LCSW, Ph.D. Example of family diagram and family processes.

8. Wesley Sime, Ph.D., Director, Stress Physiology Laboratory, University of Nebraska, Lincoln, NE. Photograph shows Dr. Sime working with an elite athlete. The objective is to help the athlete recognize stress responses during film review sessions as a means of discrete awareness training. The ultimate transfer of training skills are generalized progressively to the field of competition in order to maximize performance while minimizing obstructive stress responses.

9. Edward Taub, Ph.D., School of Social and Behavioral Sciences, The University of Alabama at Birmingham. Stroke patient attempts to pick up a (simulated) sandwich and bring it to her mouth with her affected upper extremity. The uninvolved arm is restrained in a sling and hand splint in an effort to overcome learned nonuse of the affected limb.

(B) THESE PHOTOGRAPHS ARE INTENDED TO SHOW EXAMPLES OF SITUATIONS WHEN BIOFEEDBACK MIGHT BE USEFUL. THEY DO NOT IMPLY THAT BIOFEEDBACK WAS USED OR IS ENDORSED BY THE PHOTOGRAPH PROVIDERS (courtesy of):

10. C & P Telephone, Washington, D.C.

11. Georgetown University Hospital (surgery)

12. Georgetown University (commencement represents many years of stress)

13. National Institute of Allergy and Infectious Diseases, National Institute of Health (HIV "budding" out of a HIV-infected T-cell; courtesy Dr. Tom Folks).

14. Transportation Research Board, National Research Council Washington, D.C. (courtesy of Dan A. Rosen).

15. University of Maryland, Department of Intercollegiate Athletics, College Park, Md.

16. Georgetown University.

INTRODUCTION

When I established the Biofeedback Program at the Georgetown University Family Center in 1975, the word "biofeedback" was mostly unknown, and often elicited questions like "bio-what?" from lay and professional people. The term "biofeedback" is now in the dictionary. It is criticized by some, applauded by many. In 1986 my daughter told me that a question on biofeedback was on her SAT. This is an indicator of a remarkable leap in the development of biofeedback. Today biofeedback is used to enhance physical, emotional, social and cognitive functioning.

The invitation to write this book provides the opportunity to describe the new frontiers in which biofeedback is used to (1) enhance responsibility for self, (2) increase belief in the possibility and facilitate voluntary physiological self-regulation, (3) manage difficult life problems, disorders and processes, and (4) optimize even high-level performance. I want to familiarize the reader with:

- the exciting frontiers in practice and theory;
- the new work reflecting that the body/mind is one;
- the "feedback" process between what happens inside and outside the body;
- the importance of professional training and certification;
- the cost-effectiveness of biofeedback.

In addition I want to present:

- my enthusiasm for biofeedback as an intervention and as an exciting lens that allows seeing new dimensions;

- my view that the theoretical orientation determines clinical practice, professional training and research;
- my theoretical orientation (natural systems thinking);
- my perspective that the concept of reactivity in all natural systems (evolutionary thinking) is a core concept in biofeedback training;

This book is intended for consumers and professionals and is organized so that readers may select those portions of interest. Unlike a "how to" book, it does not provide quick interventions. Instead, the information, motivation, and appropriate professional consultation may facilitate personal success with voluntary self-regulation.

Many biofeedback applications are for women including PMS, "hot flashes" during menopause, and easing childbirth (Chapter 12). To the extent that women do what men do as executives, athletes, professionals, and astronauts, and women suffer as men do with a variety of psychophysiological disorders and relationship problems, this book is for women and men.

It is of interest to health care professionals including physicians, dentists, vision care specialists, nurses, speech pathologists, physical and occupational therapists, clinical social workers, health educators, pastoral counselors, psychologists and family therapists. I have also written this book for medical, dental and other students who wish to explore body/mind issues and the frontiers of health care. Several specialties in medicine use biofeedback including endocrinology, dermatology, neurology, gastroenterology, urology, obstetrics and gynecology, oncology, rheumatology, anesthesiology, immunology, psychiatry and cardiovascular medicine. Educators with audiences of all ages, and athletic coaches will see opportunities for including biofeedback in their work. Biofeedback is used as a part of or an adjunct to a variety of psychotherapies. Biofeedback-assisted stress management is used in private and government organizations and in small and large corporations; executives, administrators and personnel specialists will want to consider biofeedback. Health care planners, policy makers, and insurance organizations will be curious about the cost-effectiveness and potential of biofeedback for prevention, intervention and for optimizing human functioning.

This book can be started at the beginning or at the end with Chapters 11 and 12 on frontiers. Chapter 11 brings together new, imaginative, biofeedback research and applications for superior performance and various dysfunctions. These include managing diabetes and cancer, modulating psychoneuroimmunological functioning, managing a variety of psychophysiological disorders, improving vision care, maximizing physical therapy, managing pain, rehabilitating prisoners, controlling nausea in space travel, decreasing medications where possible, and facilitating the peak performance of superior athletes. Preliminary impressions suggest that biofeedback may help manage and possibly alter the course of the HIV virus and AIDS. Any frontier I have left out may reflect lack of space or that it is now so well known it is "standard." Being selected out of this volume may be as much a tribute as being selected in. Biofeedback frontiers are not only technical applications but also new conceptualizations (Chapter 12) and ways of thinking about the human phenomenon.

Biofeedback is cost effective (Chapter 10). It can lead to reduction in medication, calls and visits to physicians, fewer and shorter hospitalizations and rehospitalizations, and significant decreases in expenses. It encourages self-reliance and responsibility for self and enhances the quality of life.

The emphasis on natural systems and family therapy theory (Chapters 5 and 6) is not intended to limit the book to clinicians who now use that approach. Although some pioneering work with biofeedback and family psychotherapy is based on family system theory, therapists with other orientations provide biofeedback. Outstanding clinicians around the country with a variety of other orientations do superior bio-feedback interventions. Natural systems is a way of thinking rather than a "how to" technique. It elucidates functioning in human and other living organisms. The theory (Chapter 6) and the purpose of the intervention also determine the instrument choice (Chapter 4).

Professionals and informed consumers can evaluate the "state of the art" and the clinical and personal relevance of research (Chapter 9). Conceptual thinking determines research methodology and interpretation of the findings. Clinicians and investigators are encouraged to think conceptually and to ask the clinically important questions rather than those which can only produce statistically significant results.

To become biofeedback practitioners (Chapters 8 and Quick Questions and Answers) or researchers requires learning physiology, electronics, and relevant fields. BCIA's intent in its early deliberations (in which I participated as a Board member) was not to create a new profession but to expand possibilities at all levels in a variety of professions. The practitioner's and researcher's theory and way of thinking determine how life and the human phenomenon are perceived and to a significant extent, biofeedback interventions, professional training, and research interpretations. This volume seeks to make explicit some aspects of the natural systems theoretical framework as I use it. "I "coach" or "teach" rather than "treat." The example is explicit as a recognition that one's thinking affects one's technique, not that it is the best or the only theory; simply, I know it best and use it with worthwhile results.

An important theme is the concept of reactivity or what biologists refer to as responsivity, the capacity of protoplasm to respond to stimuli (Chapter 3). I examine reactivity at various levels of complexity including the single-cell, the psychoneuroimmune system, the human organism and larger relationship systems such as the family and the work organization. Reactivity is also a basic theme in frontiers (Chapter

11). What makes reactivity so important in a book about biofeedback? The evolutionary origin of reactivity provides a way of thinking about and working with symptoms. Responsiveness (reactivity) is an indicator of life and essential for survival. However, chronic over or under responsiveness can be dysfunctional in living systems. Reactivity is one conceptual link in the functioning of seemingly disconnected phenomena such as the immune system, psychophysiological disorders, family, societal problems, and the processes involved in maximizing human potential. Family systems theory proposes that the behavior of all natural systems is connected and has some fundamental bases. Reactivity is one of those biological bases. The voluntary self-regulation of reactivity can be facilitated by biofeedback. Decreasing over reactivity and increasing flexibility seems to affect the reactivity of subsystems in the individual (e.g., immune system, neuroendocrine system). The decreased reactivity of the individual also seems to decrease the reactivity of larger suprasystems including family and work. That is, optimizing reactivity has an effect in both directions – "inside" and "outside" the skin. Appropriate reactivity enhances self-direction and more self-initiated behavior rather than reflexive, knee-jerk reactions. The person can be more him/her self.

Family systems theory, an awareness of natural systems and of the evolutionary origin of reactivity provides a way of thinking that influences biofeedback interventions. A natural systems orientation facilitates a broader perspective about the symptom and the reason for biofeedback training. It places the individual and the living systems within and outside him/her on a continuum with all living systems. It observes the dysfunction as an indicator of system functioning, rather than solely as a problem in the individual. Neither the individual nor the systems are believed to be the cause of dysfunction. Human reactivity is determined by both the state of psychophysiological arousal of the organism (person), as well as the state of the field (family) of which the individual is a part. Observing the effects of relationship processes on the physiology adds a new dimension to understanding human functioning, and promotes a conceptual approach — natural systems. Humans have some of the same material of single celled-organisms. This knowledge and awareness of one's own position facilitates a thought guided rather than an automatically, reactive approach to life. Enhancing responsible, voluntary self-regulation can be an active way of participating in the forces that influence evolution, living systems, and life itself.

An extensive literature has developed on biofeedback's history, instrumentation, psychophysiology, applications, and research. I include over 300 references but this is not a literature review. Self-regulation techniques, exercise and nutrition are mentioned briefly because readers can readily find those elsewhere. To preserve anonymity, the examples are appropriately altered composites which represent more than one person's situation, except my own experience.

My enthusiasm for biofeedback is not intended to be confused with irresponsible endorsing or implying that all the work I describe has been "proven" effective. Some studies are only of a few individuals and some fields, such as psychoneuroimmunology, are so new that even definitive findings have to be considered cautiously. Conflicting findings do not always reach the literature immediately. However, frontier work suggests that a variety of phenomena in health, performance and cognitive enhancement are possible and that they merit further study. The field is so dynamic that it demands periodic updating. My enthusiasm for biofeedback is also not intended to suggest that it is the only path to change. However, improved functioning and self-regulation of the body/ mind is a major frontier, and biofeedback has an important role in this evolutionary human endeavor.

My thinking and practice are influenced by the theory and expertise of many, including Murray Bowen, Paul MacLean, John Calhoun, Candace Pert, Stephen Locke, Stephen Suomi,

E.O. Wilson and Charles Darwin. Their diversity has a common theme–reactivity. Understanding reactivity (responsiveness), balance, and an evolutionary perspective on natural systems is one door to life and can enhance responsible personal functioning.

1
HISTORICAL SURVEY

Imagine teaching a rat to blush in only one ear or conducting your own symphony of brain waves. What is its significance for you? For medicine? For Olympic athletes? For astronauts? Twenty years ago, amidst much excitement, biofeedback research showed that self-regulation of physiological functions typically thought to be out-of-awareness, is possible. Blushing and brain waves are automatic responses normally considered to be out of voluntary control. Pioneers of mind/body research demonstrated that these and other functions could in fact be learned and self-regulated. It is possible to learn to make brain waves faster or slower, larger or smaller. So began biofeedback self-regulation. "Bio" for biological, "feedback" for information fed back to the animal or person. Since these pioneers were in the United States, it is not surprising that the information that made voluntary control possible was provided with electronic instrumentation. Ancient cultures "knew" thousands of years earlier that the mind could control the body. With training, preventing bleeding, controlling one's heart rate, lying on nails without injury, or walking on fire without burning was possible. But the Western mind is technologically oriented and not widely cognizant of ancient Eastern traditions, so these findings seemed "new." Self-regulation is not new, but biofeedback is an innovation.

Definitions

Biofeedback is the process which provides immediate and continuous information (through auditory and/or visual signals) about physiological responses of which individuals are ordinarily unaware. This information facilitates physiological self-regulation. Biofeedback instruments detect physiological responses such as skin temperature and blood pressure, and are typically noninvasive (sensors placed on skin surface) when used for stress and symptom reduction. The BCIA adopted this meaning for clinical biofeedback:

> ... a therapy in which several efficacious self-regulation techniques are used such as autogenic training and desensitization, imagery and breathing exercises, cognitive behavior modification, and stress management. Biofeedback instrumentation is used to enhance learning of these self-regulation skills. The instrument provides verification of the strategy used.[270]

For me the term biofeedback includes the above and more. It is also a process which affects self-regulatory natural systems at many levels of complexity including the cell, the organ, the psychoneuroimmune system, the individual, the family and society. As I use biofeedback it implies a perspective on health and illness, function and dysfunction (See Introduction and Chapters 3 and 5), evolution, reactivity and life. It is not a panacea, but in the context of family and natural systems thinking, it is exciting, rewarding and productive. The relatively few situations in which it does not facilitate the expected results can be as instructive for the consumer as the majority of situations in which the changes are impressive, often beyond the expectations of both the consumer and the provider.

Early Development

Early biofeedback researchers discovered that physiological functions previously considered out of the realm of voluntary learning could in fact be modified. Their contributions led researchers and therapists in the 1970s to view physiological and psychological processes as aspects of a single process[335] or as two interrelated aspects of the organism. The reliability of the intervention sparked the growing interest and acceptance of biofeedback, which later helped create the field of behavioral medicine.[27]

Biofeedback developed from several fields, especially electronics and psychophysiology. As sometimes happens in the history of ideas, biofeedback was developed by several researchers working independently seeking interventions for a wide range of disorders. Behaviorist research traditions, such as shaping behavior and operant conditioning, influenced the development of a number of techniques. A variety of studies emerged in operant conditioning of human heart rate, human galvanic skin response, and human alpha brain wave control as well as curarized (drug-induced immobility) animals. The idea was to show that involuntary responses could be learned and could come under voluntary control. In the 1950s, Whatmore and Kohli[325] used electromyography (EMG) to feed back information on muscle tension to patients. In the early 1960s, Kamiya[136] showed that biofeedback methods could be effective in teaching individuals to control their alpha rhythm voluntarily. Brown[38] found that individuals could recognize different brain waves in their own electroencephalograph (EEG). Budzynski and Stoyva[40] used biofeedback to relax muscles and relieve tension headaches.

In 1969 Miller's landmark paper suggested that animals could learn visceral and glandular (autonomic) responses.[185] This influenced speculation about the possible wide range of human psychosomatic or psychophysiological disorders. Shapiro and co-workers[267] demonstrated that biofeedback and operant conditioning techniques are effective in teaching individuals to increase and decrease heart rate and blood pressure. Engel and Melmon[74] began using biofeedback to treat cardiac arrhythmias. Others began using biofeedback techniques for various psychosomatic disorders.[291] In those early years, as a clinician who came to biofeedback with family systems theory, I wondered how learning endocrine and other "involuntary" responses takes place in the context of important relationships (See Chapter 12).

The Important Question Is Answered

The important question researchers asked during the late 1960s was: could subjects given information (biofeedback) about their own physiology control that physiology? If the information tells them that their electroencephalographic (EEG) brain waves are within the alpha range, that their heart is beating slowly, or that their blood pressure is low, can they learn to prolong the occurrence of the alpha rhythm, or keep their heart rate slow, or maintain a low level of blood pressure? Could individuals learn to control a single motor unit (which later had a great impact in the improvement of physical performance and physical rehabilitation)?[12] A series of investigations provided affirmative answers.[291]

In 1969, researchers joined formally together and organized the Biofeedback Research Society, emphasizing research, now known as the Biofeedback Society of America (BSA). BSA currently has 2,100 members (clinicians and researchers) and serves as the central source for biofeedback communication in the U.S.A. and abroad.

Early Applications

The range of clinical applications of biofeedback for the treatment of psychophysiological disorders has expanded in the past two decades[250,24,100,120] and includes muscle activity,[12] tension headache,[42] autonomic learning,[266,303,227] hypertension,[199] drug dependency,[316] seizure disorders,[288] irritable colon,[322] bronchial asthma,[148,202] and bruxism.[245] Some of these were case reports or small series of cases which required further research. Butler's[46] biofeedback literature bibliography has over 100 applications including the management of insomnia, Raynaud's disease, sexual dysfunction, and weight control.

Another biofeedback application no longer on the "frontier" is treating masticatory pain and dysfunction (MPD) and temporomandibular joint (TMJ) syndrome. Although still unknown to many dentists, biofeedback is successfully used and some dental schools include at least an introduction to it. Rugh,[245,246,247,248,249] a pioneer, developed a portable EMG unit for patients to observe their responses in the "natural environment" rather than only in the laboratory. His work integrated biofeedback in dental schools.

Recent Literature and Clinical Guides

Advances in biofeedback research and practice have been reviewed by Yates.[340] Additional works include diverse clinical texts on physiology,[6] on clinical applications of biofeedback,[100,195,81,164,13,90] and articles on the use of biofeedback in family,[334] family practice medicine[223] and evaluation or efficacy.[102,289,326,123] A substantial recent guide to clinical practice includes a strong chapter on evaluation.[261] BSA published several volumes for beginning and advanced clinicians, including the practical *Foundations of Biofeedback Practice.*[259] I found the chapter on the effects of drugs (prescriptions) on biofeedback especially useful. Another BSA primary document is *Applications Standards and Guidelines for Providers of Biofeedback Services.*[262]

Updating the Literature Periodically

The BSA organized a series of Task Forces to study major biofeedback advances and to publish a number of reports in 1978 on the research[51] and clinical applications of biofeedback in psychophysiological disorders,[93] vasoconstrictive syndromes,[302] gastrointestinal disorders,[327] vascular headache,[67] muscle-contraction (tension) headache,[42] physical medicine and rehabilitation.[88] A series of 20 reports, published between 1978 and 1980, included topics such as instrumentation[246] and athletic applications of biofeedback.[254]

A recent bibliographical analysis[122] of the growth and developed of biofeedback from 1964 to 1985 produced references to 2,431 journal articles, 102 books, 79 popular magazine articles, and 551 doctoral dissertations. Citations found from 35 countries are in 18 languages. More articles were published annually in medical journals than in journals of any other discipline or all specialty journals combined. *Biofeedback and Self-Regulation,* is published by BSA quarterly.

Frontiers in Biofeedback

Major applied and conceptual innovations include research and applications for diabetes, cancer, AIDS, aspects of physical rehabilitation and pain, education, vision disorders, improving performance in space and in superior athletics (See Chapter 11), and physiology of relationships (See Chapter 12). In two decades, the work begun by fewer than a dozen pioneer investigators and continued by a variety of frequently interdisciplinary teams changed disease and health concepts, improved the treatment of disease and enhanced human potential.

2
BODY/MIND, STRESS, AND PSYCHO-NEUROIMMUNOLOGY

Ms. J. admitted herself to the hospital to improve her control over diabetes. Diagnosed in her teens, she had many occasions to be out of control. Now she had the beginning of typical complications including high blood pressure and mild neuropathy. She was also very upset. Her husband's restaurant was in serious financial trouble, and he was having a relationship with another woman. Her mother was ill, and her daughter was taking her father's side. As the endocrinologist and attending physicians tried to stabilize her diabetes, she kept asking for help with stress. She knew that if she could manage her anxiety, her blood glucose would stabilize. Three of her physicians called me in one day to refer her. She began biofeedback with family theory about twice/month; within six months, she stabilized her diabetes to a "near normal" (hemoglobin Alc of 7.0%). She had learned over many years of observing herself that the body and mind are one. Biofeedback maximized her body/mind functions.

That the body and the mind are one is a very old idea,[138] but only recent research has shown some of the two-way connections between the endocrine system and the central nervous system, as well as between the immune system and

8

the central nervous system and the autonomic nervous system. Other main ideas in this chapter are (2) the evolution of the brain inherently determines the human needs for connectedness with and separateness from others; (3) degrees of emotional and social isolation have an effect on health; (4) understanding these forces is relevant to understanding the person in the context of natural systems (e.g. family and work); reactivity in one person can be manifested in symptoms in another person in the relationship system; (5) the brain's main task, in addition to survival, is the restoration and maintenance of health; and (6) there is an intricate connection among all physiological systems in the body.

Ideally biofeedback can maximize the functioning of the organism at all levels. A person's functioning occurs at many levels: at the level of the neurotransmitters, of tissue, of organs, of one system such as the endocrine system, of many systems such as the endocrine, immune, and nervous systems (called the psychoneuroimmunological system), of the total person including physical, emotional, social and cognitive manifestations in terms of feelings, thoughts, and behavior, and at the level of the family and other important relationship systems. No response, and especially not the so-called "stress response" occurs in isolation. All coping responses, and thus all responses that maintain, restore, or improve health also occur in the context of a variety of natural systems.

"The brain minds the body."[197] The brain is a healing instrument, the largest organ of secretion. The neuron, far from being like a chip in a computer, is a small gland that produces hundreds of chemicals. The main task of the brain is to restore and maintain health. Producing rational thought is one function but not the main one. The brain is a collection of small brains which evolved over time; they function in harmony and in conflict. The basic connectedness of people to each other has its basis in the evolution of the brain.

Basic to the evolution of the brain is our early attachment and dependency on other people. Our social nature links us fundamentally to others throughout our lives. When these links are strained or ruptured, the health consequences are profound.[197]

This perspective, like Bowen's natural systems view[143] (See Chapter 5), emphasizes the importance of providing biofeedback training in the context of the person's family and other social systems. This view of physiology intricately links the responsiveness of one person to the functioning of others.

Biofeedback training can facilitate those natural functions of the brain that restore and maintain health. Understanding some of the functions of the brain and physiology increases the likelihood of success by raising the motivation and willingness to practice. Research may also show that anatomically accurate visualization and imagery also facilitate physiological changes.

HUMAN PHYSIOLOGY

Excellent references for studying the physiology implicated in reactivity include an introductory explanation of the nervous system and the stress response,[81] an in-depth description of the physiology of stress with special reference to the neuroendocrine system,[6] a detailed textbook of biological feedback with specific pathways implicated in various disorders,[90] and a scholarly and detailed description of processing in the central nervous system.[343]

The physiology monitored by biofeedback instrumentation is summarized below: (1) the cell, the basic electrochemical activity; (2) the central nervous system (CNS) (brain and spinal cord) the most valued "biofeedback" system; (3) the peripheral nervous system (much physiological activity happens at this automatic level); (4) the endocrine and (5) the immune systems which under certain circumstances become involved in the stress response.

Central Nervous System

The CNS consists of the brain and the spinal cord. Anatomically the human brain has three major parts: cerebrum, cerebellum and brainstem. MacLean[167] has called it the "triune brain" because of its three functional levels: reptilian, limbic, and neocortical (See Chapter 3).

Cellular physiology is important because some of these electrical events are measurable and thus are the basis of biofeedback. It is also fascinating that changes in one person's cellular physiology can affect the cellular physiology of another person in the relationship system (See Chapters 5 and 6).

The neuron consists of three basic functional subunits: the dendrites which receive incoming signals, the neuronal cell body which contains the nucleus of the cell, and the axon, which conducts signal impulses away from the cell body and relays the signal to another dendrite or target organ. The impulse is transmitted across a space (called a synapse) by a variety of neurotransmitters (chemical substances). The transmission along the neuron itself is based on a complex process of simultaneously occurring electrical and chemical changes resulting in a changing membrane potential (relative voltage). This electrochemical activity occurs by the movement of ions across the membrane of the axon. During the transmission process, the electrical potential inside the cell with respect to the outside generally reverses itself and becomes positive. (Some cells may just depolarize and not reverse this polarity.) This is called depolarization, and this depolarization wave can spread down the axon. The conduction of impulses yields a measurable electrical event, seen as the increase in voltage occurring in the action-potential spike during depolarization. Almost immediately the action potential is restored, called repolarization. The action potential is of short duration and the whole electrical event, both onset (depolarization) and recovery (repolarization) occurs within milliseconds. These measurable electrical events are the basis

for electrophysiological measurements such as those monitored in biofeedback, as for example in electromyography.[6,81]

Peripheral Nervous System

The peripheral nervous system comprises all the neurons
that are not part of the CNS. It is divided into the somatic
and autonomic nervous systems (ANS) and is coordinated by
the hypothalamus in the limbic system.

The ANS has two branches, the sympathetic (thoracolum-
bar) and the parasympathetic (craniosacral). These have anatomical and functional differences. The anatomic differences
arise from their outflow from the spinal cord in the CNS.[6] The
ANS regulates basic body processes, including the regulation
of heart rate, respiration, blood pressure, hormonal balance,
metabolism, and reproduction. During stress, the sympathetic nervous system (SNS) is activated; its general effects
on the organs it innervates ("end-organs" meaning the expanded end of a nerve fiber in a peripheral structure or an
actual organ that manifests dysfunction as the result of
chronic stress) are arousal and escalation of activity. In contrast, the parasympathetic nervous system (PNS) is concerned mainly with restorative activities and relaxation of
the body. It counterbalances the activity of the SNS by
slowing down the body and returning it to a resting level
following the emergency response.[6] The PNS can also be
activated during a stress response. Its effects are more local
(e.g., blushing, increased gastrointestinal motility) whereas
the SNS response is more generalized.

At times under stress the organism shows altered or reverse responses in autonomic system activity. Gellhorn[103] described these phenomena and studied various circumstances
that alter the organism's responses. He called them tuning
and reversal. He attributed these responses to altered states
of the centers that control sympathetic and parasympathetic
activity in the hypothalamus and was able to demonstrate

such alterations. Under certain conditions, then, stimuli that would normally produce a generalized sympathetic response might produce a very limited sympathetic response and/or a more exaggerated parasympathetic response. The opposite is also possible. When the balance is shifted chronically in one direction or another, he refers to the process as "tuning" of the ANS. The outcome is often a "reversal" of the anticipated autonomic response.

Endocrine System

It has long been known that the endocrine system and the brain communicate with each other. One implication for biofeedback training is that since the brain can "instruct" the endocrine system, a voluntary cognitive instruction from the person can have direct consequences on the endocrine system.

The main endocrine organ involved in the "fight or flight" response is the adrenal medulla. Sympathetic stimulation of the adrenal medulla results in the release of the catecholamines epinephrine (adrenaline) and norepinephrine (nonadrenaline). The initial activation of the brain structures, along with cortical and affective integration have already occurred at this point. The catecholamines intensify the general adrenergic activity of the sympathetic nervous system. However, since they are hormones they are released quickly. There is approximately a half-minute delay in the onset of their activity. They also prolong the effects of the adrenergic sympathetic response and thus represent a more chronic phase of the stress response. Increased secretion of the hormones of the adrenal medulla can have significant effects on the physiology of the organism. The respiratory, circulatory, and gastrointestinal systems, as well as the CNS, the blood and metabolism are affected by these hormones.[6,7]

The prolonged phase of the stress response includes the activation of the endocrine axis. A longer time is required for endocrine hormonal release and transportation throughout the circulation system as compared to a direct neural response of the ANS. The main endocrine glands directly influenced by stress are the adrenal cortex and the pituitary.[6,7]

Immune System

Only recently has it been known that the immune system also has a two-way communication with the brain. As with the endocrine system, this implies that with biofeedback and cognitive self-direction the brain can direct the activity of the immune system.

The immune system is the body's built-in biochemical defense against disease and infection. One of its important tasks is to distinguish self from non-self. Elements that play an important part in immunity include certain types of blood cells, the lymphatic system, the spleen, and the thymus gland. The immune system has no identifiable center. It has two broad strategies for defending the body. Cell-mediated immunity uses a team of specialized cells to alert the immune system to the presence of an invader and to organize an attack. Cell-mediated reactions specialize in fighting off viruses and attacking tumors. Humoral (fluid) immunity relies on special molecules, such as antibodies, present in body fluids. It moves quickly against infection.

In cell-mediated reactions the immunity team includes two types of white blood cells, or lymphocytes, and other cells. Some cells summon others to attack, others mark the victims, and others destroy. Still others call off the attack or clean up the microbial debris. These include T-cells (which include Helper T-cells, suppressor T-cells, and Killer T-cells), B-cells, phagocytes (scavengers), and auxiliary cells (including the null cells and the mast cells). The null cells include the natural killer (NK) cells. These recognize tumors and viral infections, and destroy them without destroying the normal cells.[161]

The finding that the CNS and the immune system have two way communication has implications for the role of psychosocial factors on the immune system. Levy,[159] formerly chief of the Behavioral Medicine Branch at the National Cancer Institute and colleagues conclude that the hypothalamus may mediate psychosocial influences on the immune system.

> . . . psychosocial and CNS processes can modify both humoral and cell-mediated immune processes. An extensive network of endocrine and autonomic processes may be involved in these effects. The multiple pathways linking limbic and higher cortical areas with the hypothalamus suggest that the hypothalamus may be of central importance in mediating psychosocial influences on endocrine, neurotransmitter, and immune functions.[159]

Emotional forces (even perceptions of clinical status and prognosis) can lead to accompanying changes in hormonal status.

> Since virtually all tumors are subject not only to growth regulations but also to alterations in their degree of differentiation and interactions with their environment by changes in their endocrine milieu, it seems inescapable that psychic factors which can evoke such endocrine changes will have effects on actual tumor biology.[159]

STRESS RESPONSE

The term stress has multiple meanings in biology, medicine and the social sciences. It can mean stimulus, response, consequence, event or process. Hans Selye[264] thought that the disease state arises from gradual, cumulative stressors which act on a relatively passive organism. I use "stress" to mean the organism's response or reactivity to events or processes; the events or processes are the "stressors." However, where I cite the work of others, I use stress as they do.

Levine[157] provides a comprehensive history of the development of stress concepts and the work of important investigators including Hess, Levi, and Berkman and Syme. Almost 40 years ago Hess coined the terms "ergotropic" and "trophotropic" (generally heightened SNS or PNS activity). The terms make clear that behavioral and neural systems are linked. Over 20 years ago Levi showed that the attitude of the person or the meaning attached to the situation affect the excretion of catecholamine levels more than the physical characteristics of stress (noise, light). Berkman and Syme more recently showed that people who lacked social and community ties were more likely to die prematurely from various causes than people with better social contact. And, having a sense of control increases resistance to stress.

It is now well known that broad physiological patterns are initiated by the brain as adaptations to environmental circumstances (or the interpretation of the circumstances). In the 1920s Cannon[49] recognized certain patterns related to arousal as in preparation for fight-or-flight mediated through the activation of the SNS on the adrenal gland. His work emphasized the role of the SNS and the adrenal hormone epinephrine. In the 1950s Selye[264] showed that another adrenal hormone, cortisol, is also secreted during arousal.

However, the studies of Cannon, Selye and others were limited to technically difficult indirect measurements of the specific hormones they knew. This limitation and the relative insensitivity of hormonal assays led them to study animals and humans under extreme and acute stress conditions. In the 1970s blood assays of every known hormone were available and that, as well as the sensitivity of the tests, made it possible to study animals and humans in more ordinary circumstances. Mason,[174] for instance, found shifts in patterns of hormones. Most of the hormones that increase during arousal promote disintegrative or catabolic processes. In contrast, anabolic processes promote renewal, repair, maintenance of surveillance against external infectious agents and against the body's own malignant cells. The hormones that increase during arousal are those that promote catabolism. The ones that are suppressed during arousal promote anabolism.[287] Prediction, control, and feedback about the effectiveness of coping are some of the factors that decrease catabolism.

There is a time sequence in the stress response process: the most immediate response to a stressor occurs through direct innervation either on other nerve cells or on various end-organs. Those end-organs are innervated by the SNS or PNS. In the chronic stress response, the endocrine system and immune systems are involved through the chronic elevations in the blood stream of certain stress hormones such as cortisol.[6]

The stress response is evoked initially by external or internal stimuli perceived as threatening. The organism responds in predictable ways. I observed that the response depends on: (1) the state of reactivity of the organism or the initial level of physiological activation (arousal at baseline), (2) the state and history of the fields (family, work, social) it is part of, (3) the type, duration, frequency, intensity and emotional significance of the stressor, and (4) the individual's pattern of physiological responses.[230] Individuals have a tendency to exhibit characteristically similar patterns of psychophysiological reactivity called response stereotypy[290] to a variety of stressors.

The best intervention may be prevention by increasing resistance to stress (such as through social connectedness), by maximizing coping skills and by increasing the level of functioning of the person and the family unit. Once the dysfunction appears, however, biofeedback and related self-regulation can be used safely with a few precautions (See Chapter 6). Understanding the physiology of the stress response is an important first step to voluntary self-regulation.

Even in predictable shifts in hormonal patterns during arousal, there are individual differences. For instance, in a study of parents of children with leukemia, parents who had been high excretors of cortisol during their child's illness showed low cortisol excretion after their child died. In contrast, parents who were low excretors during their child's illness had elevated cortisol excretion for a long time after their child's death. That is, arousal patterns are not tied to the "objective" situation but to the interpretation that elicits coping behaviors.[287]

Each organism, single-celled to human, exhibits different degrees of flexibility in recovering to .baseline levels. The family can also be thought of as an "organism" or a unit with different degrees of flexibility. Coping patterns, whether physiological, social, emotional or cognitive, influence the response to stress. These determine how the stress response proceeds to dysfunction. In humans, the response has physical, emotional, cognitive, and social characteristics which are all part of relationship processes.

Usually medical treatment of "arousal pathology" is endstage treatment. The person is treated when the chronic arousal has contributed significantly to the symptom. In spite of the advances in medical technology, the endstage treatment of chronic disease is only marginally effective. For instance, the life expectancy of adult white males age 50 was the same in 1900 (73.1 years) as in 1970 (73.2 years).[287]

PSYCHONEUROIMMUNOLOGY (PNI)

Communication Among the Nervous, Endocrine and Immune Systems – Implications for Biofeedback

The term psychoneuroimmunology reflects that psychological processes and the nervous, endocrine, and immune systems are intricately interdependent. It is not only a new term, but a new way to understand the person having broad implications for health and interventions such as biofeedback training.

A gradual, revolutionary discovery is that the CNS and the immune system have two-way communications. It had been known that the endocrine and the immune systems are closely connected. For example, the stress response increases ACTH production by the pituitary. ACTH enhances the release of glucocorticoids (cortisol) by the adrenal cortex. Large amounts of cortisol profoundly influence certain blood cell types which in turn influence the immune mechanisms of the organism.[6] But until relatively recently it was thought that the CNS and the immune system were not connected. The discovery that the immune system and the CNS communicate provides a rationale and an opportunity to influence, cognitively through biofeedback, the delicate immune system.

It is now known that (1) there are direct links between the immune and central nervous systems; the immune system (i.e. thymus gland, spleen, and bone marrow) is touched by nerve endings that reach the brain; (2) an indirect link of the CNS and the immune system is through the hypothalamic-pituitary-adrenal-cortical axis that results in the release of cortisol; (3) the cells of the immune system have receptors for neurotransmitters from the CNS; (4) immunotransmitters transmit information from the immune system to other systems including the central nervous system;[137] the immune system communicates back to the CNS through thymosin and endocrine-like substances known to affect immunocompetence;[137] (5) the immune system can create new cells, remember, make decisions and learn;[137,197] (6) there is evidence that the morphine analogs, the endorphins secreted by the brain, have immunosuppressive or immunoenhancing effects; (7) some consider the immune system a "sixth sense." Elkes calls the immune system the "liquid nervous system."[161] There are functional similarities between the immune and the nervous systems:

> ... both are primarily concerned with responding to outside information and with the regulation of the body; both respond

to a great variety of stimuli; both receive and transmit signals, which are either excitatory or inhibitory; both exhibit learning and memory. It has been called a 'liquid nervous system,' only a small exaggeration.[197]

Spector,[161] neuroscientist at the National Institute of Health, considers that research will clarify that the immune and nervous systems "control each other;" (8) stimulating (or damaging) the brain can affect immunity.

The immune system may serve as a sensory organ in response to noncognitive stimuli such as viruses, bacteria, and tumors. Lymphocytes may then signal the neuroendocrine system through production of an immunoreactive hormone. The complete regulatory circuit between the neuroendrocrine and the immune systems operates via peptide signals (hormones) and receptors common to both systems (Figure 2.1). This allows for easy communication within and between the two systems. Recognition of cognitive stimuli by the CNS results in similar hormonal information being conveyed to and recognized by hormone receptors on lymphocytes, and an immunologic change results. These molecules can also regulate their own production. The two systems represent a totally integrated circuit.[25,26] If the immune system can learn to be "sick" can it learn to be well? (See Chapter 11).

Immunity in Animals: The Immune System Learns

The processes reviewed above were preceded by decades of sophisticated, carefully designed animal research. As early as 1926 Metal'nikov and Chorine[179] reported that the immune system could be conditioned in dogs to the point of obtaining an immune response with a placebo. The first evidence of a flow of information from the activated immune system to the hypothalamus was reported in 1977 suggesting that the brain is involved in the immune response.[23] Immunoregulation is mediated by the SNS.[22] Vessey found in 1964 that

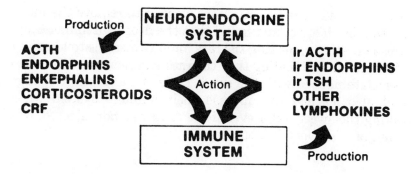

Figure 2.1 A Complete Regulatory Loop Between the Immune and
Neuroendocrine Systems

From "A Complete Regulatory Loop Between the Immune and Neuroendocrine Systems" by J. E. Blalock and E. M. Smith, 1985, *Federation Proceedings, 44*, 110. Reprinted by permission from the authors and publisher.

grouped mice had significantly lower titers of circulating
antibody (concentration of a certain substance in a known
volume of a solution) than did isolated mice. Dominant mice
had significantly higher titers than the other mice in their
group.[319] Immunological responsivity of adult mice was modified by the experience of being handled during infancy.[281] This
provides supporting evidence that the hypothalamus has a
regulating role in immunity. These and other findings clearly
show that social factors (e.g. handling, social rank, early
experience) affect immunity.

Fifty years after Russian investigators had determined
that the immune system can learn through conditioning,
investigators in the United States made the same discovery:
behaviorally conditioned immunosuppression in rats.[1] Rats
were taught to avoid saccharin-flavored water by pairing it
with cyclophosphamide, a drug which produces nausea. The
rats were given the saccharin water and then were injected
with the drug. They learned after one time to associate the
sweet taste of the water with the nausea from the drug.
Unexpectedly, they also seemed to learn to die from drinking
the saccharin water even when the drug cyclophosphamide

was not used. The investigators wanted to remove the unexpected death effect and found that the drug had immunosuppressant effects, making the rats more vulnerable to a variety of diseases. The finding that the rats had not only learned to associate nausea with the sweet taste of saccharin, but they had also learned to suppress their immune system when taking the sweet water even if the drug was *not* injected, was a major discovery in neuroscience.[197]

Immunity in Humans: Effects of Social and Emotional Connectedness

The individual's or family's susceptibility to streptococcal infections was significantly determined by acute life stress or chronic family disorganization.[180] Depressed lymphocyte function was found in bereaved spouses.[11] In a four-year prospective study of 1,400 cadets at West Point Military Academy, psychosocial factors (such as overachieving fathers) were significantly related to the development of infectious mononucleosis.

Women who had separated from their husbands had significantly poorer immune function within a year than demographically matched married women.[146] Among married women, a poorer state of the marriage was associated with more depression and a lower response on three qualitative measures of immune function. Significant declines in natural killer (NK) cell activity in blood samples from 75 medical students during final examinations were found. Lonelier students had significantly lower levels of NK cell activity. There is a comprehensive review of the literature on psychosocial factors, immunologic mediation, and human susceptibility to infectious diseases.[131] An annotated bibliography with over 1,300 scientific papers on mind and immunity is useful.[162] Human immunity is affected, in part, by emotional, cognitive and social factors, that is by feelings, thoughts, and behavior.

This suggests that to some extent it is possible to influence the immune system by biofeedback facilitated changes in feelings, thoughts and social behavior.

"Lock-and-Key:" Neurotransmitter and Receptor Molecules

How do neurotransmitters "fit" into certain receptors?

When these molecules reach the target-cell membrane, the postsynaptic membrane, they attach to chemical receptor molecules that are a part of the postsynaptic membrane. These are large protein molecules that stick out from the membrane. They have particular shapes. The chemical transmitter molecules raining down on the postsynaptic membrane also have particular shapes, shapes that fit into the receptor molecules, much as a key fits into a lock.[196]

How was this "lock-and-key" concept established? Morphine, the major active ingredient of opium ("poppy juice"), reduces pain. "Why should a molecule derived from a plant affect the human brain?"[197] (This section draws from Ornstein and Thompson[196] and Ornstein and Sobel.[197]) Goldstein's data in 1971 suggested the existence of opiate receptors in the brain and how to search for them. In 1974 Snyder and Pert demonstrated that there must be opiate receptors in the brain. They used special radioactive procedures with a then new drug, naloxone, which blocks (antagonist) the action of morphine and other opiates. They showed that naloxone produced its effect by tightly attaching to the opiate receptor sites, and thus preventing the opiate molecules from fitting into the receptors.[207,278,185] This very old receptor system is present in all vertebrate brains and apparently developed long before the poppy plant. Why is it there? Scientists around the world assumed that the brain must produce its own "opiates" and that the receptor system is there to be acted on by them. The search for these natural opiates was on.

A substance from animal brains that had the same action as morphine was isolated and named "enkephalin," meaning "in the head." Since then other natural brain opiates that relieve pain and anxiety have been found.[197]

Pain can have survival value by inducing withdrawal, reduced action, and rest. Yet this response can be counterproductive if the organism has to fight or flee. So the pain cannot be too great. The organism must be able to ignore the pain to deal with the immediate situation. One of the main neurotransmitters involved in the transmission of pain messages to the brain is a peptide called "Substance P."[244]

Pain and anxiety are physical events and emotional sensations. The immune, nervous and endocrine systems interact, and what we think, what we tell ourselves and what instructions we give our brains may affect basic physiological processes (e.g. pain) at the "lock-and-key" level. Research may show that biofeedback and related self-regulation have an impact on the "environment" in which the "lock-and-key" events occur, or may even affect the "lock-and-key" mechanism itself. Research in this field may also expand the understanding of evolution (See Chapter 3).

Psychoneuroimmunology and Biofeedback

Psychoneuroimmunology represents a shift in thinking about health and disease and about the relationship between the immune and other systems. Based on meticulous research with both animals and humans, it suggests a way of thinking about the response of organisms in terms of reactivity, self, and non-self, which I believe is useful in the broader context of family systems. And it suggests a major potential for biofeedback and voluntary self-regulation if human thoughts (cortical activity) and the immune system can influence each other.

However, many studies are still in preliminary stages, and conflicting evidence sometimes does not get reported in the literature. As in other new fields, some findings have not yet passed the test of time. But, with caution and enthusiasm, research continues. A large number of "information substances" directly communicate between and within several subsystems, including the endocrine and immune systems.[208] These also communicate with the psychoneurological system, which means, for instance, that a thought or a cognitive instruction could be translated directly to the immune system.[210]

Psychoneuroimmunology has implications for biofeedback. A shift in arousal is a basic step in changing physiology which may also provide an opportunity to affect, directly and cognitively, the delicate balance of the immune, endocrine, and nervous systems, and thus is of central importance for biofeedback and self-regulation training.

Biofeedback training, especially with a perspective on natural systems forces, can optimize the balance of over or under reactivity at the emotional, social, cognitive and physiological levels. It facilitates difficult actions that further increase the level of functioning. It may facilitate optimal balance and action among the nervous, endocrine and immune systems. And it may enhance the overall balance of health in the person and in the family. The balance and order of the universe of neuronal, endocrine and immune systems is as intricate as that of the universe of planets and stars.

BODY/MIND

Biofeedback makes it clear that thoughts and emotions not only affect the body but in a sense are the body. That is, the body/mind is one. Pert[208,209] believes that the mind and body are bound together by the "talk" of neuropeptides and are best understood as an integrated entity which she called "bodymind."

What is the biochemistry of emotions? The body's "information system" has two major elements – the chemical substances known as neuropeptides and the receptors into which they fit. These are the keys to the biochemistry of emotion. Pert and her colleagues speculate that neuropeptides are the likely candidates for the biochemical mediation of emotion because of (a) the pattern in the distribution of neuropeptide receptors in mood regulating areas of the brain and (b) their role in mediating communication throughout the whole organism. These speculations are based on fascinating findings, many from her laboratory. Every neuropeptide receptor they have looked for is also on human monocytes (immune system). These emotion-affecting biochemicals (the neuropeptide receptors) appear to control the direction of the migration of monocytes. They communicate with B-cells and T-cells, and interact in the whole system to fight disease and to distinguish between self and non-self. The cells of the immune system not only have receptors for the neuropeptides, they also can make neuropeptides themselves; that is, they make the same chemicals that are thought to control mood in the brain. Certain neuropeptide receptors, like CCK, have been found in the gut, the brain, and spleen. Insulin is not just a hormone; it is a neuropeptide made and stored in the brain; and the brain also has insulin receptors. When insulin is "mapped," it is concentrated in the amygdala and the hypothalamus (in the limbic system). The limbic system, known as the "seat of emotions in the brain," is also the focal point of receptors for neuropeptides[208] (See Chapter 3).

What does all this mean? "Emotions" exist not only in the head but in other parts of the body. For instance, the entire lining of the intestinal tract from the esophagus through the large intestine is lined with cells that contain neuropeptides and neuropeptide receptors. When people say they have a "gut feeling," maybe they do. Pert believes that the three classic areas neuroscience, endocrinology, and immunology are actually joined to each other through information "carriers" called neuropeptides.[209]

Biofeedback instrumentation makes clear that thoughts, emotions, feelings and verbalizations produce observable and measurable physiological changes. The body/mind is one. "Emotions" are in the limbic system, in the brain. But to the extent that neuropeptides and their receptors are elsewhere in the body, emotions are also distributed. All physiological and biochemical systems within the organism are intricately linked to each other. They are also linked to other important persons in the relationship system. The connections are between the living, but also through thoughts and feelings with past generations even if dead, and with future generations, even if unborn. The brain's main task beyond survival is the restoration and maintenance of health. This task is performed in the context of natural systems within the body/mind, and outside the body/mind. Degrees of emotional and social isolation have an effect on health and can be influenced by biofeedback training with family theory. The functional and structural evolution of the brain inherently determines the human need for connectedness and separateness from others.

Metaphysics is beyond the scope of this book, but it is worth considering that the mind/body concept and the understanding one has of the nature of being is an underlying, yet rarely explicit issue in biofeedback. It is important because it affects intervention and consumer behavior. Whether Ms. J.'s diabetes (described at the beginning of this chapter) was in the control of her mind, her body, both, or an entity called body/mind is part of larger issues which touch on metaphysics, the ultimate nature of existence. Ontology (in Greek means discussion of being) is the branch of metaphysics that studies the ultimate nature of being. In general, an ontological position may be appraised in terms of materialism, idealism or realism. Materialism states that all being is ultimately matter; idealism holds that mind and "spirit" are the basis of being; and realism maintains that no single principle explains the ultimate nature of being.[34] Metaphysical philosophers include Plato, Aquinas, Descartes, Spinoza and Hegel.[73] There are a number of theories of the relation between mind and body and they are usually monistic or dualistic. Monistic theories identify the body and mind as one, dualistic as separate. The monistic theories include (a) the theory of mind as bodily function advanced by Aristotle and the behaviorists, (b) the theory of body as mental appearance, and (c) the "two-aspect" theory, as of Spinoza and others, which considers mind and body as manifestations of a third reality, neither mental nor physical.[251] Fortunately, an academic understanding of metaphysics is not a requirement for biofeedback or other self-regulation efforts. At some level, Ms. J. "knew" her mind and body were intertwined. She "knew" that to improve control of her diabetes she would have to balance her thoughts, emotions, feelings and behavior and in addition continue to balance nutrition, insulin, and exercise. Philosophy influences one's perception and understanding of natural science. Health care professionals have a responsibility to define their own philosophical position and how it affects evaluation, intervention and research.

3

EVOLUTION, BALANCE, AND REACTIVITY

Balance and Reactivity

Biofeedback training can help restore physiological balance within the body/mind and between one person and another when used in the context of family systems theory. Sustained physiological imbalance usually indicates lack of health or less than optimum functioning.

Fundamental to biofeedback frontiers is the concept of reactivity in nature. Reactivity is the human aspect of what biologists call responsivity—the capacity of protoplasm to respond to stimuli. Responsivity is one of the four basic characteristics of living systems, along with metabolism, reproduction, and growth.[252] Life is a series of interacting processes always associated with and taking place in a biological system—a complex organization of anatomical structures. Responsiveness or reactivity is thus part of life. It is required for survival and occurs automatically. However, chronic over or under responsivity can be dysfunctional. Balance depends on the degree of reactivity of each living component to the others.

Automatic responses that have a survival value occur at different levels of complexity within a cell, organ, system (such as the immune system), individual, family, social group, and society. Although the automatic nature of responsiveness is essential for survival, it also can be a liability for optimum functioning. Examples of automatic, unbalanced and dysfunctional responsiveness include unlimited cellular reproduction (cancer), physiological over-reactivity in the autonomic nervous system (ANS) and associated systems (as in diabetic hyperglycemia), psychological overeaction in an individual (phobia), and functional overeaction within the family system (child abuse). Reactivity includes physical, emotional, social and cognitive responses. The dysfunction may occur when the automaticity of the response prevents a more appropriate alternative response. The intricate balance is astonishing — and so is the fact that more symptoms or disorders do not occur routinely. Biofeedback can help restore some balance when an organism or some of its subsystems are over or under reactive. It can improve functioning by facilitating greater flexibility and less automaticity for voluntary self-regulation.

Some of the person's physiological subsystems in various degrees of balance include: (1) central nervous system and autonomic nervous system, (2) parasympathetic nervous system and sympathetic nervous system, (3) right and left brain hemispheres, (4) neocortex, limbic, and reptilian "brains," and (5) nervous, endocrine and immune systems.

Within each system is a vast number of components with their own intricate balance, from the single cell to larger systems. The organism survives because a normal internal environment is maintained, commonly referred to as homeostasis. The organism also lives and survives as a component of larger natural systems, including family and special relationships. Some imbalances in the family system (like the death of an important person) can contribute to, and be expressed in, dysfunction of the person or even death of another person in the family or relationship system.

Much biofeedback is based on the rationale that one of the first and important systems to stress is the ANS. The imbalance is appropriate when the physiological fight-or-flight changes are necessary for survival,[49] but inappropriate when the organism is not in any real physiological danger. In a calm organism the activity of the sympathetic nervous system SNS and the parasympathetic nervous system (PNS) are in balance. Biofeedback can help restore that balance by calming the overreactive SNS and facilitating PNS activity.

The ANS is coordinated by the hypothalamus in the limbic system. Since the hypothalamus has direct connections to the pituitary, sustained imbalance of the ANS activates the pituitary and other functions of the endocrine system. Sustained or extensive endocrine changes produce changes in the immune system. For instance, cortisol in large amounts suppresses lymphoid tissues resulting in a decrease in lymph organ production of leucocytes and antibodies. The general level of immunity of the organism to foreign substances decreases. Cortisol decreases the plasma levels of eosinophils and lymphocytes.[6]

Biofeedback interventions viewing the individual as a part of the "family organism" take into account the family system reactivity. The individual is coached to use the voluntary self-regulation skills not only to calm self, but to deal with complex family and relationship processes and to enhance functioning. A calm state is not necessarily an end itself, but a means to facilitate differentiation and to deal better with self in difficult situations and relationships. This calm facilitates pursuing a self-driven, self-initiated, life direction.

A possible explanation of how biofeedback facilitates decreased over and under reactivity is that it may help to bring the reptilian, limbic and neocortical brains into functional balance. The activity of each is required for optimum functioning. Reptilian brain activity is essential for survival but it is not enough for optimum functioning. Someone primarily responsive with limbic system activity is so "emotional" that he/she is unable to plan for self or others. The neocortex can also over function to the extent that it becomes so focused on details that appropriate messages of the limbic system are ignored. Fortunately reptilian and limbic activity is usually automatic, allowing a whole range of functioning and behavior that does not require attention. The organism is then free for other processes such as thinking, working or enjoying nature rather than making sure to breathe. But, if the reptilian and limbic "brains" are over or under reactive, the organism cannot function optimally.

The effect of biofeedback on physiological processes is even more impressive, considering that the intricate balance of the triune brain and the ANS is responsive to tiny shifts in the balance within another emotionally important individual. When biofeedback instruments are used to monitor the other person(s), some physiological changes based on relationship processes can be observed. For instance, the heart rate or muscle tension of one person may be responsive to the respiration rate or the muscle tension of the other. That is, an individual's reactivity is determined by the state of the organism and the state of the emotional field (family) of which he/she is a part of (See Chapter 12).

Underreactivity can be as much of a problem as overreactivity. An undereactive immune system can succumb to infection from outside the body or to cancer from within the body. An undereactive person may be depressed or dysfunctional. An undereactive family unit may be more vulnerable to societal processes.

Fight-or-flight responses are controlled by the ANS. According to Calhoun, [47] cortical activity is also required for the response to occur. In his studies on crowding he found that mice become so stressed they underreact to the point of becoming what in humans would be described as autistic. The animals self-destruct. Behaviors necessary for survival, such as mating and parental care disappear. Adult male mice respond to increasing population density by huddling together in small groups. Calhoun calls the well-groomed, asexual males "barflies." Overcrowded female mice often wandered about and trailed behind novel objects, including Calhoun's feet when he would enter their living structure. He calls the restless females "pied pipers." When both sexes withdraw, he calls it "universal autism," as these processes lead to extinction. I speculate that while the behavior is undereactive, the physiology is overeactive and may contribute to the extinction process.

Evolution of the Nervous System

The importance of the ANS in governing overall behavior was first introduced conceptually by Eppinger and Hess in 1915 and later experimentally by Hess in 1925 and Gellhorn in the 1950s.[157] Yakolov[157] proposed in 1948 that the central nervous system and behavior evolved from "within outward" in evolutionary terms.

Central to Gellhorn's work were his concepts of autonomic reciprocity, states of relative sympathetic or parasympathetic dominance, and states when the normal reciprocity breaks down and one branch of the ANS becomes "tuned" at the expense of the other. Animals left in the wild, after intense excitation, almost always exhibit species-specific behaviors that tend to restore homeostasis. Twenty years ago Goddard showed that daily, weekly or even monthly stimulation with single, brief, low-intensity currents of limbic structures in rats produced a chain of long-lasting neurochemical events. He called this "kindling,"[157] whereby the neocortical and limbic systems influence each other in a two-way interaction integrated in the hypothalamus.

MacLean[170] proposed in 1955 that the hypothalamus is central, a sort of driver at the wheel of the brain stem, regulating ANS activity. He suggested that the hypothalamus organizes and directs the behavior of the organism as a whole.[157]

Triune Brain

MacLean's seminal concept of the triune brain describes how the brain developed phylogenetically in three stages: reptilian, limbic system and neomammalian cortex (Figure 3.1). Human behavior is determined largely by the older brains, and much of what is thought to be typically human behavior (e.g., family) is actually shared with our evolutionary ancestors. The human reptilian brain (oldest level) is the same in structure and function as in our ancestors the reptiles. It includes the reticular formation (complex network of nerve fibers within the brain stem that functions in arousing the neocortex) and the brain stem, and is concerned mainly with maintenance of vegetative functions such as vasomotor activity, respiration, and heartbeat. The reptilian brain conducts impulses through the reticular formation and relay centers of the thalamus to the neocortex.[168,6,81]

As evolution proceeded, the reptilian brain developed a primitive cortex which in mammals is in the limbic lobe. MacLean named it the limbic system to include the limbic cortex and the structures in the brain stem with which it has primitive connections. The limbic system consists of several neural structures including the hypothalamus (which sends messages to the pituitary), thalamus, hippocampus, septum, and amygdala and cingulate gyrus. It serves as the emotional or affective control center. The human limbic system is the same in structure and function as in the more developed animals, the non-human mammals. The limbic system developed as a kind of cortex for these earlier ancestors.

The limbic system has three nerve cell subdivisions: (1) the amygdala deals with self-preservation including feeding, and fighting, (2) the septal division cells deal with primal sexual functions and sociosexual expression involved in procreation, and (3) the mamillary bodies, the newest and largest subdivision which achieves a regulatory role in three fundamental aspects of a family situation—maternal care, play, and the isolation call. The isolation call is probably the most primitive and basic mammalian vocalization, which served origi-

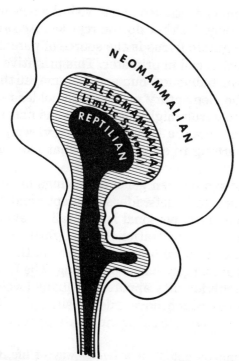

Figure 3.1 The Triune Brain

The three basic types of brains which in the evolution of the mammal became part of man's inheritance. The paleomammalian brain corresponds to the limbic system or "visceral brain" has been shown to play an important role in emotional behavior. From "Cerebral Evolution and Emotional Processes: New Findings on the Striatal Complex" by P. D. MacLean, 1972, *Annals of the New York Academy of Sciences 193,* 137. Reprinted by permission of the author and the publisher.

nally to maintain maternal-offspring contact and later on, contact of individuals within a group.

Research with hamsters in which the neocortex is destroyed shows that these animals growing up with only the reptilian brain and limbic system are capable of engaging in all the species-typical forms of behavior. They mate, breed, rear their young, and develop play at the appropriate time. If, however, the cingulate gyrus (the primitive cortex of the limbic system) is destroyed along with the neocortex, they do not develop play. Neither do the reptiles. According to Mac-Lean, the cingulate gyrus is the source of parental care, play, and the isolation call in primates. This primitive cortex of the limbic system ballooned out and became further differentiated from the elementary cortex of the older reptilian brain. The cingulate gyrus might be imagined as nature's device for providing an animal a better means of viewing the environment and learning to survive, somewhat like an early television set.[170]

The limbic system can generate feelings of conviction that humans attach to beliefs, ideas, concepts and theories. This suggests that most personal issues talked about in biofeedback training are not "rational," thoughtful comments, but may originate in the rudimentary cortex of the ancient limbic system and are largely based on feeling. The forces of togetherness and individuality apparent at many levels of life are in part the forces which have existed since the limbic system and its primitive cortex, the cingulate gyrus, were formed.

> When mammals opted for a family way of life, they set the stage for one of the most intense forms of suffering. The condition that makes being a mammal so painful is having to endure separation or isolation from loved ones and, in the end, the utter isolation of death.[170]

These ancient forces of togetherness and individuality are also reflected in human reactivity in behaviors like mating, breeding and rearing young, playing, and the "isolation call." In short, human family life is determined to a large extent by the older brains. The history of the evolution of the family as a biological institution is the 180 million year history of the evolution of mammals.[169,170]

Prefrontal Cortex

The neocortex is the most sophisticated and recent part of the brain. Its functions include: decoding and interpreting sensory signals, gross control of motor activities (musculoskeletal), imagination, decision making, memory, problem solving and planning. Only humans evolved the prefrontal cortex, the newest development in the neocortex. This is a uniquely human structure which looks inward at the limbic system, at the emotions and feelings within self.

The neocortex is relatively new in this history. In the progress from Neanderthal to Cro-Magnon man, the human forehead evolved from a low to high brow. The prefrontal cortex developed underneath and is the only neocortex that looks inward to the inside world. Significantly, it establishes strong connections with the third division of the limbic system concerned with parental care. The prefrontal cortex makes possible the foresight to plan for the needs of others as well as for self.[170] Thus humans have some choice about how those emotions and feelings affect them. In a sense, it functions as a kind of biofeedback instrument.

Reptiles never developed a neocortex; mammals did. We carry the neocortex of early mammals as well as the specifically human part of the neocortex (prefrontal cortex) which developed sometime as Neanderthal became Cro-Magnon. Only humans evolved the prefrontal cortex. It is the first development in evolution allowing inward attention, to the limbic system, and to our feelings and emotions. The activity of the prefrontal cortex and the third division of the limbic system may be apparent in parental over-concern for children, to the point where the over-concern itself triggers or magnifies problems in the child. The prefrontal cortex can also plan ahead and is probably active when biofeedback is combined with family systems therapy to observe the "inner" limbic self, emotions, feelings and thoughts. By attending to, observing and planning, the prefrontal cortex assists in gaining more self-control of the world within as well as outside.

Unlearning or Suspending a Response
According to MacLean, evolution is unlearning ancestrally determined behavior. Unlearning some ancestral responsive-

ness is necessary for evolution. That is, physiological inhibition of an otherwise automatic response is in part what evolution is about.[171] Bowen believes that biofeedback facilitates new learning rather than unlearning. Neither of them has described the basis for this distinction which might clarify the implications for biofeedback training. Neither has biofeedback clinical experience. I believe they are both correct and are viewing different aspects of complex processes. Both reptilian and limbic system activities are automatic and produce ancestrally determined behavior. In some circumstances reptilian and limbic system activities can come under voluntary neocortical self-regulation. This can occur in at least three ways: (1) suspending a response, (2) learning specific voluntary control of some aspect of one's own physiology or (3) optimizing the arousal of the two older brains and allowing increased neocortical input to determine behavior. This means optimizing the balance between the three levels of the brain.

To change an evolutionary pattern of physiological responsiveness requires, in my view, complex change process:

(1) being aware of the physiological response;
(2) reducing arousal;
(3) suspending the automatic response;
(4) learning a new response;
(5) practicing the new response;
(6) substituting the new response;
(7) observing changes in self;
(8) observing changes in important relationship systems;
(9) anticipating the dysfunctional physiological response;
(10) preventing the physiological response when appropriate;
(11) allowing the process of "growth." Biofeedback can minimize the dysfunction as well as facilitate the recovery from the overresponse or the dysfunction.
(12) triggering, creating, and facilitating changes in the

biological and social systems by choice (even if there is
a temporary increase in dysfunction).

Essentially, changing physiological responsiveness can improve self-regulation at the physiological level as well as at
the levels of individual and family functioning. Biofeedback
with family systems therapy can facilitate those processes.
As the two older brains may become more balanced, the
newer brain may have more options and more control. This
increased voluntary control itself further optimizes and balances the reptilian and limbic system, and so a spiraling
process is in motion that gives the organism a greater range
of flexibility and choice of response to internal and external
cues. The control also encourages new behaviors, initiating a
position or activity, even if difficult and even at the price of
temporary symptoms.

Whether ancestral responses are inhibited, eliminated,
overridden or otherwise processed, it does appear that biofeedback with family therapy allows automatic reactions to
come under voluntary (cortical) control by choice. People
seem to become more thoughtful, more flexible physiologically, cognitively, and behaviorally. That is, there is more
choice of whether to allow the automatic response or whether
to self-regulate it. People do not become less spontaneous.
They become more flexible and have a wider range of responses with which to react physiologically and cognitively.
These persons can be considered to be more "differentiated"
(See Chapter 6). By choice, with time, motivation and practice, the new response can become increasingly automatic.
However, given enough stress (anxiety) in the person and in
the emotional fields of which the person is a part, the old
automatic response is likely to reemerge at least temporarily.

Understanding the role of the prefrontal cortex which plans
forward and attends inward, as well as the role of the thalamus as a way-station of neural signals from the spinal cord
and brainstem on their way to the forebrain, are a challenge

to understanding biofeedback and human functioning. Biofeedback to calm down the limbic and motor systems and family systems theory to activate the prefrontal cortex can result in changes which either alone may not achieve.

Neuropeptides: "Information" Substances as Indicators of Evolution

That humans are part of the evolutionary process is reflected not only in the triune brain level but also at the microscopic, molecular levels. Some of the complex processes the human body can perform—produce insulin and beta endorphins—also occur in one of the simplest protozoa, the tetrahymena.

Pert[209,210] describes the neuropeptides as "signaling molecules." The components that "talk" are the neuropeptides and the components that "hear" are the neuropeptide receptors.

> How can fifty to sixty neuropeptides be produced, float around, and talk to fifty or sixty types of listening receptors which are on a variety of cells? Why does order rather than chaos reign?[209]

Her laboratory data suggest that there is actually only one type of molecule in the opiate receptors, one long polypeptide chain. This molecule is capable of changing its "conformation" within its membrane to assume a number of shapes. She describes this as the "molecular unity" of the receptors. In that unity is the evidence of evolution. The tetrahymena, a protozoa that is one of the simplest organisms, can do much of what humans do: eat, reproduce, and make the same neuropeptide components. The molecule of the rat-brain opiate receptor is identical to the human-brain receptor and also identical to the receptor components in the tetrahymena.

This finding gets to the simplicity and the unity of life. It is comparable to the four DNA-based pairs that code for the production of all the proteins, which are the physical substrates of life ... in this substrate there are only 60 or so signal molecules, the neuropeptides, that account for the physiological manifestation of emotions ... the receptor molecules do not become more complex as an organism becomes more complex. The identical molecular components for information flow are conserved throughout evolution.[209]

Awareness that one of the simplest living organisms, the tetrahymena, produces insulin and beta endorphins is an example of how an evolutionary perspective influences my thinking and clinical work with biofeedback. The production or release of insulin can be affected by biofeedback. First, these microscopic processes are not new, only the measurements are; second, a biofeedback intervention can reach back into evolution to processes humans have in common with the earliest living organisms.

Materials that resemble hormonal peptides and neuropeptides, previously thought to be restricted to multicellular animals, are present in protozoa, bacteria, and higher plants ... we suggest that the molecules of intercellular communication probably arouse much earlier in evolution than the endocrine, nervous, and immune systems.[243]

Emotions and Reactivity: Neuropeptides in the
Limbic System
Neuroscientists have thought for a long time that emotions are mediated by the limbic system. Wilder Penfield and other neurologists used electrodes to stimulate the cortex over the amygdala (in the limbic system) to evoke a variety of emotional responses such as grief, pain and pleasure. Recent receptor-mapping in Pert's laboratory expanded the psychological experiments that defined the limbic system. The lim-

bic system is "highly enriched with opiate and other receptors."

Biofeedback and the Perspective of Evolution

The evolutionary perspective that human responses are part of the continuum back to early forms of life is basic to Bowen natural systems theory. This is the perspective I use when providing biofeedback training (See Chapters 5 and 12). Some aspects of the instinctual and emotional forces of togetherness and individuality are apparent in all living organisms, including the earliest forms of protoplasm. Emotional processes within and between humans are partly derived from the activities of our ancient reptilian brain and limbic system. Many human dilemmas such as marital discord, behavioral problems of adults and children, issues of territoriality and rituals, have precursors in our ancestors the reptiles. Indicators of individuality and togetherness, as reflected in reactivity, are monitored by biofeedback instrumentation and are sometimes displayed even when talking, thinking about, or imagining these processes.

The concept of reactivity is based on the notion of biological responsiveness and can be observed in organisms from the single plant cell, to the multi-cellular animal, to individuals, family, and society. Patterns of responsiveness are based in part on the function and structure of the system, and not only on individual functioning. Responsiveness can be observed and predicted (See Chapters 5 and 12). Bowen's important contribution is emphasizing the commonalities of human functioning with other forms of life.

Biofeedback and Evolutionary Direction

Over or underactivity, then, can affect evolution to the point of extinction. The concept of evolution is important to biofeedback. (1) It is useful for maintaining clinical perspective and is a challenge for integrating theory. (2) Human physiology can be understood as direct evidence of evolution and thus an effort to change one's physiology represents an effort to intervene in ancient regulatory processes. And (3) some aspects of biofeedback training may enhance evolutionary processes; that is, biofeedback helps regulate the body by increasing the influence of the neocortex and possibly by further developing the neocortex itself. Biofeedback interventions work on structures and processes (e.g. triune brain, neuropeptides) which developed through, and affect evolution. Thus, biofeedback might advance or modify the very process of evolution.

Understanding human ties to early evolutionary forms of life brings into perspective the idea that when a person changes his/her level of reactivity with biofeedback training, he/she is involving processes deeply imbedded in nature over eons.

It may be that biofeedback training's major contribution is that it facilitates homeostasis, or balance, at many levels. It affects "tuning" and "kindling;" it affects the balance of the parasympathetic and sympathetic branches of the ANS; the balance of the reptilian, limbic and neocortical processes; the balance within and between systems such as the psychoneuroimmunological system; hemispheric (right, left) balance in the brain; the increased use of the prefrontal cortex and balances its potential to attend inward as well as to attend to the future and plan; and balance of reactivity not only within but also between people. As biofeedback modifies physical, emotional, cognitive and social processes, it encourages people to optimize their evolutionary potentials. Biofeedback training serves to harness the untapped capabilities developed during the course of evolution.

4

NEW CONCEPTS ABOUT INSTRUMENTATION

The telephone rings during a session. The receptionist informs me that Dr. M. says it is important. I do not know Dr. M., who says, "My agency is finishing its budget, and wants to buy biofeedback equipment. Should we get a temperature unit or an EMG?" Over the years improved screening does not interrupt the activity of the moment with dozens of such calls. When the Coordinator of Biofeedback Professional Training or I later respond with questions about how the instrumentation will be used, the professional training of the person using it, the understanding of physiology, motivation to obtain BCIA certification, and the goals of the program, frequently the caller is impatient or annoyed. These are essential, difficult, issues which when defined, make purchasing instrumentation relatively easy. Just as some patients search for a "quick cure," some aspiring biofeedback providers search for a "quick practice." Responsible professionals know better.

A variety of complex issues determine which instruments are effective for a given purpose, and what variables in each instrument must be considered. Excellent sources for instrumentation information include the BSA Task Force Report [246] with about 60 references. It reported that wide variability was found in the functional characteristics of commercial feedback devices manufactured by different companies. Variability was found in filter characteristics, input impedance, sensitivity, noise rejection, type of feedback, battery life, calibration, time constant, and resolution. However, this wide variability does not appear to be related to therapeutic effects. Whereas the usual laboratory device is intended to monitor a physiological function accurately without influencing it, the biofeedback instrumentation is intended to facilitate altering the function it monitors. For information on biofeedback instrumentation sources contact BSA which is compiling a directory of manufacturers and suppliers of hardware, software, books, tapes and other self-regulation materials.

The technical characteristics of biofeedback instruments may be evaluated on several levels: sensitivity, accuracy and stability of sensors and transducers; amplification of physiological data with maximum fidelity and minimal distortion; and filtering capacity to reduce artifact of physiological, environmental or instrumental origin.[90]

Once New, Now Standard

Some biofeedback instrumentation, new twenty years ago, is now considered standard. Instrumentation to feed back skin temperature, muscle tension, brain waves, heart rate and blood pressure levels are examples. This chapter describes some of the now standard instruments which are frequently improved and modified for specific purposes. In addition, this chapter describes new biofeedback instrumentation, some medical instruments which can be used for biofeedback, and some new concepts that use standard instrumentation in new ways.

Biofeedback instrumentation is an extension and amplification of the body's own form of biological feedback. Electronic instrumentation, an essential component of biofeedback, provides immediate and continuous information (through auditory, tactile, or visual signals) of physiological responses of which the individual is ordinarily unaware. This information facilitates physiological self-regulation. Special sensors placed non-invasively on the skin, measure electrical, mechanical, thermal, and biochemical signals. Physiological functions are transformed into electrical signals, amplified, and analyzed.

Frequently monitored responses include the electrical potential from the muscles measured by the electromyograph (EMG), skin temperature which indicates peripheral vasodilation and vasoconstriction, electrodermal (EDR) which indicates tonic and phasic changes in the electrical activity of skin moisture (perspiration and chemical surface conditions), heart rate, blood pressure, and respiration rate. Plethysmographic techniques measure blood volume changes. By 1979 other instruments measured and fed back information on stomach acidity, penile erection, mastication, nasality in speech, anal sphincter pressure, and respiration.[246]

EMG: Muscle Activity Biofeedback

The electromyograph (EMG) measures the electrical activity of both striate and smooth muscles. The basis for EMG biofeedback is the recording of electrical impulses from muscles which connect (synapse) at the neuromuscular or myoneural junction. Action potentials are transmitted from the cerebral cortex down through the spinal cord via a complex series of nerve pathways to individual motor units in the muscles. When a significant number of action potentials is generated in a particular time period over a given area, contraction of the muscle occurs. In other words, contraction occurs as the result of a convergence of temporal and spatial summation of action potentials. Conversely, muscle relaxation represents a decrease in the firing or electrical discharge of motor units.[90] This is measured in units of "microvolts" (Uv), which are millionths of a volt. Surface electromyography as utilized in biofeedback is an indirect measurement of striate muscle activity.

Thermal: Skin Temperature Biofeedback as Cardiovascular Indicator

The physiological basis for thermal feedback is the cardio-vascular system. The feedback is either audio (the equipment converts the biological signal into a sound) or visual (usually a number, a light, or a meter needle). During stress, the body's survival system automatically alters blood flow in various organs of the body to make it ready for action. Peripheral (hands, feet) blood flow decreases which causes a decline in skin temperature. Thus skin temperature is an indicator of cardiovascular function. More specifically, the sympathetic branch of the ANS exercises significant control over peripheral skin temperature through electrochemical changes stimulated by norepinephrine and other neurotransmitters. Sympathetic activation leads to many changes in the body's smooth (nonstriated) musculature. One of these changes involves the contraction of smooth muscles surrounding the peripheral blood vessels (arterioles). This vasoconstriction results in lowered skin temperature as peripheral blood flow decreases.[90]

Electrodermal: Skin Changes Related to Perspiration

Different states of arousal induce changes in perspiration. These changes alter the electrical resistance on the surface of the skin. The electrical measurement of the resistance changes in the skin is the basis for electrodermal response (EDR) biofeedback. Although the EDR has been used as a measure of anxiety for more than a century, it has only recently been discovered that skin responses could be modified by purposeful "non-effort" or "letting go." The specific chain of events resulting in electrical skin events has not been completely identified. However, the fact that perspiration produces an increase in skin conductance appears to be one of the important factors in the production of EDR. When a person is more aroused, there is less resistance on the skin. The skin is more conductive. When a constant voltage is applied to the surface of the skin, the electrical conductivity or "skin conductance" can be used as a measure of anxiety. This factor is measured in (umhos). The lower the electrical conductance on the skin's surface, the lower the "physiological arousal." Electrodermal activity can be measured in skin conductance level (SCL), skin conductance response (SCR) and skin potential response (SPR).[90] Other measurements include skin resistance level (SRL), skin resistance response (SRR), spontaneous skin resistance response (SSRR), and spontaneous skin conductance response (SSCR). The measurement of skin potential (SP) consists of measuring the skin's natural electro-chemical activity, rather than introducing an electrical current to the surface of the skin as in GSR.[81]

EEG: Brain Wave Biofeedback

The electroencephalograph (EEG) measures brain wave patterns.[90][120] Measurements of cortical electrical activity can be displayed as brain wave frequencies and amplitudes. At any one time EEG reflects a fluctuating mixture of frequencies and amplitudes. EEG varies according to the region of the brain which is being recorded, age, level of consciousness and alertness, blood chemistry, and other metabolic variables. Different subjective experiences may in certain circumstances be associated with different predominant frequencies. For example, narrowly focused attention may be associated with predominant beta frequences (14 Hz and above) in certain brain regions. Meditative states or passive non-focused attention may be associated with dominant alpha frequencies (8-13 Hz) from the posterior head regions.[6,91] In adults theta frequencies (4-7 Hz) are common during periods of falling asleep or waking up ("twilight sleep"), or during some active mental states in front brain regions. During a normal night sleep in the adult there are several stages of brain wave activity showing marked variation with predominant low voltage beta activity, theta activity and delta rhythms (less than 4 Hz) of variable morphology (form and structure).[91] Dreams have been associated with rapid eye movements (REM) and low voltage beta activity.

Medical Instrumentation Used as Biofeedback

Another important biofeedback source is medical instrumentation. In fact, early biofeedback developed in part with medical instrumentation such as EEG and blood pressure. Recent instrumentations enrich biofeedback opportunities. The Biostator is a "computerized pancreas" which monitors blood glucose and insulin and automatically provides either dextrose or insulin (See Chapter 10). Reflectance meters monitor blood glucose at home and are also a form of biofeedback before and after a session. While not continuous, this feedback is relatively immediate (1 minute). Blood tests can also provide endocrine and immune system indicators of reactivity. The respirator, which feeds back tidal volume, and the ECG's heart activity can be biofeedback in the Intensive Care Unit. The Inspirix, which measures the volume of inhalation, is used in asthma treatment to increase tidal volume while breathing diaphragmatically.[202] The BioTherm Infrared Thermometer measures skin temperature without making contact with the skin and was used with Olympic and other athletes.[206]

Themography consists of an infrared camera which detects subtle changes in skin temperature. These reflect underlying changes in blood flow caused by peripheral vasodilation or constriction. Thermography has been primarily used in the diagnosis of pain associated with nerve root injuries, and sometimes in the diagnosis of cancer. The entire body, or large segments, can be seen at the same time and, depending on the blood flow, (the skin temperature) different colors can be seen on the screen. In contrast, the usual thermal biofeedback monitors skin temperature in tiny areas (the thermistor is usually less than 1/499 in diameter). Randomly selected people learned to warm their skin more easily with the thermography than the thermal biofeedback instrument.[118] This research provided valuable information regarding the patterns of skin warming and the most appropriate placement of thermistors. Thermography can also be used for diagnosing difficult conditions, and as a form of feedback for people with special difficulties. This is another creative use of medical equipment to provide information on the state of the arterioles.

Instruments for Home Training

The use of biofeedback instruments loaned to use at home is another example of how the conceptualization of the biofeedback program determines the use of instrumentation. Many programs discourage home instruments and use audio cassettes (commercially available to fit the program or individually made for each person) to practice. If used indefinitely, home training instrumentation like tapes can get in the way of the individual paying attention to his/her own body signals. The goal is that the person not become dependent on the equipment for feedback, but to begin to use his/her own body as a "biofeedback instrument" as soon as possible. On the other hand, the now standard, portable, transistor-radio-size EMG instrument to monitor facial and jaw muscle tension, innovated years ago,[245] is still very helpful to use even for short periods of time. The person becomes aware during daily activities at home, work, and even while driving, which events increase the muscle tension. Portable instrumentation to be used at home and work is small and best used in conjunction with a comprehensive biofeedback program. The clinician's theory determines how this and other instrumentation is used at home, work or school. The goal is to maximize physiological awareness and optimize functioning.

Consumer's Thinking

Ultimately, the consumer's thoughts are the most meaningful for biofeedback success. The consumer's expectations, hopes, fears, and previous treatment disappointments significantly influence the success with biofeedback instrumentation.

Instrumentation (1) acts as an amplifier of the body — it helps to see, hear, and sense functions not at all or not easily discernible otherwise; (2) provides a window to one's own physiology during rest and motion, upset or calm, alone and with others; and (3) is a temporary extension of the brain to facilitate learning functions which become permanently available and can be used by choice. Like riding a bicycle, one does not forget how; one only chooses if and when. When properly used with professional coaching, the instrumentation can facilitate flexibility, adaptability, decreased reactivity, and increased self-regulation of physiological, emotional, social, and cognitive functions.

Professional Training

Personal training is essential for the professional (see Chapter 8 and "Quick Questions and Anwers").

Clinician's Thinking and Instrumentation Advances

In addition to basic professional training, the way the clinician thinks about the processes being monitored becomes a crucial factor. The theory determines the use of the instrumentation for demonstration, treatment, education, and training. The clinician's brain is in a sense an important part of the biofeedback equipment and is the integrating "instrument" when planning an intervention. Theory determines, for instance, how to use the equipment so that the person does not become even more symptom focused and thereby more dysfunctional. I used Biofeedback Systems, Inc. (Boulder, Co.) and J&J Enterprises (Poulsbo, Wa.) instrumentation much before their computer capabilities became available. Nevertheless, the physiology of relationships and other concepts were studied (See Chapter 12).

Biofeedback is used to balance and optimize general reactivity and arousal. A specific change, for instance in skin temperature, may be associated with general changes in the cardiovascular, endocrine, and/or immune systems. It is also used to learn to shift a specific function for a specific purpose, such as to reduce temporomandibular joint disorder and to improve incontinence. A biofeedback "plug" containing EMG electrodes is inserted in the rectum to learn to manage anal incontinence.[175] Perry's[211] electronic perineometer provides specific information on pelvic muscle function. Perineometer biofeedback applications include problems of sexual functioning such as anorgasmia, vaginismus and dysmenorrhea, pain, and several varieties of urinary and fecal incontinence. Biofeedback for fecal incontinence was effective for 72% of patients, and 85% of urinary incontinence patients improved[328] (See Chapter 10). EMG electrodes and the perineometer also decrease pelvic pain by insertion into the vagina or applied near the anus in males and monitoring the activity in the pubococcygeous (PC) muscle during biofeedback sessions.

Telemetry, a process for determining distance from a remote object, permits innovative biofeedback instrumentation that leaves the person free to move within a certain distance.[308] The sensors are placed on the muscle, the sensors (wires) go to a small box (held by a belt) which transmit the signals to the computer without being physically connected to it. This is particularly useful in neuromuscular re-training and variety of applications including training athletes, and simulating work or other situations in the biofeedback laboratory. Financial, technical and other considerations at Georgetown have not made it possible to observe physiology and differentiation indicators when people are not at rest.

Brain topography or brain mapping (See Chapter 11) is a new, evolving technology which makes it possible to observe brain function and use the observations as biofeedback. The process uses spectral analysis which is a mathematical technique that can be used to examine any complex wave form. Four to 20 EEG channels, phase and coherence sensitive, produce a color electronic "map" of brain activity in "real time" and in an easily comprehensible form. "Real time" means that the brain activity represented on the monitor has occurred not more than ½ second earlier and as the consumer changes brain activity, the colors on the map change. This new instrumentation has the capability of simultaneously recording 8–16 channels of other physiological variables such as skin temperature, blood pressure, heart rate, electrodermal activity, and muscle activity. By looking at brain activity in real time color topography as well as autonomic activity, it may be possible to determine if the brain signals are primarily from the brain stem, midbrain, or the neocortex. I believe it may be facilitate further understanding MacLean's triune brain function model (See Chapter 3); and, using natural systems concepts (See Chapter 5), one intriguing possibility would be to attach the surface electrodes at the same time on more than one person in the family and observe the family as a whole organism, with the activity of each triune brain as a component of the field. NeuroMap,[189] used 8 years to study the relationship between brain activity and stress responsivity, became available for purchase at the time of this writing, and Capscan[50] was about to be distributed. One salient feature of these innovations is the opportunity to observe and self-regulate mind/body integration.

Biofeedback with microcomputers is new but for many clinicians microcomputers are now a given. The capabilities of the computer itself provide additional feedback by interpreting data and feeding back not only raw data to the learner (client, trainee, patient) but also graphs and other displays. Simultaneous feedback and recording of several aspects of the physiology of one or several people allows accurate information on responsiveness within a family or emotional system. In children's computerized biofeedback "games," "winning" depends on changing a physiological function. However, too much feedback can be as limiting to the learner as not enough.

Beyond these uses, microcomputers are absolutely essential in the derivation and analysis of more complex functions such as brain topography and integrating several physiological functions into either a profile or single index of responsivity.[198] Professional objectives and theory of human behavior are important factors in selecting computer hardware and software.

Applications to Family Systems

Theory guides new uses for existing instrumentation. For instance, in 1973 while observing changes without biofeedback, I decided that biofeedback instrumentation might be used to monitor and possibly facilitate changes in reactivity in family members. I wanted to see if changes in one person's thought, feelings or actions affected the physiology of the person and the thoughts, feelings and actions of family members. In fact, when I set up the biofeedback laboratory in 1975, my primary purpose was to monitor changes in reactivity. Biofeedback services for symptom relief were a vehicle to observe responsivity in relationships (Chapter 12). The following uses of existing biofeedback instrumentation developed:

(1) Biofeedback is used during psychotherapy sessions so that, in addition to learning to shift arousal or a specific function, the person becomes aware of the connections between physiology, emotional and cognitive processes.

(2) The physiology of relationships is monitored. More than one person in the family is monitored simultaneously but separately. For instance, a child's hand temperature is monitored while observing fluctuations in the parents' degree of emotional over or under-involvement in their child. Sometimes reciprocity is observed: when skin temperature is high in the parent the child's intense responses can change from cool to warm. An emotional process, or a change in reactivity, in one person has consequences in the reactivity of another person. Changes in family physiology become part of the learning process about self in relation to others. The goal with natural systems thinking is to enhance each person's psychophysiological and emotional functioning in the context of their own family system. Microcomputers can facilitate observation.

(3) The use of biofeedback with video is another new way of providing the person or family comprehensive feedback of their behavior and psychophysiology.

Biofeedback instrumentation can monitor activity in various ways, but not yet the processes whereby thoughts or feelings in one person change the physiology of another. Is the study of reactivity in a family system in part also the study of the changes in permeability in neurons, tissues, organs, and persons? Reactivity is in part the activity of the transmission of electrical signals along the neuron (See Chapter 2). The transmission occurs because of simultaneous complex electrical and chemical changes which result in changes in the membrane potential. That is, cell exitation results in changes in cell membrane permeability to ions (sodium and potassium).[6] (An ion is an electrically charged atom or group of atoms. The electrical charge results when a neutral atom or group of atoms loses or gains one or more electrons during chemical reactions.) When the potential at the neuron hillock reaches a critical value, an electrical impulse is transmitted from one neuron to another or to an end-organ (end-organ is any specialized structure at the peripheral end of nerve fibers having either sensory or motor functions). This transmission involves changes in the terminal membrane permeability to calcium ions, release of neurotransmitters, and changes in sodium and potassium permeabilities of the next (postsynaptic) membrane. How is this process which occurs at the atom level in one person transmitted to another person in the family, organization or athletic team?

One continuing challenge is assessing not only the momentary reactivity but also the basic level of functioning or differentiation over time. Is there a way to use physiological processes such as electrodermal skin responses (EDR) as an indicator of differentiation? Differentiation is too complex to reduce to one physiological indicator. But the characteristics of physiological membranes are interesting. The cell membrane of an amoeba represents a well-defined boundary between that organism and its environment and is the primary screen controlling the interaction of the protoplasm and the external world. In mammals, although many functions have been taken over by mouth, lungs, gastrointestinal tract, eyes, ears and nose, the skin still defines the external physical limit of the body.[70] Is a person with well defined functional boundaries (differentiated) also a person whose skin measures less conductance? Unlikely as a single measure. However, I believe that sometime it may be possible to see that degree of skin conductance can be a small aspect of a complex *pattern of processes* which do reflect not only over or under reactivity, but also the degree of maturity or differentiation of a person. Possibly a *pattern* of indicators must be understood since it is known that people vary in the responsivity (lability) of different physiological activity. I focus on conceptual questions regarding functioning in family, organization and other relationship systems in order to extend my understanding of differentiation and reactivity.

5

SYSTEMS CONCEPT OF DYSFUNCTION

NATURAL SYSTEMS

A film shown in Washington, D.C. at the Smithsonian's Air and Space Museum facilitates an understanding of the intricacy of a natural systems view which goes from the cells in the body to the stars in the Milky Way. The film starts with a couple having a picnic. Viewers are given the fabulous opportunity to see one person's hand at this picnic, and slowly back away to greater distances so that they see the hand of the person who is in a field, in Florida, in the U.S.A., on Earth, in the Milky Way. Viewers then come closer and closer, with ever more powerful lenses, until they come back to the hand, through the skin, and finally observe the activity of one cell in that hand. While I cannot reproduce the experience of seeing this film, it helps highlight that: (1) reactivity at various levels determines the responsiveness of the organism (person) observed and for whom biofeedback training is provided; (2) the presenting symptom or reason for biofeedback training is only an infinitesimal aspect of interrelated, mutually regulated natural systems. A symptom, like the couple at the picnic, is only an aspect of natural systems.

What natural forces drive lemmings periodically into the sea? Is it a total coincidence when someone dies on or near the anniversary of the death of another important member in the family? What forces operate such that most families have a functional "runt?" What forces drive a person who marries and divorces three alcoholic spouses? What patterns emerge when examining personal and family events two years preceding and two years after the diagnosis of a serious illness? What paradigms can be developed to understand illness or dysfunction in terms of forces in natural systems?

Family systems theory[31] provides a way to think about symptoms, illness, and dysfunction (physical, social, emotional and cognitive) which takes into account all levels of natural systems and their basic forces. Systems thinking is not linear, cause and effect thinking. Systems thinking looks at the organized whole, at the interrelationships among its elements and processes, at its driving forces and how the forces balance. The family is conceptualized as a unit or system.

Intrigued by marine life, I think of the human family system and some similarities with the coral colony system. Coral colonies[268] are comprised of many individuals called polyps. All the polyps in a colony are derived from a single fertilized ovum that matured and then formed new polyps. Polyps attach one end to a hard surface on the ocean bottom. The other end or "mouth" is open, surrounded by beautifully colored tentacles which capture tiny bits of food such as plankton and bacteria that float by. As the individual polyps die, their flesh is washed away, leaving only their skeleton. The remaining living polyps stay attached to the skeleton, and in turn produce buds. Thus the coral formations that people are familiar with are skeletons of many generations stacked one on top of another. Coral colonies rarely grow in isolation. Usually vast numbers of colonies clump together into three basic types of formations. Their beautiful colors, which range through the color spectrum, are intensified by the algae that lives within the soft polyp tissue. The algae, small one-celled plants, live under the "skin" of the tiny coral polyp animals. Algae absorb carbon dioxide produced by the coral, and releases oxygen used by the coral, each dependent on the other for existence. These tiny primitive animals build coral reefs which provide the foundation for a complex and interdependent society which is the support of all sea life.

The reality of interdependence, the importance of association, collaboration and space, the difficulties of isolation, the building of one generation upon another, the specialization of function, and the fact that the living coral is but a minute representation of an incredibly long "family history," all have a counterpart in human families.

Bonner[28] organized natural systems by size, from the known "upper limit" of the universe, to a galaxy, a star, a planet, the crust of the earth, a community, a population, an organism, a tissue, a cell, macromolecules, molecules, an atom, and the "lower limit" of the elementary particles. Science is not philosophy. It is about "things" which used to be called "Nature with a capital N." He observes fascinating facts, including the variability in speed of motion each object has related to its size. Science describes. It also is concerned with order and with the history of the natural things being ordered.[28]

Bowen family systems theory can be in the direction of science in the sense it helps to order phenomena. It seeks to understand, describe and order the functional connectedness of living systems and their evolutionary history.

Some explanations here of that theory gained clarity from others.[15,96,143] Concepts from family systems and from the literature on biofeedback are described as I use them.

Mr. N. was referred by his physician for biofeedback training for blood pressure. Over 200 lbs., 5' tall, he had no weight losing plans. He was interested in biofeedback but during brief family process questions he saw no relevance of family to his blood pressure. The responsible oldest of six brothers and sisters, he was under pressure to take in his mother due to his father's recent death. His wife was against this plan.

His construction business was slow. He emigrated from Europe shortly after World War II, but he still frequently thought about the hunger he had experienced. He would never diet, he announced. In subsequent biofeedback training sessions he learned, a little each time, about some of the family system concepts described below. He also learned to reduce his reactivity and to observe it go up when he either thought about family issues, or when he talked about what he eventually called the "triangle" (his mother, himself, and his wife). Since financial pressures were high, he limited himself to about 10 sessions and periodically for follow-up. Six months later, his blood pressure decreased enough that his physician had taken him off the antihypertensive prescription. Although his weight was unchanged, he had calmed his "triangle." He practiced the biofeedback skills at least once/day for 20 minutes, and several brief times through the day, and he had begun to observe triangles and other systems processes while at work.

Family Systems Theory

As I understand Bowen's thinking, the core concepts that were later to become family system theory or "Bowen theory" were all "in his head about 1947–49." The terms natural systems and living systems have been used to reflect the notion that the basic concepts in family systems theory may be applicable to all living systems. Since the term living system excludes what is presumed to be non-living, the term natural systems is probably more accurate. The most important criterion for whether a concept ultimately has been retained in the theory is whether the concept is consistent with evolution. It is thus not surprising that as family systems theory became better understood, thinking about the applicability of those concepts for understanding all natural systems became possible. The limitations of observing the applicability of the concepts is with the observer, with the personal attachment of the human to the event.[32]

From the beginning Bowen looked for concepts which reflected not only that the human species is unique, but also that it is in many ways like other forms of life. In the 1940s Bowen developed systems thinking, in order to replace conventional psychiatry and individual psychology with evolutionary theory. A natural systems theory was conceptually more useful. Later, in the 1960s, some people confused general systems theory with evolutionary systems theory. To differentiate from general systems theory, the term "natural systems" was then used.[32] Webster's definition of "natural" includes:

> ... of or arising from nature; in accordance with what is found or expected in nature ... not artificial or manufactured ... without man-made changes ...

In the long struggle of the human species to become the dominant species, it tended to forget that it is also part of the other species. Mankind tended to focus on its uniqueness and not on its commonality with other species. Natural systems theory takes evolution into account. Family systems is thus one segment of natural systems. Since family systems theory was derived from evolutionary thinking it is not surprising that concepts from that theory apply in varying degrees to other natural systems. "Family systems therapy" is only a small subset, and in some ways an incidental development, of natural systems thinking.[32]

Differentiation is one of the indispensable concepts of family systems theory. How does one cell differentiate from another, one coral from another, one neuropeptide from another, one bird from another, one person from another, one family from another, one planet from another? How does each become more "itself"? What distinguishes me from you?

According to Bowen, it is a "fact" that better differentiated people are less automatically reactive and have better control over their brains. Processes which augment the opportunity to increase the brain's control over itself increase differentiation. Biofeedback is one such process.

The following concepts of family systems theory were applied in my biofeedback work:

(1) A symptom is an indicator of the functioning of the system(s).

A symptom is an indicator of forces out of balance in one or more levels of natural systems. The same patterns influence the development of physical, emotional, social and/or cognitive dysfunction. The person in the most vulnerable family position, absorbs the relationship system problems and is the one that becomes relatively dysfunctional. The symptom itself can also be an additional trigger for more reactivity and more problems in the person, family, or work system. A well differentiated, flexible, mature person is better able to cope with the vulnerability in the system and less likely to become as dysfunctional.

Although a symptom can be evidence of dysfunction, it can also be a part of the process of adaptation of that system. It can also be evidence that one person is trying to change self, while the system tends to maintain itself as it is. When a system is stressed, the usual balance of forces is disturbed. To adjust, all biological systems have adaptive mechanisms. However, symptoms develop (a) when the intensity, frequency or duration of stress or anxiety is too great, (b) when the person, a subsystem (such as the immune system), or the relationship field (such as family or work) is particularly vulnerable (either over or under reactive), (c) when the coping skills are few, weak, or not used, and (d) when a person attempts to change self to become more mature (or "differentiated"). The imbalance of forces can overload adaptive mechanisms and symptoms emerge. The type of symptom that develops is frequently (not always, as in some symptoms which develop after an injury) a complication or exacerbation of the mechanisms that exist to preserve the balance.

(2) The "system" includes the individual, the family, work school and other larger social organizations of which the person is a part of, as well as the smaller systems within the individual, such as cells, organs, regulatory systems as the ANS, the endocrine and immune systems.

The idea of balance of forces is central to systems thinking. A cell, an organ, a person, a family, an organization, a society is each a system within natural systems (Figure 5.1). The notion of balance at all levels is appealing to me as a scientific thought as well as a personal orientation transmitted through my father who spoke of choosing the "golden middle road." The systems view of physical illness takes all natural systems into account and the balance within and among them. In one direction (out) the person is observed with a wider and wider lens to include larger systems. In the other direction (in) the individual is observed with a series of lenses that focus on smaller and smaller components within. Reactivity is one unifying concept at all levels of natural systems. When providing biofeedback with a system orientation, the *thinking* is focused on understanding all systems, even though initially the attention may be specifically on the symptom.

(3) Differentiation and the life forces of individuality and togetherness.

Bowen[31] defined two counterbalancing life forces – a force towards individuality and a force towards togetherness. These natural forces of closeness and distance can be observed at all levels of life. Plankton too far apart or too close together do not grow. Humans too intensely fused (merged) together emotionally or those too emotionally distant from each other also

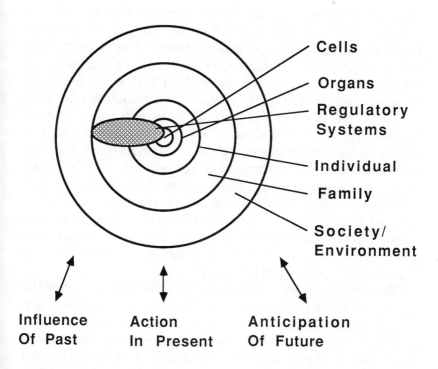

Figure 5.1 Natural Systems

do not function maturely. In cells, the process of specialization is known as cellular differentiation. Cells differentiate, become specialized, when they organize into relationships with other cells. This suggests that cellular differentiation is related to the forces cells have on each other. Humans also differentiate, become themselves, in relation to others.

The balance of these two forces within an individual is one indicator of the level of differentiation of self. This balance is affected by the degree of over or under reactivity of the individual and of the systems of which he/she is a part. Well differentiated people are responsible for self as well as respectful of others and of the differences between self and others. Other characteristics of differentiation are functioning with integrity and principle, knowing the difference between feelings and thoughts, and having the flexibility to choose when to act based on feelings and when based on thoughts, when purposefully and when automatically. That does not preclude spontaneity. It does not mean "rugged individualism" or "selfishness." At the togetherness end of the continuum most physiological, emotional, social and cognitive responses are automatic; at the opposite end, individuality, most responses have some degree of flexibility. At that end, family members can be effective team players as well as well-defined individuals. Families whose members maintain a higher level of differentiation are more adaptive under chronic or acute stress, less vulnerable to symptom development, and more flexible in their coping responses.

Differentiation, in my view, is also characterized by: the degree of balance between individuality and togetherness, the flexibility of the organism at physiological, emotional, cognitive and social levels, the rate of recovery from imbalanced states, the groups the person is part of, integrity and principles, ability to deal with the past, present and anticipated future, the capacity to be objective and have perspective about self, the ability to recognize one's dependency on others, and the capacity to deal with one's own inevitable eventual death.

Complex variables are involved in increasing differentiation (maturity) and decreasing symptoms through biofeedback and family systems therapy (Figure 5.2). If the initial family reactivity is low, level of differentiation is high, coping skills are strong and stressors are few, the person is likely to increase differentiation and to decrease the symptoms (Figure 5.2.a). In contrast, a person with high family reactivity, low initial differentiation, weak coping skills and many stressors has a much smaller likelihood of increasing his/her differentiation but still has a strong likelihood of decreasing symp-

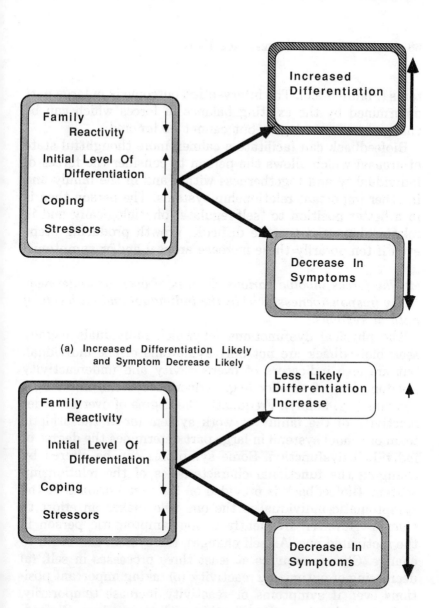

(a) Increased Differentiation Likely
and Symptom Decrease Likely

(b) Increased Differentiation Less Likely
Yet Symptom Decrease Likely

Figure 5.2 Processes Affecting Differentiation Increases and
Symptom Decreases

toms (Figure 5.2.b). The intervention outcome is in large part
determined by the existing balance of forces which can be
changed to some degree but cannot be ignored.

Biofeedback can facilitate a calmer, more thoughtful state
of arousal which allows the person to consider the forces of
individuality and togetherness within and in the family and
in other important relationship systems. The person then is
in a better position to "self-regulate" physiologically and in
relationships and to take difficult, growth producing steps
even if temporarily these increase arousal and/or symptoms.

*(4) The forces involve various degrees of over- or under-reac-
tivity (responsiveness) within the individual and all levels of
natural systems.*

The physical dysfunctions for which individuals usually
seek biofeedback are not only symptoms of the individual,
but are also indicators of overreactivity and underreactivity
(dysfunction) of smaller (e.g. endocrine system) and larger
systems (e.g. family). Frequently the degree of over or under
reactivity of the family or work system (or of the athletic
team or school system) in large part determines the degree of
individual dysfunction. Some symptoms can be altered by
changing the functional characteristics of the relationship
system. Biofeedback is provided on the assumption that the
symptomatic individual is the one who makes an effort to
change. However, frequently a non-symptomatic person is
the motivated one. As self changes, the system can begin to
change. Change requires at least three processes in self: (a)
decreasing or optimizing reactivity, (b) taking important positions even if symptoms or reactivity increase temporarily,
and (c) staying in communication with the system. Biofeedback assists people to develop their own ways of monitoring
reactivity, a personalized "instrument" or set of indicators.
Biofeedback facilitates awareness of the physiological manifestations of one's thoughts, feelings, images, behaviors,
hopes, beliefs, and anticipations. Under stress, however, a

person can ignore, not recognize, or recognize but not be able to (or not choose to) act based on the indicators.

(5) A symptom is in part the product of the nuclear family emotional process.

A systems concept of dysfunction considers the symptom an indicator of the nuclear and extended family emotional processes. Other indicators or mechanisms for managing distress in the family are (a) emotional distance (Figure 5.3), (b) marital conflict (Figure 5.4), (c) over adaptiveness of one spouse (Figure 5.5) to the extreme of becoming symptomatic, and/or (d) parental focus on one or more children (Figure 5.6). These four mechanisms are determined in part by the degree of reactivity in the person and in the relationship system.

Emotional distance is used by people who seek to preserve a sense of autonomy in an intense relationship and to avoid the discomfort (or loss of self) associated with too much closeness. Marital conflict provides a relatively stable "solution" to needing emotional closeness to maintain the relationship and emotional distance to maintain autonomy. Over adaptability or dysfunction reduces reactivity in one spouse (or single person) who consistently adapts to the other(s) in marriage, family, or work. If the stress is sustained and/or high, the over adaptability pattern may gradually impair (emotionally, physically, socially or cognitively) one person in the system. Child focus occurs when the emotional reactivity between the parents becomes focused in one or more children who become more vulnerable to emotional, physical, cognitive or social problems. The more relationship-oriented child (rather than goal-oriented child) is more responsive to relationships, absorbs more family reactivity, and may become symptomatic. The development of symptoms (regardless of which kind, and regardless of whether in an adult or a child) is influenced by the basic level of differentiation and level of reactivity. A person who can be in contact with important

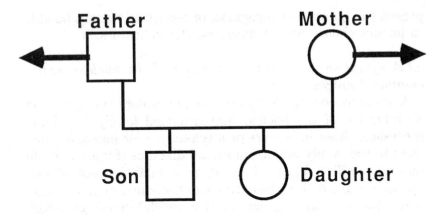

Figure 5.3 Emotional Distance

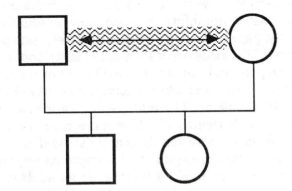

Figure 5.4 Marital Conflict

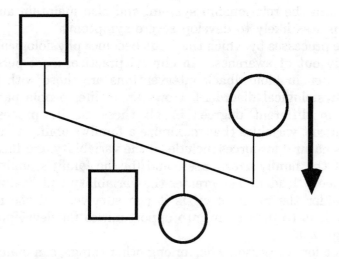

Figure 5.5 Overadaptiveness of Spouse

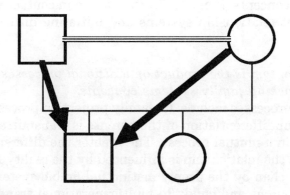

Figure 5.6 Parental Focus on Child

others in the relationship system, and also maintain autonomy is less likely to develop severe symptoms.

The processes by which the focus becomes physiological are mostly out of awareness. In clinical practice, most persons interested in biofeedback interventions are those with psychophysiological disorders. However, in life, people participate in different degrees in all these family processes. Important variables that maximize a family's ability to draw on its natural resources include (a) the variability and flexibility of the family's responses, and (b) the family's ability to produce a "leader." The greater the variability and flexibility, the wider the range of crisis it can survive, and the more likely it is to turn them into opportunities for development and growth.

A leader is a person who, among other things, can maintain a perspective on alternatives, can maintain his/her own integrity, can remain reasonably calm during personal and family (or work system) crises, and can remain in contact with the relationship system even when the system is reactive. Biofeedback can facilitate, particularly if provided in the context of family theory, these processes. It can increase the flexibility and variability of responses, it can facilitate self-regulation of responsiveness and, with coaching about basic family systems concepts, it can facilitate staying in contact with the important relationship systems and initiating difficult positions.

(6) A symptom is the product of additional processes defined as interlocking family systems concepts.

Other processes include: (a) family projection process or the way the undifferentiation of the parents is transmitted to the children in a mutual process. The greater the differentiation, the more the relationship is influenced by the reality needs of the child than by the deeply instinctual limbic system needs of both parent and child; (b) multigenerational transmission process, the transmission of family processes through many

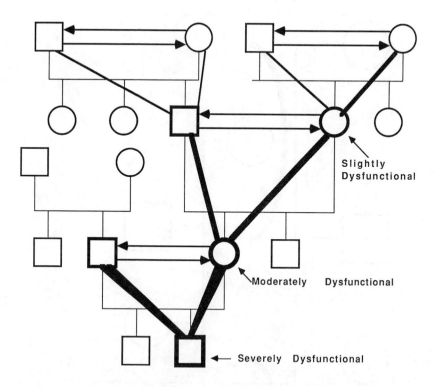

Figure 5.7 Multigenerational Transmission Process

generations (Figure 5.7); (c) emotional cutoff refers to the
quality of emotional contact between people who deal with
unresolved attachment to their families of origin by cutting
themselves off physically and/or emotionally from them and
from current important relationship (Figure 5.8); (d) triangles
in nuclear family which describe the process driven by emotional reactiveness of people and the level of emotion that
gets attached to a particular issue. With increasing tension,
other people than the first three (Figure 5.9) may become
involved in a series of interlocking triangles which can reach
outside the family system to include work, social, educational, legal and health care systems (Figure 5.10); (e) sibling

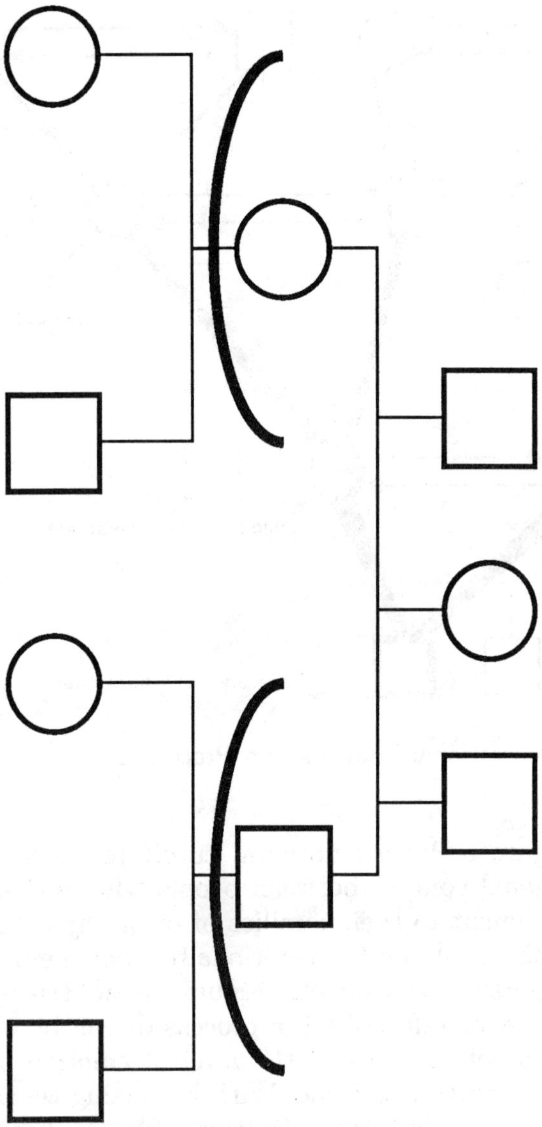

Figure 5.8 Emotional Cutoff

74

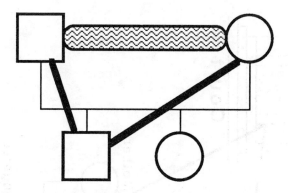

Figure 5.9 Emotional Triangle in Nuclear Family

position,[307] which describes that rank and sex determine functioning in many ways (Figure 5.11); and (f) societal emotional process, the concept which describes how forces towards individuality and togetherness counterbalance each other on a societal level the same as in families and individuals.[31,145] The degree of reactivity plays a part in all these processes.

(7) A variety of diseases may be understood, in part, as different expressions of the same kind of family system processes.
    Over a century ago Darwin[62,63] observed a process of earlier age of onset and increased severity in succeeding generations of seemingly inherited conditions. Bowen theory suggests a non-genetic transmission of family emotional processes. A balance between the need for emotional connectedness with others (togetherness) and the need to be oneself (individuality) is transmitted. Imbalance in these forces and high anxiety in the system, can manifest symptoms. The variety of physical dysfunction may be different versions of the transmission process, called "uni-disease."[145]

(8) Human behavior and functioning is a natural process which has much in common with other forms of life.
    Bowen theory uses biological rather than pyschiatric or psychological terms to highlight the similarities between the

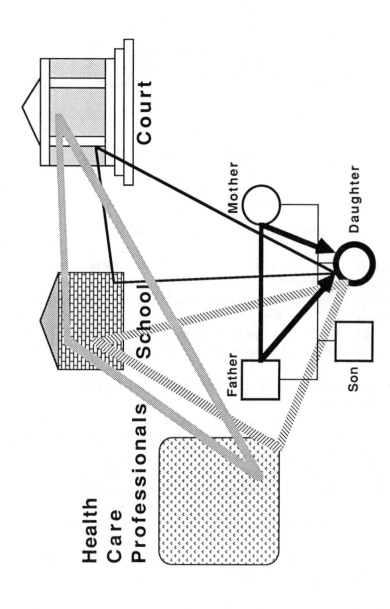

Figure 5.10 Triangles in Larger Systems

Influence Of Sex And Birth Order

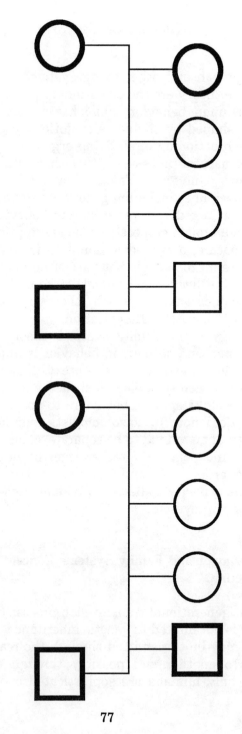

Figure 5.11 Sibling Position

human organism and other living systems. The foundation stones of the theory are the evolutionary process and natural systems. Human behavior, while having many unique aspects, was shaped by the same evolutionary processes that shaped the functioning of all living organisms. Disease is an outcome of natural processes rather than of specific causes.

Georgetown University Family Center has reached out to scientific disciplines including genetics, immunology and animal behavior in order to place human behavior and human problems in a broad perspective. One assumption is that man is part of nature; a related assumption is that clinical dysfunctions are a product of that part of humans they have in common with other forms of life.[31,145] The main focus in therapy is to reduce anxiety (which relieves symptoms) and to increase basic level of differentiation.

Sociobiology[329] and family systems theory both assume that all human and subhuman behavior is understood most objectively in an evolutionary context. However, there are differences between sociobiological theory and family theory. Sociobiology links specific behaviors to specific genes. Family theory does not. To sociobiologists individuality means the capacity of an animal to be separate, competent, and able to function independently rather than be governed by the needs of a group. In family systems theory individuality refers to the capacity to be an individual while being part of the relationship system.[143]

Animal Behavior and Family Systems Concept of Dysfunction

The multigenerational transmission process (Figure 5.7) includes but is not limited to genetic inheritance. Processes and behaviors may be transmitted through the reactivity of one organism to another and possibly through differentiation level. Not only humans are sophisticated enough to be affected by their mothers' and grandmothers' reactivity. Below are descriptions of family transmission in rat families and reactivity in rhesus monkey families.

When pregnant rats were placed in an enriched environment, their offspring exhibited a thickening of the brain's cortex.[66] When females were impregnated by males who had also been in an enriched environment, succeeding generations had increasingly thicker cortices. Vertical transmission of acquired ulcer susceptibility occurs in rats.[277] An altered susceptibility acquired by environmental manipulation (premature separation) during postnatal development in one generation, is transmitted to the offspring in the next. Behavior of adult rats was modified by the experiences their mothers had as infants, whether the mothers were natural or foster mothers.[65] The experiences which an animal has in early life influence her unborn descendants two generations away by nongenetic transmission mechanisms.[64] It seems to me that transmission is determined in part by reactivity.

If the rat is too distant a mammalian cousin, consider Suomi's[299] fascinating studies on the reactivity of our closer cousins, the rhesus monkeys. Suomi's work is relevant to human reactivity, and thus to biofeedback training which monitors and facilitates a change in reactivity. The systems concept of dysfunction in humans and its transmission across generations between people in important relationships is in some ways similar to physiological and emotional processes which are transmitted in rhesus monkeys' important relationships. The implications for combining biofeedback and family therapy are mine.

Reactivity Similarities in Rhesus Monkeys and Humans

Human and monkey infants and children have similar responses to new or challenging situations, and also have some

responses which are stable over time. Human infants and
children withdraw in the face of novelty, adapt poorly to
environmental changes, and are extremely intense in their
reactions. Some tend to inhibit exploration. Some characteristics are highly stable over as many as twenty years. "Highly
inhibited" children showed unusually low variability in heart
rate under challenging conditions, and high levels of urinary
cortisol.[299]

Long-term studies of laboratory-born and raised rhesus
monkeys also show individual differences in response to environmental novelty and/or challenge. Behavioral and physiological measures consistently distinguish "high-reactive"
subjects of various ages from those less reactive. The behavioral characteristics change with age although the physiological characteristics seem stable during that time. Behavioral
and physiological differences in response to challenge carry a
strong genetic component but their expression can be consid-
erably modified by specific environmental factors.[299]

(a) Neonates (1–4 weeks old) who are highly reactive display
poor visual and auditory orienting responses to test stimuli,
have relatively poor muscle tonus, and neonatal motor reflexes which appear and subsequently disappear later than in
low reactives. They also show "difficult temperaments." (b)
Infants (1–6 months) who are highly reactive show extreme
and prolonged rises in plasma cortisol and ACTH following
short-term separation from their attachment objects (mothers, surrogates, or peers) as well frequent "self-directed" behavior and infrequent or nonexistent locomotion, exploration,
play and vocalization. ("Self-directed" behavior refers to behaviors directed towards self, such as clasping, grasping,
mouthing.) Their heart rates are high and stable during the
initial hours of separation. (c) Juveniles (6 months–3 years)
who are highly reactive reveal similar responses to separation
and new environments; however, their "self-directed" behavior
is less frequent and their cortisol and ACTH levels are lower
than earlier in life in response to similar environmental chal-

lenges. Highly reactive juveniles also exhibit stereotypic
(fixed, unvarying pattern) motor activity. During periods of
separation they have lower levels of CFS norepinephrine (NE)
and higher levels of metabolite MHPG than the less reactive
subjects. (d) Adolescents (4–5 years) who are highly reactive
continue to exhibit the basic patterns of hypothalamic-pitui-
tary-adrenal activation and increased CSF NE turnover in
response to separation as occurred in earlier life. Their behavioral reactions are characterized at this stage by general agi-
tation and excessive activity, usually involving stereotype
movements.[299]
Of particular interest to me in terms of biofeedback and
family therapy is that Suomi and his colleagues report they
have not yet found any behavioral or physiological indices
that reliably discriminate between high-reactive monkeys and
normals *during stable* baseline periods. Behavioral and physiological parameters differentiating high-reactive subjects of
all ages from their normals are observed only during times of
environmental challenge. These physiological and behavioral
patterns of difference in response to challenge among high
and low reactive rhesus monkeys are similar to those observed in human infants and children.[299]

Effects of Mothers' Reactivity on Infants' Reactivity
Caretaking and personality characteristics of rhesus monkey mothers as well as their infants' temperamental qualities
are the same basic factors that appear in humans. A mother's
characteristic reactivity to stress could affect her infant's
reactivity. Infants of highly reactive mothers: (1) might learn
to react to certain events as a result of their mothers' "predictable disruption" after those events; (2) might model their
mothers' patterns of responses; (3) might be unusually sensitive to the emotional arousal state of their mothers and tend
to "match" that state; (4) or, highly reactive mothers may be
more likely to rear highly reactive infants. Siblings and half
siblings are much more likely to have similar reactivity than

are individuals who are not close blood relatives. There is significantly more similarity in levels of cortisol, ACTH, heart rate and levels of both disturbance and coping behavioral patterns following challenge among siblings and half siblings than among unrelated individuals.[299] Individual differences in the intensity and duration of the reactions, as well as in the range of conditions that trigger these reactions may in part be genetically determined.[298]

The fact that the mother's reactivity affects the offspring's reactivity (in rhesus monkeys) has also been observed in clinical situations of family therapy with and without biofeedback. One family systems theory explanation for the similarity in biochemical and psychological measures between mother and offspring may be the level of functioning of the mother. In humans this would be referred to as level of differentiation. Biofeedback instrumentation monitors the reactivity of both mother and child, or of any persons in an important relationship system, as part of the therapeutic process. Biofeedback for parents to decrease their reactivity decreases the reactivity and symptoms in children (See Chapter 12).

*Effects of Foster Mothers' Reactivity on
Infants' Reactivity*

Rhesus monkey infants of different genetic pedigree are raised by foster mothers who were selected based on their own relative reactivity during the environmental challenges, and the patterns of maternal care they had displayed toward their own offspring.[299] In neonates, genetic pedigree was a more important factor in determining their reactivity than the characteristics of their foster mothers. However, later in their first 6 months of life, the infants' genetic pedigrees were of little or no importance while in their home cages with their foster mothers. That is, when the infants were in stable housing, in a familiar environment and in the presence of a "competent" (not over-reactive) caretaker, genetic pedigree was of very little or no importance.[299]

Differences occurred when, beginning at 6 months of age, these infants were separated from their foster mothers for four 4-day periods. During the separation these highly reactive infants returned to their presumed biological predispositions. However, in the presence of their foster mothers, reactivity differences between infants almost disappeared, even though major differences were displayed just before and right after each reunion. The availability and/or activities of the foster mothers overrode the different reactive tendencies of the infants. Infants with highly reactive foster mothers had higher levels of disturbed behavior during the separations. Their high level of disturbed behavior carried into the reunion periods, especially after the later separations.[299]

Reactivity of Caretaker Is Key

Suomi[299] and colleagues conclude that under familiar, stable, and generally nonstressful circumstances an infant's patterns of behavioral development were better predicted by the style of caretaking than by genetic pedigree. However, in environmental challenge while separated from its mother or foster mother, the infant's characteristic behavioral and physiological reactivity responses were most determined by its genetic pedigree. When the infant was returned to its caretaker, still during somewhat stressful circumstances, the caretaker's reactivity became the predominant influence on the infant's behavior, apparently overriding both infant reactivity and caretaking style.

In a nutshell, these findings suggest that rhesus monkey infant reactivity most likely has a genetic basis that is clearly expressed under conditions of challenge, but that is largely irrelevant in the absence of challenge and that can be overridden — even under stressful conditions — by the behavioral reactions of its caretaker, especially when the caretaker is physically present . . . both theoretical and empirical efforts to predict and understand individual differences in reactivity -- be they monkey or human – must go beyond simple models and single-factor experimental designs . . .[299]

These findings fit with family systems theory and biofeedback clinical observations. People's behavior at different levels of differentiation can appear similar in periods of calm. However, in periods of "challenge," those less well differentiated may become symptomatic, overeactive, or dysfunctional.

Suomi's observations are similar to those seen in human clinical biofeedback. For instance, (1) reactivity is more readily seen during chronic or acute stress, but not necessarily during stable periods of life. Physiological biofeedback baselines (See Chapter 6) do not necessarily show significant differences unless the baseline includes a "challenge" or stressor. (2) A person's characteristic reactivity (high or low) seems to remain stable over time. (3) Reactivity of one person affects another, such as between parent and child, between spouses or lovers, employer and employee. (4) In humans, as in Suomi's rhesus foster mothers, the non-anxious person can over-ride the anxiety or reactivity in another person in the system by staying calm and in close contact. (5) Biofeedback and family therapy to reduce the over-reactivity of one person can optimize the reactivity or health of another person in that unit. (6) Clinical change is facilitated by a non-anxious or non-over-reactive clinician or coach.

Over or Under Reactivity in the Immune and Family Systems

Behavior and physiology are determined in large part by the reactivity of those important in the emotional system. These complex forces also act on natural systems within each individual, such as the immune system. The immune system is an exquisite example of the delicate balance of forces, and of the consequences of too much or too little reactivity. If the immune system (See Chapter 2) either undereacts or overeacts, the person becomes ill. Parallels exist with over-under reactivity in family systems processes.

Through the immune system, the organism distinguishes self from non-self. For instance, if the immune system is overeactive in response to an antigen from outside (exogenous) the body, the result is allergy. If it is overeactive in response to an antigen that is in the body (endogenous), the immune system attacks its own body's healthy tissues such as cartilage in joints and the result is an autoimmune disease such as rheumatoid arthritis. If it is underactive, or unable to destroy an outside antigen, for example bacterium, the result is infection. And, if it is underactive to an abnormal antigen inside the body, the result may be cancer.[161]

Family emotional processes may have indirect and direct effects on immunity.[106] Basic assumptions to conceptualize a direct biological link between family emotional process and susceptibility of family members to diseases resisted by the immune system are that (1) the family emotional system plays an important part in the emotional process of individual family members, (2) a family member's emotional process can affect his/her immune status, and (3) observed emotionally-induced changes in immune function are clinically significant in the onset and course of immune-associated diseases. Rigorous research is urged to determine if

> ... the same experiences which can promote the lifelong behavioral characteristics of lower differentiation may also promote lifelong immune characteristics of inhibited immunity.[106]

In summary, family systems theory helps to view the individual in evolutionary terms both within the larger natural systems of which he/she is part, as well as the smaller natural systems within each individual. Like the viewer at the

Smithsonian's Air and Space Museum, a biofeedback clinician who uses this theory, has both a wide and narrow lens
through which to understand symptoms and coach the person.

6

THEORY AND PRACTICE

Importance of Theory – Any Theory

Around the country hundreds of centers and thousands of clinicians are providing biofeedback training based on a variety of theoretical models. However, many do not have their own theoretical base and tend to use whatever is new or has worked elsewhere. One risk to this approach is that, without realizing it, inherently conflictual techniques may be used inappropriately together. Quality programs around the country are guided by clearly conceptualized theoretical models which are internally consistent and which help determine what, when, how and where something is done. These models also make it possible to collaborate productively with other disciplines such as medicine, dentistry, physical rehabilitation, and physical education. In addition, theory makes clear the boundaries of biofeedback as an adjunct to physical, emotional, social or cognitive changes. Below is an example of a program I developed (1975–1988) based on theory.

Rosenbam's Biofeedback Program: Self-Regulation and Family Systems Theory

This program is described in detail not because it is the "ideal" or the "only" useful one, but because I know it best

87

since I established and directed it. I used techniques developed by investigators and clinicians elsewhere, as long as the techniques were consistent with family systems theory (See Chapter 5). My Georgetown Biofeedback Program was the first of its kind in the Washington metropolitan area. Almost 3,000 people have received clinical services (See Chapter 12). The clinical work was initially based upon the model[40,292] developed by Thomas H. Budzynski, Ph.D. and Johann Stoyva, Ph.D. which focused on optimizing physiological balance. Other techniques (e.g. quieting reflex,[294] open focus[84]) which fit conceptually in systems thinking were included later. Budzynski and Stoyva's approach was attractive because of the notion that biofeedback could facilitate an arousal change. This relates to the importance in family systems theory of reducing overreactivity. My clinical goals are to honor the specific physiological dysfunction or presenting problem of the person, facilitate changes in arousal, and keep the broader natural systems framework as a blueprint.

At the time I established the Georgetown program, biofeedback was provided in relatively few centers around the country and often only in research. It was my intent to establish the best possible biofeedback clinic with a focus on symptomatology, yet also think and use family systems theory, considering the family and other relationship systems as the intervention unit. Bowen theory suggests that it is not possible to change the functioning of someone else directly. It is, however, possible to change one's own functioning and thereby, in certain circumstances, change some aspects of the system(s) of which one is a part. Modulating one's own reactivity is essential in this effort. To maintain or enhance the change, it is very useful to observe and understand the part that important systems (e.g. family, organization, athletic team) play in the course of the disorder and the part that the dysfunction plays in the system(s).

Becoming more observant about automatic physiological, emotional, social, behavioral, and cognitive patterns of functioning increases self-regulation. Self-regulation is not only managing one's physiology enhancing cognitive functions, and optimizing performance, but also regulating one's self in relationship to family and the other systems of which one is a part of. Biofeedback clinicians have studied family systems. Patients already in psychotherapy elsewhere may continue with their clinician which requires extra coordination and caution that the goals of each intervention do not conflict. Comprehensive care includes attention to (and referral to specialists when appropriate) nutrition, exercise, and myotherapy.[214] Coordination with primary care physicians and/or with physicians at Georgetown University Medical Center is also part of comprehensive care.

Biofeedback Training: Family Diagram; Baselines; Frequency, Duration, Follow-up

Before biofeedback training begins, a family diagram is done and a baseline with biofeedback instruments is performed as part of the intake process. I start the family diagram by asking information about the person seeking biofeedback and include demographic data, the history of the person, the history of the problem, and the efforts to treat it. Then I broaden the questions to include information on at least three generations. Usually people who come for biofeedback for a physiological symptom are more open to providing the family history if the questions initially focus on health. Then I expand the questions to include education, occupation, religion, geographical moves, concerns, and emotional processes. Gathering additional extended family (great grandparents, uncles, aunts, cousins and others) information can begin at intake and is continued throughout the intervention process in subsequent sessions. Level of reactivity in the family, level of reactivity and differentiation in the important individuals, level of functioning, previous problems and how

the family (including some who have died) coped are among
the processes examined. Belief systems, fears, expectations
and hopes all play a part and are inquired about at intake or
later. An experienced clinician who knows both family theory
and biofeedback can do an initial family diagram and obtain
significant information in 10–20 minutes (Figure 6.1). A clinician without the theoretical orientation can not use the diagram even if the information is collected.

With repeated or chronic life stressors and incomplete recovery from the overactivity in the person and in the family
system, eventually a symptom is manifested (Figure 6.2). The
symptom can be physical, emotional, social or cognitive (See
Chapter 5).

During baseline the sensors are attached to the person as
during biofeedback training, but the person does not receive
feedback (information) of the physiological activity until the
baseline is completed. When a person is under acute stress,
or when a person is presented a laboratory stressor during
baseline, the physiological recovery pattern (Figure 6.3) can
manifest itself in several ways. Indicators may recover
quickly and the person returns to homeostatic balance (Figure 6.3.a). Other patterns exist: the recovery may be partial
(Figure 6.3.b), or recovery does not occur and the person's
reactivity remains high long after the stressor is terminated
(Figure 6.3.c), or the reactivity may continue to escalate even
after the stressor is eliminated (Figure 6.3.d). This physiological variation in patterns can also be observed in the way a
person deals with relationships. The individual either is flexible and "recovers" from the stressor and/or relationship process quickly, or is less flexible and the other patterns occur.
The least flexible, most adaptive person also absorbs the
anxiety or reactivity of the important others in the system.

Extreme difficulty in recovery results in sustained, intense,
frequent, and long lasting symptom(s) in that person.
During biofeedback sessions, the sensors (for muscle activity,
blood pressure, skin temperature and others) are placed on

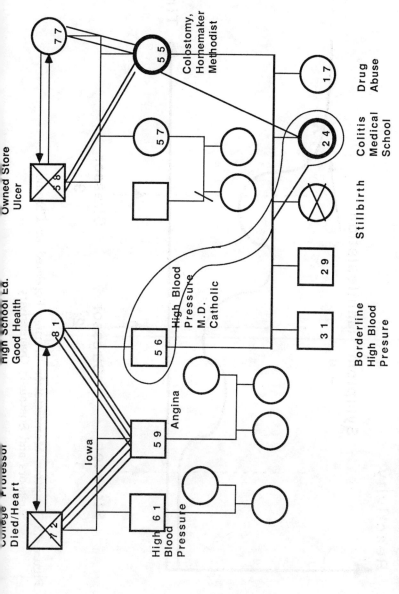

Figure 6.1 Initial Family Diagram

91

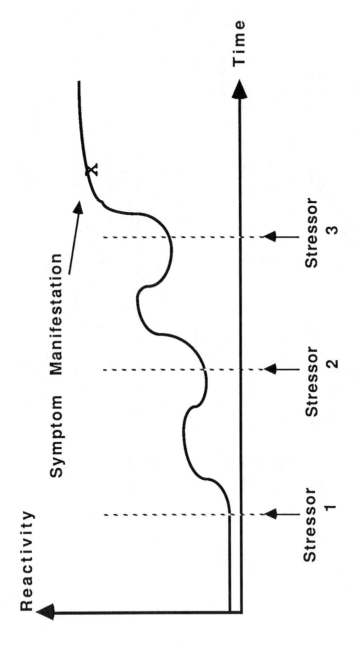

Figure 6.2 Symptom Manifestation During Repeated or Chronic
Stressors and Sustained Overactivity

92

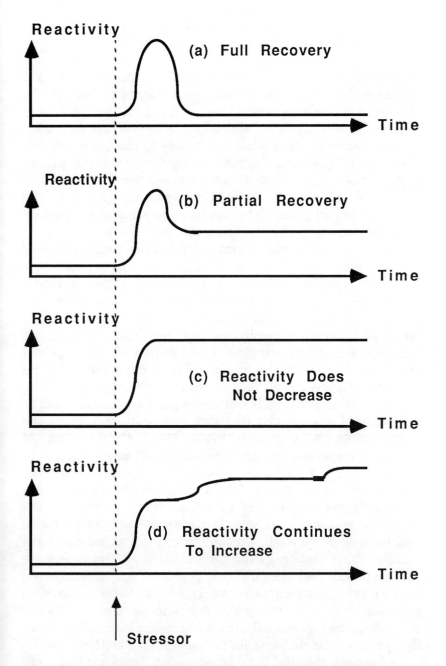

Figure 6.3 Psychophysiological Recovery Patterns after Stressors without Biofeedback.

93

the person. The biofeedback instruments amplify biological signals and display them as auditory, visual or tactile signals. The signals, such as sounds, are recognized by the person learning to self-regulate. Normally the person sits in a comfortable reclining chair when the goal is to change reactivity. The type of feedback depends in part whether the person prefers to learn self-regulation with eyes open or closed. The person, by learning to regulate a signal (e.g., decrease the sound), is in fact learning to regulate a physiological function such as increasing skin temperature.

Figure 6.4 shows psychophysiological reactivity, recovery patterns after a stressor, and the effect biofeedback can have on reactivity. Biofeedback, by facilitating self-observation and awareness of some of these automatic responses, can assist in their self-regulation and thereby decrease pain, stress and some psychophysiological problems. Biofeedback can facilitate recovery (reduce the duration of the response) and thereby prevent the involvement of more physiological systems (Figure 6.4.a), it can reduce the intensity of the reactivity (Figure 6.4.b), it can decrease that person's usual or chronic level of reactivity (Figure 6.4.c), or it can prevent the overeactivity and symptom (Figure 6.4.d). Combinations of the above responses are also possible as well as a reduction in frequency of the response. Mastery to criterion means the person has learned to regulate a physiological response to a certain degree within a certain time. This, as well as the ability to regulate reactivity and recover from overeactivity can be useful by itself. In addition these skills can be a vehicle which encourage the person to "grow," become more differentiated, and take difficult positions and actions, even at the risk of becoming temporarily symptomatic. Progress is evaluated then not only by the ability to be calm, but by the willingness to proceed with one's life course even if temporarily symptomatic and unable to "master" physiology.

Biofeedback training is designed to facilitate long term self-regulation in daily life without instrumentation. Daily home

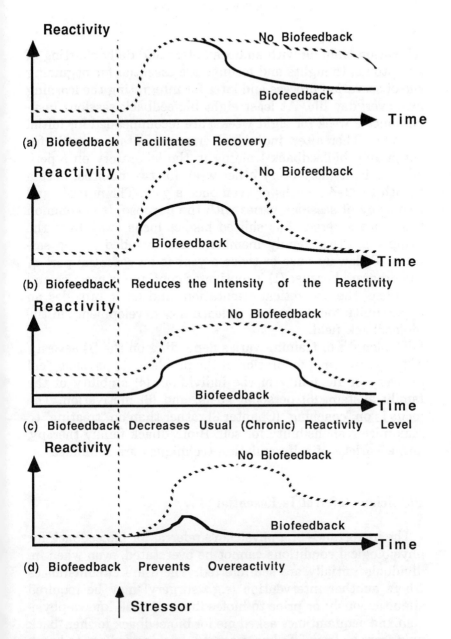

Figure 6.4 Reactivity. Recovery Patterns, after stressors, and Possible Effect of Biofeedback on Reactivity

95

relaxation training with audiocassettes and daily charting of symptoms, thoughts and feelings are essential for beginning the observation process and later for integrating the learning into everyday life. At least eight biofeedback sessions (usually once a week for eight weeks) are recommended for initial training. Thereafter, individual arrangements are made for continuing biofeedback training in the laboratory on a periodic basis, usually every other week for two months, once a month for 2–4 months or even once a year. The number and frequency of sessions varies with the purpose. It is common that once a person has shifted his/her focus away from the symptom, other family member(s) are included in the sessions. Follow-up once or twice a year is an essential part of the program because (1) it motivates continuous practice and broadens the theoretical orientation, and (2) it provides an opportunity for the person to learn new developments in the biofeedback field.

The length of training varies depending on the (1) severity of the symptom, (2) duration of the problem, (3) physiological recovery or flexibility of the individual, (4) stability of the family system, (5) personal goals, and (6) motivation. The focus is on "coaching" (Chapter 8) rather than on "treating" to maximize responsibility for self. Biofeedback family therapy, and a variety of self-regulation techniques are combined.

Physician Referral Is Essential

The importance of a physician's referral for biofeedback for physiological conditions cannot be overstated, even when individuals initially are self-referred. There are circumstances where another intervention (e.g., surgery) may be required simultaneously or prior to biofeedback. A well known-physician and acquaintance asked me for biofeedback for her "back pain from a strain." I almost agreed, but decided not to break my own rule and insisted on her physician's referral. She was diagnosed with advanced lung cancer and died a few months later. While it would have been possible to work with biofeedback for pain management for cancer, or even to see if the immune system could be enhanced, it is not the same as working on pain from a "strained back."

Although biofeedback is often provided in a medical setting, there are potential medical implications or precautions. The physician referral may be acceptable with less intense screening requirements in some circumstances, for instance, (1) for children and adults in educational institutions, (2) for athletes, (3) for musicians or artists looking to maximize their functioning, (4) for people in psychotherapy who are being monitored to understand emotional patterns in relationship processes but who are not trying to change physiological conditions, or (5) for executives and/or staff in organizations.

Optimize Exercise and Nutrition

Exercise and nutrition are important factors reviewed as part of the biofeedback training. It is common that appropriate exercise leaves one "feeling better." Research shows that exercise has a positive effect on stress indicators including neuromuscular tension, resting heart rate, anxiety, and some stress hormones. Exercise has been successfully used to treat mild to moderate depression. A well-conditioned heart can better withstand the effects of stress. Exercise, as a part of daily lifestyle, is a coping strategy with concomitant health benefits.[71] Comprehensive overviews can be consulted.[215,186]

Many gaps exist in the research linking exercise and improved emotional state. For example, the question of how exercise mediates stress, is controversial. The impact of individual differences and the question of optimal dosage are unanswered. To study the effects of different intensity of exercise on the relaxation that follows exercise, Edwards[71] and colleagues are comparing post-exercise relaxation measured by two-site EMG, oxygen consumption, and psychological questionnaires following 15 minutes of treadmill exercise at low, moderate, high and maximal intensities.

How best to maximize nutrition effects and combine exercise and biofeedback is important. Dietary guidelines vary[82,188] and include government recommendations and less common approaches such as the macrobiotic diet.[150] The clinician provides assistance to coordinate the medical, exercise, nutrition, biofeedback and family systems effort.

Precautions and Contraindications

Biofeedback is one of the safest procedures ever developed for facilitating physiological and other changes in self, but it is necessary to take into account potentially harmful iatrogenic effects. Iatrogenic effects are those symptoms or ailments, though unintended, that are caused by the medical treatment itself. These are uncommon in biofeedback, and common in medical treatment. For instance, diuretics to treat hypertension can produce compensatory mechanisms. Anti-vasoconstrictors such as hydralazine and reserpine have serious side effects often requiring additional treatment. The compensatory increases elicited by diuretics and anti-vaso-constrictors must then be suppressed to prevent the return of high blood pressure. This can be accomplished by beta-blockers such as propranolol which block the "beta-receptors" for epinephrine and norepinephrine. But, beta-blockers themselves evoke new compensatory mechanisms and iatrogenic effects.[286]

Precautions for biofeedback are much less complex, and include: (1) understanding enough about the symptom, the person and the family system in order to anticipate otherwise unexpected physiological and/or relationship changes directly or indirectly related to the presenting problem, (2) communicating this and any other important information to the person (and, when appropriate to significant others to maximize responsibility for self), (3) collaborating with primary care or referring physician(s) and other appropriate health care professionals, athletic coaches, and teachers, (4) explaining that biofeedback itself is not producing the result; rather, biofeedback provides an opportunity to observe and learn to alter self, and (5) teaching an understanding of the relevant physiological mechanisms. With these provisions, biofeedback is a cost-effective, efficient, harmless procedure for enhancing responsibility for self, health and functioning.

The importance of thorough examinations before biofeedback and at subsequent appropriate intervals by the primary care physician cannot be over stated. For instance, it is theoretically possible that a person receives medical attention for an injured arm and then continues with biofeedback as part of the treatment plan. If that person has been doing biofeedback relaxation for years and been feeling well from it a simultaneous but separate condition (such as lung cancer) might stay undiagnosed. Theoretically it is possible to temporarily mask an undiagnosed condition and thus delay proper medical attention. In sickness or in health, biofeedback is best used in collaboration with appropriate medical attention.[101]

Another issue is the notion that because self-regulation is possible, anything and everything can be regulated, and if not, the person is creating the problem (See "Over-under Responsibility" in this chapter). Symptoms and dysfunctions, viewed with a natural systems perspective (Chapter 5) are not "caused" by any one factor. A variety of processes, within and outside the individual, past, present and anticipated future contribute to function and dysfunction of the system and of the individuals in it.

Prescribed, Over-the-Counter, and Illicit Drugs;
Other Substances

Luthe[166] and the BSA Medical Precautions and Complications Committee warned that if biofeedback improves homeostatic balance in the organism, an individual may require less medication of any kind, and maintaining the same dose could in fact result in a technical overdose. Such medications include those routinely used for essential hypertension, diabetes, or hypothyroidism.

The use of other substances such as caffeine in medications, methylxanthine in chocolate, alcohol and tobacco are sometimes strongly discouraged from the beginning of biofeedback training. The interaction of substances with biofeedback may affect the laboratory training sessions, home practice, and long-term aspects of self-regulation depending on what substances have been used, how much, and when.

Biofeedback cannot be expected to be useful during the actual period of intoxication or over-medication. Of course the effects vary. Having two cups of coffee just prior to a biofeedback session prevents a deep shift in physiology. Being totally intoxicated prevents everything other than sleep. Being dependent on small but daily use of tranquilizers may make each session less productive but may in the long run have a positive cumulative effect and make it possible for that individual to decrease or eliminate the unwanted medication and/or illicit drugs.

Paradoxical effects of prescription drugs and withdrawal symptoms must also be considered. For instance, some tranquilizers taken over an extended period of time actually produce hyperarousal (over excitation). Some prescriptions for headaches, especially if they contain caffeine, seem to produce or trigger the next headache even though they produce some relief of the headache experienced at the moment. Withdrawal from the medication can also initially trigger more severe and frequent headaches. Frequently when people are referred for biofeedback they are unaware they are taking a drug that increases SNS activity. Those medications some-time contribute to the problem and make biofeedback train-ing difficult. The *Physician's Desk Reference*[213] is a very valuable tool for the biofeedback clinician. Sometimes I en-courage people to read the side effects description to moti-vate them to practice biofeedback, to encourage them to discuss this with their physician, and to understand the limi-tation the prescription may present towards successful bio-feedback training and long term self-regulation.

This chapter briefly summarizes some precautions, but I wish to emphasize that it is precisely the harnessing of this potential for change which is one of the greater challenges and accomplishments of biofeedback.

Precautions for Specific Conditions – Examples:

Diabetes. An important precaution is to have orange juice, sugar, or commercially available dextrose available to use after a biofeedback session to prevent a hypoglycemic epi-sode. An additional precaution for some persons at risk for hypoglycemia is to have a responsible adult nearby during self-regulation practice. This precaution is modified as the person becomes more expert at recognizing important cues in his/her own body. Physician collaboration is essential.

Ocular hypertension. A person with systemic hypertension (in the entire body) may also have ocular hypertension, which is a specific and different problem. In the eye, the person can have ocular hypertension, which shows higher than normal intraocular pressure (IOP), or if the IOP is even more ele-vated, it can be an indicator of glaucoma. If the systemic hypertension is decreased with antihypertensive medication (or with biofeedback) and there is also ocular hypertension, the pressure within the eye may remain high and the im-balance between intraocular and blood pressures can cause restriction of blood flow to parts of the optic nerve. The person could thus lose visual function.[342] Again, collaboration with a physician, and in this case also with a vision care specialist, can determine whether there is ocular hypertension and how to treat it separately to prevent complications from providing biofeedback for systemic hypertension.

Psychiatric and Other Contraindications

Biofeedback may be contraindicated in profound mental retardation, some congenital disorders, or chronic organic brain disease. It may likewise be contraindicated in conditions where the brain is affected by some external agent such as a CNS infection, certain head injuries, and poisoning.[90]

The idea that biofeedback is contraindicated for some psychiatric problems (e.g., psychoses and paranoia) varies based on the theoretical approach. Biofeedback and especially imagery may promote further loss of contact with reality. Deeply disturbed children and adults can benefit indirectly from biofeedback with family therapy provided to responsible persons in the family to improve the system function.

Precautions Related to Family Systems

It is important to keep in mind that the symptom, although lodged in one individual, can be an indicator of family functioning, not just of individual functioning. Thus, if the symptom changes in one person, the family system may experience changes in balance. Some members of the family may find the change in certain family system processes pleasant or uplifting; others difficult or at least surprising or unsettling. Change sometimes triggers unexpected reactions in the person changing or in other emotionally important persons. For instance, Mr. B. had made very good progress with biofeedback training for a severe back problem which had required surgery twice. His pain had decreased, and his mobility increased. It became clear that one of the deep conflicts and anxieties was that his sister, whom he had not seen for 14 years, was in state mental hospital. He felt responsible because his now deceased parents had expected him to "look out" for her. He was afraid he would not have the "heart" to leave her there if he saw her. His wife's position was that he had to choose between bringing the sister home or having the wife stay. It became clear that a visit to the sister was essential. As he prepared to go, his back pain became acute again and was as intense as when he had needed surgery, but he nevertheless decided to go. After an emotional reunion with his sister, he offered to visit again, but did not invite her to live with him and his wife. He experienced enormous relief and noticed he was relatively pain free. The family system precautions for biofeedback do not imply abstaining from either biofeedback or family systems "interventions." The precautions imply need of knowledge about biofeedback, physiology, and family processes.

Whether the symptom is physical or manifests itself in relationship problems, when one person is making an effort to change, the system may change too. If a person with severe migraines gains some control over them, a spouse who previously was primarily a "helper" may now develop a discomfort or symptom such as mild hypertension. This is usually a temporary "exchange" or "traveling" of symptoms and both persons (such as spouses, or parent/child) improve their functioning with enough family systems work and biofeedback. In general, in my clinical practice experience regarding symptom change, I have found that the symptom in one person in the family does not travel to another person when one self-regulates with biofeedback. On the contrary, when one person in the system has improved his/her own functioning and decreased symptoms, the system can function better. It would be interesting to study families in clinics where family systems theory is not used and see if the findings are the same. That is, when one person decreases symptoms, does the functioning of other persons also improve?

Traditional psychoanalytical orientations posit that when biofeedback helps remove a symptom in one person, there is no real change because the symptom will re-emerge differently in the same person. A similar opinion[143] is that biofeedback may result in an "exchange" of symptoms within the family. That is, that a symptom will emerge or re-emerge in a different person in the family. This is transitory if the intervention is thorough, and can be an indicator of progress in the system.

Paradoxes in Self-Regulation: Over-Under Responsibility

The notion that a dysfunction happens by itself and is unrelated to anything that the person does reflects a sense of under-responsibility which makes it unlikely to initiate or maintain biofeedback training. On the other hand, a sense of over-responsibility (that the condition arises primarily or exclusively out of one's own doing) is also immobilizing.

The concept that some form of self-regulation is possible tends to trigger conflicting and/or contradicting responses. The relief that a condition might be ameliorated or eliminated is sometimes accompanied by guilt that one may have played a part in its development or course. A corollary to that response is anxiety that one may not be able "to do" the self-regulation well enough to change the course of the condition. The anxiety can then slow the training process. This heightened awareness and erroneous sense of over-responsibility can be further complicated by family systems processes. In different but complementary ways biofeedback and family theory focus on observing and changing self, which can, if inappropriately managed, increase dysfunctional over-responsibility.

The challenge and precaution is to find a way to assume responsibility for self in a way that enhances freedom, sense of self and life direction, without assuming the guilt, self-blame and anxiety which make self-regulation very difficult. Personal experiences provided me these lessons: self-blame or accepting others' view of the possibility that one intentionally creates a dysfunction is counter-productive; a sense of omnipotency is dysfunctional; mortality is certain; and, biofeedback self-regulation with an appropriate perspective can be extremely useful.

Applications

Biofeedback can be used for the following broad categories (See "Quick Questions and Answers"): (1) to facilitate and enhance peak performance, for instance, of athletes, astronauts, musicians, performers, surgeons; (2) to improve cognitive processes; (3) to manage stress; (4) to manage pain and chronic disease; (5) to promote physical rehabilitation; (6) to decrease the intensity, frequency, severity of psychophysiological disorders; (7) to alter the psychoneuroimmune and neuroendocrine systems; (8) to alter autonomic responses in healthy people; and (9) to manage relationship processes.

People without a specific physiological disorder do biofeedback in conjunction with family systems work to better observe and regulate their own responsiveness. Becoming more observant about automatic physiological, emotional, social, behavioral and cognitive patterns of functioning increases the ability to regulate one's self in relationship to family and organizations.

In summary, biofeedback with a systems way of thinking is used for a variety of symptoms. The goal is to honor the specific physiological dysfunction or presenting problem of the person, yet always keep the broader natural systems framework as a blueprint. Harnessing the potential for change is one of the greater challenges and accomplishments of biofeedback interventions. The emotional, psychophysiological, cognitive or behavioral symptom that a person brings to the biofeedback laboratory is the product of processes in a variety of natural systems: (1) between subsystems, (2) between emotionally important individuals in the same generation, (3) between larger family, work, and social systems in the same generation, and (4) between and across two or more generations. A sense of under- or over-responsibility (that the condition arises primarily or exclusively out of one's own doing) can lead to immobilization and prevent successful biofeedback training. A natural systems view of the problem provides a balanced perspective about the symptom. An explicit theory, a research orientation, and a well defined self are essential for a clinician to keep the processes on target.

7

RELATED
SELF-REGULATION
TECHNIQUES

Biofeedback-assisted relaxation often includes a variety of self-regulation techniques which can also be used without biofeedback. Some believe that when biofeedback is used with other self-regulation techniques that it is no longer "real" biofeedback (See Chapter 9). That is a limited view. The effectiveness of the techniques is in part related to the severity of the problem. Mr. G., is a computer scientist, recently married, age 32, and his wife had just become pregnant. He had unsuccessfully tried relaxation on his own. All day he felt he could not breath, often gasped for air, had rapid heart beat, felt dizzy and unable to concentrate, and his productivity declined. A thorough cardiac and pulmonary workup revealed good health. The Georgetown pulmonary specialist noticed that he was hyperventilating and referred him for biofeedback.

During the biofeedback intake I obtained his three generation family diagram (See Chapter 5). His mother had died instantly in a car accident when driving to her parents' home when he and his siblings were children 20 years ago. His parents were then separating. His younger brother and baby sister had some injuries. He managed to get out of the car, and gasping, ran for help. When I gently asked about some connection between gasping and the current stress, he saw none. However, he was very interested in biofeedback as a technique to deal with his symptoms, learned to decrease arousal with relatively few sessions, and then generalized it to work. He learned diaphragmatic breathing and other relaxation techniques. He talked about his past and current life situations during part of each session. He began to observe that his physiological readings on the biofeedback instrumentation changed when he talked about certain topics. His wife came twice and they talked, while connected to the instrumentation, about both families of origin, the problems, the strengths, his mother's death, their hopes for their own marriage and the expected baby. He did very well with less than 10 sessions. The gasping stopped except when under considerable stress at work, during which he could decrease the intensity and frequency.

Many self-regulation books and tapes are available and can be used with or without biofeedback. The intent of this chapter is to provide an orientation to the kinds of techniques that can be combined with biofeedback. People who are interested in relaxation techniques without biofeedback may want to examine those before beginning biofeedback. However, even self-regulation techniques without biofeedback can be more productive with the coaching of a professional.

The term "biofeedback-assisted relaxation" usually refers to using biofeedback instrumentation to facilitate low arousal. In addition, relaxation cassettes and the other exercises can be used for home practice to augment the effects of biofeedback training and facilitate the transfer of the learned response to everyday situations. Examples of self-regulation techniques include progressive relaxation,[130] autogenic training,[166] relaxation response,[19] quieting reflex,[295,294] open focus,[84] systematic desensitization,[337] imagery,[155] cognitive restructuring[176] and stress inoculation,[177] blends of physical and mental exercise,[30] and a variety of breathing techniques. Biofeedback clinicians use none, one, or a combination of these techniques depending on the problem, the intervention and the theory.

Combining family systems theory with biofeedback I developed a self-regulation blueprint which guides one to: (1) become aware of family patterns and processes which trigger over-responsiveness; (2) become aware of type of physiological responsiveness; (3) become aware of early signals of it; (4) plan a strategy; (5) visualize a difficult situation while maintaining a calm physiology (or while observing physiology with biofeedback instrumentation); and, (6) act with a plan in specific family or work system processes.

This requires an understanding of the emotional, social, and cognitive processes in addition to physiological processes. For example, a woman in a custody struggle over her daughter learned a variety of self-regulation techniques. She then developed a strategy to deal with her former husband (with whom the daughter lived) to see the daughter more often. She practiced recognizing her own reactivity and calming it down in the biofeedback laboratory. She then found ways to do the self-regulation techniques before and during visits with her daughter. She was able to deal with daughter and former husband in ways which led to greater access to the daughter.

In most circumstances a carpenter could prevent or ameliorate his headache with biofeedback skills, but he learned that sometimes only by dealing with the work system (which in this instance had similarities to his family system) could he get beyond the symptom. He learned that if he took firm positions and talked with each conflictual person separately, he could decrease a two-day pain within two hours.

A variety of cognitive exercises help clarify which aspects of a person's reactions in daily life are based on feelings and which on thoughts. The exercises include observing self and when appropriate changing automatic thoughts, "distorted thinking" and covert assertions. Techniques such as systematic desensitization, stress inoculation, visualization, covert reinforcement, covert modeling, and paradoxical intention are useful. A description of fifteen styles of "distorted thinking" includes: "filtering" (magnifying negative details and ignoring positive aspects of a situation), "polarized thinking" (situations are good or bad without a middle position), "overgeneralization" (assuming the same situation will continue to occur), "mind reading" (thinking one knows what other people are feeling without their saying it), "catastrophizing" (expecting disasters), "controlling fallacies" (either feeling controlled by others, or feeling omnipotent about others' lives), and "blaming" (inappropriately holding others responsible for one's own situation).[141] These exercises can be done with or without biofeedback. Responsible clinicians choose techniques which are consistent with their way of thinking as well as with the client's personal orientation and goal.

8

PROFESSIONAL TRAINING

Conceptual Framework Determines Biofeedback Professional Training

Dr. M., professor many years, is ready for a second career along with his second marriage. Because his wife has a special opportunity to advance her career in the Washington, D.C. area, they are moving here. He asks about the Georgetown Biofeedback Professional Training Program and the requirements to train or become associated with it. My parents would have had a spontaneous response – to be a "Mensch" (person with integrity), an important requirement in life. I think this as I elaborate with "fancy" terms about motivation, differentiation, knowing oneself, principles, integrity, beliefs, theory, certification and more.

Conceptual frameworks or theoretical orientations determine clinical and research activities as well as the direction of training programs for professionals who plan to use biofeedback in their work. I believe it is important to inquire about a theoretical orientation prior to a professional training commitment. Many programs do not describe the theory that guides them. An "eclectic" program may reflect flexibility of thinking but, as in psychotherapy, "eclecticism" may also indicate lack of direction or lack of a rationale for the curriculum. Combining activities with different conceptual frameworks can result in a mixture of inherently contradictory techniques.

Certification by BCIA

An important criterion in selecting a place to train is whether professionals are certified by the Biofeedback Certification Institute of America (BCIA). Certification and re-certification every four years became necessary in a field that includes a wide variety of professions. Preparation for the written and a practical examination can be obtained in many ways. The American Association of Biofeedback Clinicians publishes a journal and has advanced certification. The National Commission for Health Certifying Agencies approved BCIA, an independent organization incorporated in 1981, and granted it full unconditional membership in 1983. The areas of study for certification by BCIA include instrumentation, clinical interventions, physiology, professional conduct, and health and education. (See "Quick Questions and Answers" for details and BCIA and BSA address and telephone.)

Personal Training, Defining Self and Expectations

Experienced biofeedback practitioners, including the author, who participated in drafting the BCIA requirements for professional training standards considered personal biofeedback training an essential requirement for certification. Georgetown Family Center has a long tradition of requiring personal training and development by professionals who plan to practice family systems therapy. An individual's ability to define a self, and to define his/her own personal and professional positions and boundaries is essential. The more differentiated the professional, the more he/she can facilitate a change in the person seeking "coaching," treatment or training. A well differentiated, well functioning person can maintain a non-anxious presence, be flexible, and be appropriately responsive to situations and persons rather than automatically reactive.

My biofeedback training builds on defining self. The clinician's family processes can be a "resource" and a differentiation "stage." Professionals have the responsibility to know something about self and own family processes and to take this into account when "coaching." An awareness of own limits, problems and levels of reactivity is important. Flexibility and ability to self-regulate physiologically even in stressful situations is useful. A well defined self does not "inflict" that self on others and focuses on process rather than content.

The provider's expectations and beliefs about whether biofeedback training "works," even when the provider is a researcher can affect learning. For instance, in 1970 Taub[303] and his colleagues initiated a pioneer program to develop techniques that would enable most people to self-regulate skin temperature though biofeedback. He found that with one research assistant 19 of 21 consecutive subjects did learn to self-regulate skin temperature. With another research assistant only 2 of 22 subjects learned. After methodically eliminating possible factors which might explain this large difference he found that one assistant believed in the feasibility of learning self-regulation with biofeedback, and the other did not. He called this the "person" factor.

The Clinician as Coach

In a systems framework, the clinician facilitates changes and teaches rather than "treats." The term "coach" is accurate: it does not imply that one person is "healing" another. The "coach's" theory provides a blueprint for action. The

integrity, internal consistency and differentiation of the biofeedback clinician or "coach" are important forces which can
give direction to the entire process including the use of instrumentation (See Chapter 8). I believe it is a given that
psychotherapeutic relationships are special relationships regardless of the therapist's theory. Coaches of athletic teams
also have special relationships to their teams. This does not
mean that the relationship is the most important factor in
change. Kerr[143] claims, however, that in biofeedback as in
other psychotherapeutic relationships, "people may derive
more benefit from the relationship with the technician than
from the technique." That position does not seem to take into
account that early biofeedback research showed that rats
could learn to blush in one ear and monkeys could increase or
decrease their heart rate. Learning was not based on a "personal relationship" with the researcher.

   Also, biofeedback with psychotherapy, regardless of which
theory, is not provided by technicians but by licensed health
professionals who in addition are certified in biofeedback
practice. When biofeedback is *not* part of psychotherapy, it
can be responsibly provided under the direction of a licensed
health care professional (e.g. physician, physical therapist). In
my view, to assume that the effectiveness of biofeedback
depends entirely on the clinician (that biofeedback works
only because of the relationship) is the opposite but in some
ways the same as to assume that the clinician has no role
(that only the instruments contribute to the process). An
example of the assumption that only the instruments are the
essential component in biofeedback training is the recent
National Research Council[68] report which considered even
relaxation techniques to be confounding variables (See Chapter 9) rather than inherent processes. Both views disregard
essential aspects of the biofeedback intervention. Expert biofeedback clinicians and investigators know that neither view
is accurate in responsible, successful biofeedback training.

   In my experience, the clinician's self definition, cognitive belief that self-regulation is possible, personal physiological self-regulation mastery, focus on ideas, and a detached, interested observer approach facilitate changes in others. These are crucial regardless of other credentials. The relationship with the clinician or coach is not the focus of the intervention, but rather the important processes and relationships in the client's family and organization systems.

Rosenbaum's Professional Training Program

The program offers to professionals, not technicians, the resources and opportunity to develop the skills necessary to integrate biofeedback into clinical practice. It focuses on professionals who are already licensed or certified in their own diverse fields, and makes occasional exceptions based on clarity about theoretical orientation, long term commitment to biofeedback and self-regulation, and curiosity about natural systems.

The training is based on the clinical method and way of thinking I developed, anchored in family systems theory. It includes a broad range of applications in hospitals, out-patient facilities, physicians' and dentists' offices, schools, athletic programs and organizations. The opportunity to identify, observe and regulate one's own reactivity is essential for differentiation and for becoming a responsible, effective clinician. The professional's way of thinking about the instrumentation is as important as the technical aspects of the instrument. A research orientation (theory, curiosity and openness) to clinical practice is encouraged. The goal of the program is not only to train professionals, but to expand knowledge. Background in natural systems thinking is not required, but those who become interested usually participate beyond the guidelines required for BCIA certification. The Program is designed to prepare persons to take the BCIA exams and to provide opportunities to develop a consistent conceptual model for personal functioning and clinical practice.

A meaningful professional training component was the yearly meeting on "Physiology and Relationships" which was largely developed by Friesen, then Training Coordinator. It evolved, through the Biofeedback Seminar Series, out of the previous annual "Biofeedback Conference," which I began in 1976. The meeting was designed for those interested in (1) applying biofeedback within the context of family systems theory and (2) conceptualizing bridges between biofeedback and family systems theory. The meeting reflected the complexity and evolution of professional "biofeedback training" at Georgetown.

The staff made considerable efforts to use biofeedback as an adjunct to other disciplines including medicine and education. Biofeedback expands but does not necessarily substitute for any ongoing intervention and education. Interdisciplinary collaboration was encouraged in practice and research and takes into account that the human organism contains smaller subsystems and is also part of larger social systems. It invited the collaboration of the behavioral sciences as it studied the person in the context of the family and larger natural systems. Systems thinking includes the awareness of the role of interdisciplinary collaboration and multifactorial explanations of problems. However, it goes beyond and views all phenomena as part of natural systems and their interconnections. The cells, the organs, the subsystems, the person, the family, and society are all mutually interdependent systems. They are linked in the present, and through evolution, to personal family ancestors and to other forms of life over eons of time.

Biofeedback professionals can have a special relationship to medicine. Teaching medical and dental students can help integrate basic sciences and behavioral medicine and provide a broader view of the organism as a part of natural systems. Since 1975 I initiated and still continue the medical student biofeedback elective. Georgetown Medical School is one of very few in the country which offers a biofeedback elective.

A newer aspect of training is being considered to facilitate responsible psychotherapists to use biofeedback to monitor people as an additional window to observe reactivity and self, without necessarily providing biofeedback training to the client. I believe that if important BCIA requirements are met, professionals and consumers would benefit.

Consultation to Organizations

Private and public organizations are alert to the costs of stress on productivity in work and personal life. Around the country substantial programs for organizations developed. The Georgetown Biofeedback Program provides a broad range of services to organizations: (1) consultation and biofeedback intervention for individuals about their personal functioning, health and work problems; (2) biofeedback and stress management for the entire organization tailored to its goals; (3) conferences on systems theory, organizational stress and human functioning; and (4) long-term follow-up and consultation to persons and organizations.

Individuals sometimes begin with their own personal training, proceed to professional training, and then set up a biofeedback program in their organization. From this process the notion developed to require that professionals not only learn from Georgetown but contribute their own expertise in an effort to advance their goals, the program, and the biofeedback field in general. This provides opportunities for faculty and participants to expand theoretical and practical knowledge.

Clinical and Research Opportunities

The program is clearly anchored in theory and is also flexible and responsive to people and ideas. It offers a variety of opportunities for training and participating in both clinical and research activities. The opportunities are structured such that qualified, motivated persons can move to different levels from volunteer work to post graduate training, clinical internships, "research rotations" (which include development of and participation in special interest research projects) and becoming staff.

9

RESEARCH AND EVALUATION

Definitions

In research questions determine findings, and the investigator's theoretical orientation and conceptualization of human phenomena determine the questions. Evaluating the findings without thinking about the theories, concepts and questions which gave rise to the findings misses the point of clinical research and evaluation. It is also important to distinguish between limitations in research methods and ineffectiveness in biofeedback interventions.

The same methodologies that are used today to question the value of biofeedback were used forty years ago to question the value of penicillin. Small one-day doses of penicillin were not effective in treating bacterial disease and investigators claimed it did not work. Some biofeedback interventions provided without trained clinicians, with too short and too few sessions have also been judged ineffective.

"Research" loosely means at least three different kinds of activities: *Basic research* helps understand nature and is designed to examine basic questions (e.g. what happens in the body when biofeedback is used). *Clinical research* promotes clinical goals through refined observations of the effects of interventions. It can be designed to develop new or better applications, new questions, and new ways of thinking. In biofeedback research the clinician can coach the person to observe reactivity and flexibility in self, and to master self-regulation skills. Biofeedback instrumentation facilitates verification by both the clinician and the consumer. *Evaluation research* is designed to answer questions such as whether an intervention (such as biofeedback) works, under what conditions, and whether it is more cost effective than other interventions.[242,339] Much biofeedback research is in fact evaluation research, but is written as if it were basic research.

"Does biofeedback work?" requires additional clarification. Shellenberger and Green[270] state that biofeedback as such is not what "works" anymore than a stop-watch makes a runner run faster. It is the information produced by the stop-watch which, in part, provides the effect (faster running). Similarly, it is the biofeedback equipment information which provides, in part, the effect of increased self-regulation. If feedback of information is not a treatment, and if it has no specific effects, then what *is* the treatment? The active ingredient that alleviates the symptom or enhances the performance is self-regulation (the essence of clinical biofeedback) which is learned through training. Biofeedback equipment produces information that enhances the training effect through verification.[270]

Early Biofeedback Research

Approximately twenty years ago less than a dozen scientists and clinicians in different parts of the country separately developed what later became known as biofeedback. Later, others' over-enthusiasm and over-expectation was followed by appropriate and sometimes inappropriate criticism. By 1980 biofeedback had attracted thousands of clinicians and researchers. The issue of the effectiveness of biofeedback captured the attention of a wave of well-intended investigators who began to study often minute and relatively unimportant details of very complex processes. Some pains-takingly peeled off one "variable" at a time, until after peeling the onion to its final layer, they found "no treatment effect." This they reported in the scientific literature. Roberts[226] claimed that research has not demonstrated "that biofeed-back is an essential or specific technique for the treatment of any condition." Furedy[99] held that it is inappropriate to evalu-ate the overall effectiveness of biofeedback rather than the specific effects of treatment. Thoughtful health professionals, potential biofeedback users and many consumers who were already benefiting greatly from biofeedback were puzzled. Recently, a few voices doubting the value of microscopic stud-ies have been heard more clearly. In addition, some clinicians and investigators have begun to study complex biofeedback training processes.

Recent Clarification of the Crucial Importance of Concepts

Shellenberger and Green[269] made several outstanding con-tributions to biofeedback research. Most significant is their focus on conceptual issues. One of the most readable biofeed-back publications in the last twenty years, it is of interest to biofeedback clinicians, researchers, and consumers. Twelve methodological and conceptual errors led to poorly designed and misinterpreted research: (1) insufficient number of train-ing sessions; (2) insufficient length of training sessions; (3) no homework exercises; (4) failure to maximize internal locus of control; (5) failure to provide adequate cognitive support; (6) double-blind designs; (7) failure to establish training criteria; (8) use of relaxation control group for comparison to biofeed-back training; (9) failure to incorporate mental/emotional var-iables in biofeedback training; (10) failure to establish reliability measures and confidence bands; (11) failure to con-trol for adaptation; and (12) failure to train for mastery which involves mastering, through a multicomponent approach, self-regulation skills gained through practice of many techniques (such as biofeedback, breathing techniques, visualization, and psychotherapy) including physiological and cognitive ones. They describe what they consider successful biofeedback training:

> Researchers who accurately conceptualize biofeedback as a training process have the goal of voluntary control of psychophysiological process for symptom reduction. The independent variable is self-regulation.[269]

The drug research terms "specific" and "non-specific" effects have to be clearly defined for biofeedback research.

> Because the biofeedback instrument and the signals from it are not chemicals and have no power in themselves to create physiological change, it seems obvious that these elements of biofeedback training produce *non-specific effects* ... And because relaxation, motivation, expectations, and beliefs do have the power to change physiology via neurochemical links between cortex, limbic system, hypothalamus and the pituitary-adrenal axis, these variables do have *specific effects* ... 'nonspecific effect' is whatever impact the biofeedback machine might have, and ... 'specific effect' is the effect that relaxation, expectation, instructions, and all other training variables and cognitions have on physiological change and symptom reduction.[269]

Conceptualizations are the basis of accurate models which lead to correct research design, results, conclusions and advances in the field. Faulty conceptualizations lead to faulty models and confusion. Information from biofeedback equipment is scientific verification of self-regulation skills.[270]

BIOFEEDBACK EVALUATION RESEARCH

It is necessary to ask important questions, to understand the issues and to have clarity of purpose. Without these, evaluations can lead to erroneous conclusions.

Special Evaluation Issues

There are special difficulties in evaluating biofeedback. It lies at the interface of three conflicting research methodologies: psychology, medicine and biology. The evaluation has been affected in two ways: some statistical and experimental design approaches have led to overlooking important effects and, conceptual misunderstandings have stemmed from a lack of theory. I believe that an evolutionary natural systems perspective may eliminate some conflicts in the future.

Classic Experimental Design and Clinical Significance

Classic experimental design requires: (a) randomization of subjects, (b) appropriate use of statistics, (c) statistical significance of the findings, and (d) consideration of errors in statistics. This chapter draws on books[242,339] which are clear for the non-researcher and accurate for the researcher.

Randomization is the use of chance selection in the assignment of potential subjects or patients to experimental and control groups. "Random" does not mean haphazard. On the contrary, extreme care is taken that every person has the same chance as any other person to be selected for either the experimental or control groups. This method guarantees that the groups at the start of the study do not differ from each other in significant ways. Yet, a statistically significant result can be irrelevant to clinical practice if it has no substantive or clinical significance.

Another issue is treatment definition. Many biofeedback studies include as treatment failures data on subjects who had not completed the protocol. To judge biofeedback as "not working" when the person has not completed the protocol, is the same error as concluding that a medication does not work although the person did not take the prescribed amount.[285] Other important issues in evaluating biofeedback research are that (1) ignorance of a mechanism of action is not equal to a lack of clinical efficacy; (2) the administration of biofeedback training is not equal to the subject's learning to criterion (e.g. the person demonstrating hand warming to a specific temperature within a specific amount of time); (3) untrained therapists are not equal to trained therapists; (4) statistical significance is not equal to clinical significance; (5) the laboratory setting is not equal to the clinical setting.[285]

Decision Errors and Statistical Significance

In scientific research, one can never prove that a hypothesis is true. Rather, scientists must be content to reject in statistical terms what is known as a "null hypothesis" – that the intervention had no effect. There are two types of statistical decision errors. The first, called a "false positive" or Type I error, is the error in concluding that the treatment had an effect when in fact it did not. The second, called a "false negative" or Type II error, is the error in concluding that the treatment had no effect when in fact it did.[242,339] Statistical analysis helps avoid wrongly rejecting a truly valuable intervention and wrongly accepting a truly worthless intervention.[121]

Quasi-Experimental Designs

When classic experimental design cannot be done, the evaluator must choose one or some combination of procedures for approximating the "equivalence" of control and experimental conditions achieved through randomization. These procedures are called "quasi-experiments." The term does not imply that the procedure is inferior and inappropriate. When properly conducted, these experiments can provide information which is free from most, if not all, confounding (complicating, confusing) processes. [242,48]

At times it may be necessary to choose an imperfectly designed experiment that can be generalized into clinical practice rather than a well designed experiment that would produce a sure finding too narrow to be useful. Because biofeedback "treatment" has a variety of components (such as relaxation, imagery, breathing techniques), experimental designs that have not considered this are inappropriate. Designs which provide treatment, then remove it and see if the condition reverts to its original form (called A/B/A), also miss the point. In successful biofeedback intervention, learned self-regulation cannot be "removed" anymore than a person who learns to ride a bicycle can unlearn it. The person may not use the bicycle, but the learning is not "removed."

CLINICAL RESEARCH

How Much Is Enough?

The time frames of the biofeedback research studies affect the results. For example, in diabetes, short-term biofeedback treatment (less than two weeks) tends to be less effective than long-term (three months). Another example is providing two 20-minute frontalis EMG biofeedback sessions to healthy college students, perfectly randomized into experimental and control groups and then concluding the EMG is not useful for pain management because neither group changed the EMG level.

A dose-effect relationship in psychotherapy has been documented[126] in a meta-analysis synthesizing studies of over 2400 patients. By 8 sessions, approximately 50% of patients were measurably improved, and by 26 sessions approximately 75% were improved. More chronic patterns of illness tended to require more sessions. It is hard to change behavior and physiology. Attempts to change too quickly may fail to produce effective and lasting improvement.

Change through biofeedback may require 10–50 sessions spread over 3-12 months under the supervision of a trained therapist. Yet professional journals have reported findings of "no difference" based on interventions of less than 6 hours of treatment and the administration of "treatment" without trained clinicians.

Clinical Single-Case Studies

Single case experimental designs can be appropriate. Distinct from anecdotal case studies, they are well-grounded in clinical research,[124,10] and provide useful information when there are repeated measurements of physiological, behavioral or cognitive variables. For large, clinically relevant effects, single case results may be generalizable or replicated in well-designed large experiments. They are the cutting edge of clinical research.

Time-Series Designs

Time-series designs[48,124] involve periodic measurement before, during and after an intervention. They may involve single-case or large sample studies with or without a control group. They are particularly useful in biofeedback studies where frequent periodic measurement is part of the treatment process. They allow repeated measurement and help control for periodic influences such as body rhythms, current stress level, and recent health history. Time-series studies help to uncover the sources of variability, periodic phenomena in symptom and drug diaries, and diaries of reactivity to family processes over time.

Chronopsychophysiology

Chronopsychophysiology,[187,293] biological periodicities (cycles) which affect a variety of psychological and physiological processes, is extremely important in medical and behavioral research. Circadian rhythms are changes that occur in plants and animals during a 24 hour period. The responsiveness of the organism is significantly affected not only by circadian rhythms but also by ultradian (more than 24 hrs.) and infradian (less than 24 hrs.) rhythms. The rhythms (e.g., metabolic, glandular, and sleep) are associated with the earth's rotation and often persist through alterations caused by travel. Solid research takes body rhythms into account.

BIOFEEDBACK WITH FAMILY SYSTEMS THEORY: IMPLICATIONS FOR RESEARCH

Different theories (e.g., individual human functioning, family systems functioning) lead to different research questions and designs.

Research Questions Based on Family Systems Theory

Most of my clinical work is done with a theory-based research orientation. One goal is to attempt to understand and organize the complex human phenomenon in an evolutionary natural systems framework. The following are examples of the kinds of questions which emerge from this orientation: (a) How is responsivity transmitted from one person to another? (b) How can individual variability of response be accounted for? (c) How are family process patterns transmitted between and across generations? (d) What are the characteristics of families of individuals who do not master psychophysiological self-regulation? Of those who master it easily?

The theory guides clinical biofeedback questions and observations. (1) Focusing exclusively on symptom reduction or cessation in one member of the system, misses the part that the symptom and individual play in the larger system (e.g., family, work, team). (2) Reducing a symptom may be associated with a temporary increase in, or the perception of, other symptoms or discomforts in that person. (3) Reducing a symptom in one person may be accompanied by a temporary increase of psychophysiological symptoms, behavior or relationship problems in other members of the system until the system achieves a new balance. (4) Looking at changes in time perspective, long-term effects may be observed even when short-term effects are unquantifiable. Psychophysiological or other changes in members of the unit can be indicators of change in the person motivated to alter self. (5) The point in the system for which the intervention is requested is not necessarily the best place to observe the intervention impact. For example, a narrow focus on self-regulation of a headache may also decrease high blood pressure in that person. (6) Facilitating symptom decrease may only be the first step in self-regulation by motivated individuals to maximize their responsibility for self, integrity, coping capacity and performance. Similarly, improved functioning of one individual may also improve the functioning of the system of which the person is a part. (7) The family unit is the client even when only one individual participates in the intervention. Conceptualizing a "control group," "matching" family systems as well as individuals is a challenge. If the experimental design does not deal with such theory-related issues the integrity of the intervention is compromised and there may be no effect to measure.

New personal computers and biofeedback instrumentation packages can monitor several people simultaneously on a total of eight physiological parameters. Although there are technical limitations, information can be gathered while the people are relaxing (shifting arousal), or interacting. The computer automatically records physiological indicators and provides a graphic assessment of changes and trends over time. It enhances the potential for developing hypotheses and more systematically linking physiological facts with family diagram information in the context of natural systems thinking.

THE NATIONAL RESEARCH COUNCIL REPORT: A FAILED REVIEW

A recent National Research Council (NRC) report,[68] *Enhancing Human Performance: Issues, Theories, and Techniques,* reviewed evaluations of various performance enhancement techniques including biofeedback. In my opinion the report is an outstanding example of evaluation problems I described. The NRC findings were presented at a press conference and reported in *The Washington Post*[282] and *Psychology Today.*[224] The U.S. Army Research Institute sponsored the study and defined and guided the review committee's tasks regarding the Army's interests in enhancing human performance. However, the report states that the objectives of the committee were to

> provide an authoritative assessment ... for policymakers in research and development who are consumers of the techniques, as well as to consider their possible applications to Army training.[68]

The report evaluated biofeedback for two areas: improving cognitive and motor skills, and stress management.

Its general conclusion on the improvement of motor skills is that "the effects of biofeedback on skilled performance remain to be determined."[68] More specifically, biofeedback "has generally failed to clearly demonstrate biofeedback effects, because (1) the effects ... are often confused with broader therapeutic techniques such as progressive relaxation or mental imagery ... and (2) the specific performance to be enhanced by means of biofeedback is often poorly described ..."[68]

The report apparently considers relaxation and self-regulation techniques confounding or confusing variables rather than inherent components of biofeedback training.

The report cites Lawrence's later[154] review in which he concludes that subjects trained with biofeedback performed better in rifle shooting, playing stringed instruments, learning (reaction time), sleep, motion sickness and manual dexterity in cold environments, but discards the findings because they are based mostly on single case studies, and some investigators had failed to replicate the initial results. However, Lawrence and Johnson's[153] earlier review based on studies which are now old, is quoted heavily. Selected, more current, studies are also cited and the report states that EMG has been used to enhance musical skills, increase hip flexibility to prevent hamstring injury, improve sprinting performance, and improve hand-eye tracking and lateral balancing performance. With "few exceptions" EMG levels in the targeted muscle group were reduced. However, the results "must be viewed cautiously" because the results were not significantly different from those of "placebo controls (i.e., relaxation-meditation)."[68] In the end, the report agrees with the 1977 review that "EMG biofeedback offers little promise for performance enhancement in stressful situations."[68]

In my view, one major problem with this analysis, is that relaxation and self-regulation techniques are not placebos.

Experienced practitioners and investigators know that they produce real, measurable psychophysiological effects. Those techniques are also not "confounding effects" but part of the biofeedback intervention as practiced by many skilled practitioners. (See Shellenberger and Green.[269,270])

Program evaluators have to be careful not to distort the programs they are evaluating by redefining treatments. Throwing out essential parts of the program to achieve methodological purity is counterproductive.

The report uses the criterion that relaxation and related self-regulation are not part of biofeedback. Inappropriate criteria are also used for other forms of biofeedback, such as temperature. For instance, subjects learned to decrease pain and improve dexterity by increasing their digital skin temperature while in 37 or in 50 degree Fahrenheit indoor environments.[140] Personally, I find it fascinating that subjects learned to warm their hands outside an arctic tent in Alaska.[139] Although the report apparently recognizes "impressive performance gains achieved with hand warming,"[68] it criticizes that subjects in the 6 studies reviewed were not trained in the "specific skill of temperature *estimation*." Instead, the subjects were "trained to increase temperatures by *relaxing*." Of course they relaxed. Any experienced clinician knows that is the first, essential step. The important findings for the report are that people had less pain and more dexterity. That does not mean that if the Army wants to train people to estimate their finger skin temperature that it cannot be done. Studies with people with diabetes, for instance, show that people can even learn to estimate their blood glucose levels.

The report concluded:

> Until more is learned about the most effective EMG, EEG (alpha or theta), and HR levels for the execution of particular tasks, biofeedback research in these areas should not be pursued.[68]

How, I wonder, can more be learned without research?

The second area of the report concerns biofeedback for stress management. Here the report has important sections from a comprehensive and important paper on stress, arousal and performance prepared by Levine. However, the review of the studies on biofeedback and stress management concludes that (1) some studies report that subjects can decrease EMG or increase Alpha, and some not, (2) that this may or may not mean the subjects relaxed, and (3) that even when this happens, it generally has no effect on stress reduction and performance.[68(p.123)] It cites, primarily, two 1977 reviews (one is the same paper by Lawrence and Johnson, 1977)[153] and one more recent, also by Lawrence, 1984.[154] The conclusion that "There is no evidence to indicate that biofeedback training—induced reduction of EMG activity or increased percentage of EEG alpha—has any effect on stress or on performance under conditions of stress" (p. 123) is made citing only Lawrence's review of 1984. Those preparing the report apparently were not familiar with the work of others such as Manuso.[173] Manuso showed that a comprehensive stress management program at the Equitable Life Assurance Society improved the health of employees. Established in 1975, this was industry's first in-house biofeedback laboratory. People were "taught to achieve and maintain low levels of psychological and physical arousal in the face of stressors." For every $1 the corporation invested, it had a $5.52 return.[173]

The report concludes that stress has a "cognitive core."[68] I believe that a position which posits a one-cause model ignores the large biomedical literature on mind body interaction (which apparently the committee chose not to review).

Many of the studies cited as evidence that biofeedback did not work were from a review by Lawrence and Johnson[153] of papers reviewed beginning in 1970 under a five-year program supported by the Defense Advanced Research Projects Agency. (Both Lawrence and Johnson are of the U.S. Army Research Institute and both were on the NRC committee.)

Thus, aspects of the NRC 1988 findings are easily 13–18 years old. If 1970 is an approximate beginning of clinical biofeedback (BSA was formed in 1969), biofeedback is now 18 years old. Yet the NRC report is based on studies that were performed when the biofeedback field was from 1–5 years old.

Some investigators have updated their work, but the NRC report does not reflect this. For instance, the early research by Cowings and associates[58] of 1977 and 1982 is cited, but not the more recent such as I included (Chapter 11) regarding NASA's successful 1987 findings.[60]

No doubt the NRC Committee would discard those as it did their earlier findings because the training is "autogenic feedback training" (AFT), not biofeedback alone, and other findings suggest "that biofeedback may have little to do with Cowing's findings." The report considers relaxation, progressive relaxation and other similar techniques as placebos or "confounding" variables, rather than integral parts of clinical biofeedback. The committee does not refer to either BSA or BCIA. It also does not include any biofeedback clinicians.

Some positive findings are rejected on the basis that even when biofeedback produces effects, not everyone can learn the techniques. The report consistently refers to the high stress of soldiers in combat but ignores the times soldiers are not in combat and the enormous number of staff (technicians, drivers, office workers, and others) who support the combat soldier and whose performance under moderate stress may be improved by biofeedback. Recovery from stress and prevention of chronic stress-related disorders can in the long run enhance performance.

The report references stress management with EMG and EEG biofeedback only.[68] It does not reference the common use, singly or in combinations, of EDR, skin temperature training, blood pressure, and heart rate in addition to EMG for baselines and stress management. It does not indicate that people respond to stress in different ways and that good practitioners choose the type of biofeedback to facilitate appropriate individual learning. Looking at how the average person responds to a single type of biofeedback obscures effects.

In my view evaluation research on biofeedback requires comprehension not only of the content being evaluated but also of the process, theory and intent of the investigator. This applies as well to reviews of research. To evaluate whether large vitamin pills are hard to swallow when the investigator studied the effect of the vitamins is inappropriate. Otherwise, an evaluation such as the one by NRC[282] which cost $425,000 may not clarify important concerns.

Research Policy: Health Care Costs and Research Investment

The nation currently spends 2.8% of GNP on research and development but only 1.7% of health costs on health research. The total health care cost in 1985 was 400 billion dollars.[283] Some estimates suggest that 70–80% of problems for which people seek medical help are stress related disorders. A conservative estimate[37] is that 200 billion dollars (50% of the $400 billion) are spent annually treating psychophysiological disorders. If two percent of the 200 billion dollars were spent evaluating the biofeedback treatment of psychophysiological disorders the research investment would be 4 billion dollars per years.

At an average of $65/hour and a minimum of 10 hours per "patient," services of 6,000 biofeedback providers cost $390,000,000. Even investing in the evaluation biofeedback 2% of $390,000,000 would support about $8,000,000/year for biofeedback research.

Government and other institutions do not now spend anywhere near such amounts on research and evaluation of the effect of biofeedback training. But the nation may not be able to afford ignoring the 200 billion dollar potential savings from biofeedback in the light of the ever rising health care costs (now over 10% of the GNP and rising), and the cost-effectiveness of biofeedback for psychophysiological disorders.

10

COST - EFFECTIVENESS

Evidence

Biofeedback is cost-effective in a variety of fields. For instance, grounding one flier for chronic, severe motion sickness can represent over a half-million dollar loss. After biofeedback, 85% of grounded air sick fliers returned to flying. Biofeedback can also be cost-effective with very dysfunctional people. Only 12.9% of 68 prisoners were sent back to prison 1 to 3 ½ years after being released, compared to the expected 35.6% (See Chapter 11).

A comprehensive review of the health care literature on biofeedback cost-effectiveness is Carol Schneider's[260] BSA Presidential Address. Biofeedback as part of a flexible multi-component behavioral medicine treatment reduced physician visits and/or medication use, medical care costs to patients, hospital stays and rehospitalization, and mortality, and in enhanced quality of life. I draw extensively from that impressive source. Published data on cost-effectiveness have so far been collected primarily by clinicians. "Cost" and "benefit" are not easily defined. For instance, cost may not include the instrument cost and benefit may not include changes in the quality of life. Dr. Schneider used Shellenberger's and Green's[269] concepts to evaluate successful biofeedback.

(1) *Reduction in physician visits and/or medication use.* (a) Shellenberger and associates found that participants in a

biofeedback program taught in a university showed a 70% reduction in physician visits, and controls showed a 26% increase. (b) Fahrion, Norris, Green, Green and Schnar found that 58% of patients medicated for hypertension were able to eliminate hypertensive medication while reducing blood pressure an average of 15/10 mm Hg. Only 7% showed no improvement. (c) Blanchard and associates found that 64% of biofeedback patients withdrew from second stage medication costing $400 to $1,000 per year. (d) Jacobs found a 63% reduction in outpatient visits and a 72% reduction in hospital days/6 month period in a 500-bed Veterans Administration general medical and surgical hospital. (e) In Mager's retrospective study there was a reduction in medical utilization, prescription drugs, and hospital visits at the U.S. Public Health Service in Baltimore. (f) Wright's patients in the Kaiser-Permanente health maintenance organization decreased outpatient visits by 25% the year following biofeedback.

(2) *Decrease in Medical Care Costs to Patients.* Steig and Williams calculated the estimated lifetime medical savings per patient of 56% decrease in disability payments and an average treatment cost of $8,160. The average estimated lifetime savings was $312,597 per patient. Of Gonick and associates' 235 consecutive inpatients, those who completed biofeedback averaged only 2.6 days of hospital treatment in 5 years post-treatment, compared to 113.7 in 5 years pre-treatment.

(3) *Decrease in Number of Claims and/or Costs to Insurers in Claims Payments.* Steig and Williams estimated lifetime medical savings per patient to be $312,597 after a multidisciplinary outpatient pain treatment program. Charlesworth, Williams and Baer provided a group-based stress management program for 40 hypertensives during the work lunch hour which resulted in a reduction of 62% in insurance claim costs. At the 3-year follow-up 70% maintained significant blood pressure reductions.

(4) *Reduction in Hospital Stays and Rehospitalization.* Jacobs found a 72% reduction in hospital days from 1 year pre- to 1 year post-treatment of 47 chronic pain patients. At 3-year follow-up, the reduction was still 47%.

(5) *Enhanced Quality of Life.* One of the best known studies on enhanced quality of life is Manuso's, which showed that a comprehensive stress management program at the Equitable Life Assurance Society improved the health of employees. For every $1 the corporation invested, it had a $5.52 return. This was industry's first in-house biofeedback laboratory. People learned to achieve and maintain low levels of psychological and physiological arousal during stressors.[173]

Biofeedback for urinary and fecal incontinence enhances quality of life and reduces cost. Whitehead[328] reports effectiveness for 72% of fecal incontinence patients (cost each approximately $600). Biofeedback for urinary incontinence results in 85% improvement and costs about $1,200 per person. In contrast, surgical correction for either costs about $5,000 – $10,000 per person, and prophylactic treatment pads costs about $300 per year for an indefinite time. Perry and Bollinger[212] report a 98% cure rate for urinary and fecal incontinence in 56 patients. They cited Neal Miller's 1985 BSA presidential address who stated that the country could "save $13 billion annually" with biofeedback intervention for incontinence.

Potential Savings: a National Perspective

Using Schneider's review[260] and data from the *Statistical Abstracts of the United States*[284] Brown[37] calculated rough estimates on potential national savings if biofeedback would be used by more people. Extrapolating from small clinical studies to national statistics has serious limitations. However, these dramatic estimates are in line with the data just presented.

For example, in 1984, there were almost 19 million (18,976,000) persons treated for hypertension in the United States. Medication for hypertension can cost $500 per patient per year. Assuming only 50% would eliminate medication after biofeedback, approximately $4.75 billion per year could be saved in medication costs.

Successful biofeedback training may cost $1,000 per year for the **first year only**. Thereafter, follow-up twice a year might cost an average of $100 per person. If biofeedback costs $600 per year per person for the first year, and $100 for each of the next 19 years, the total cost in 20 years would be $2,200. In contrast, the total cost of medication for hypertension in 20 years would be $10,000. For other problems, the savings would be even greater with reduced hospital days.

A conservative estimate is that 50% of all health expenditures are for stress-related conditions. The national total of health care expenditures is $400 billion. Fifty percent, $200 billion, would be the national health care costs associated with stress. Assuming a 4:1 benefit/cost ratio,[260] $150 billion would be saved if all stress-related conditions were treated by $50 billion of biofeedback training. If only 20% did biofeedback, the national health care expenditure savings would be $30 billion. These very rough estimates provide a perspective of the potential advantages of widespread, expertly provided biofeedback training.

Barriers to the Diffusion of Technology

Cost-effectiveness is only one factor that influences diffusion of medical innovations. A National Institute of Health conference addressed policy, research and planning perspectives.[105]

... the relatively high technologies such as large cobalt units and heart transplant systems, which are costly and utilized less frequently, tend to be diffused relatively rapidly. By contrast, less dramatic innovations such as diagnostic techniques, laboratory procedures, and hypertensive therapies, which may be applied in the preventive diagnosis of early intervention stages, tend to be diffused more slowly.[105]

Diffusion of innovation barriers may be related to social systems and communication, as well as to existing investment in prevailing interventions.

Cost-Effectiveness, Theoretical and Research Models

The way cost-effectiveness is studied is also a function of intervention theory. Some physical, social, emotional and cognitive dysfunctions are transmitted within and across generations by family processes. If biofeedback (with family systems theory) of one person prevents or ameliorates certain disorders in future generations, studies require taking into account family transmission processes and long-term follow-up. One member of the family (or system), by changing self, can decrease symptoms and improve functioning in other members of the system (e.g. family, school, corporation, team).

National Health Care Priorities

Senator Daniel K. Inouye has been an advocate of biofeedback care for a decade, for instance during the Senate Appropriations Committee deliberations on the Fiscal Year 1978 budget. In a recent keynote address to the Biofeedback Society of America, he noted that prevention and various behaviorally oriented programs are essential to improve quality of life. With concern he reported that the nation spends "less than 50 cents per capita on prevention in contrast to $1,400 per capita on curative care." He urged BSA members as well as the Society itself to become more active in the public policy arena.

It is very difficult to predict what the next decade will bring to our nation's health care system. I personally feel that we will see ever greater attention being paid to issues such as 'accountability,' 'cost-effectiveness,' and 'quality of care.' I think that in the long run this will be in the best interest of our nation. But, there can be no doubt that in the short term, it will be unsettling to many.[128]

He believes that priority must be given to the health care services that "truly work," such as biofeedback:

It is time for fundamental change in our nation's health delivery system. We must give priority to services that truly work, such as biofeedback care.[128]

11

INTERVENTIONS FRONTIERS

The main goals in this chapter are to transmit my engrossing interest in biofeedback, to provide examples of the broad range of applications (used nationally), and to convey biofeedback frontiers in applications and conceptualizations. Reactivity self-regulation is a basic theme in a variety of intervention frontiers. It is not my intent to review the literature in every field, nor to necessarily select the most representative work. The hope is that the examples are alluring and that the reader will search the expanding literature.

BIOFEEDBACK FOR SUPERIOR PERFORMANCE: THE EXTREMELY WELL

Biofeedback is used by unusually healthy people such as Olympic athletes, pilots and astronauts to maximize performance. It is also used for public school children who are not clinically ill. Not only does biofeedback produce impressive results in treatment for a variety of clinical conditions, it now has been shown to produce positive effects in very healthy people.

Concepts and techniques developed for the unwell expanded and apply for superior performance of the "superwell." As in clinical situations, the more severe or the longer the duration of the process or condition to be changed in athletes and pilots, the longer biofeedback training is required to self-regulate the body/mind successfully. Many of the concepts and techniques which are useful for facilitating peak performance in superior athletes and astronauts are also used in other situations such as (1) enhancing performance in routine activities (school, work) and (2) enhancing the psychoneuroimmune system. The findings with the superwell, now provide reinforcement of the value of biofeedback techniques, as well as new ideas to assist the unwell.

Athletic Peak Performance

This section describes biofeedback for facilitating peak performance in superior athletes. Thoughts and feelings influence sports performance. Syer and Connolly[301] explore possible pathways between thoughts and performance, and provide practical applications to enhance athletic performance. Many of the topics the authors deal with are applicable to performance in ordinary school situations and a variety of work organizations. Themes include body awareness, relaxation and concentration, visualization, analytical thinking ("the two hemispheres of the brain . . . when the left brain hinders . . . when it helps"), dealing with anxiety, attitudes and change, team spirit, competition and motivation. The exercises can be done alone or with the assistance of a coach. Although biofeedback is only mentioned once as a technique which helps to achieve deep relaxation, it is clear that achieving rapid, deep relaxation is the cornerstone of, and point of departure for, most exercises they propose.[301]

What is known about the influence of thoughts on muscles in sports? There is evidence,[225] for instance with karate, that skill does influence muscle innervation during imagery, that this innervation appears specific to the muscle group necessary to execute the task, and that the type of imagery has different EMG effects.

To enhance the likelihood of experiencing peak performance states, the gymnast must possess basic relaxation and arousal skills.[219] When the gymnast is under or over-aroused there may be (1) excessive amounts of muscular and nervous tension, (2) self-doubts or lack of confidence, (3) inappropriate focus of attention, and (4) distractions that interfere with performance. A three stage process allows the athlete to gain control: (1) identification of specific stressors, (2) recognition of stress manifestations and (3) selection of appropriate intervention. Common categories of stressors include the coach, family members in attendance, level of competition, facilities and unfamiliar equipment.

Sime[274,275] focuses on physiological perception as the key to peak performance in athletic competition. By helping the athletes to recognize their own psychophysiological responses such as muscle tension, shallow breathing, palmar sweat, heart rate, blood pressure, and skin temperature, they move toward an objective formula for success. Biofeedback can be used to enhance the awareness and self-regulation processes.

Strong and Wenz,[296] pioneers in biofeedback peak performance, found that common stressors for athletes include (1) ambivalence about participating, (2) watching a rival warm up or perform, (3) worrying about not doing well, (4) participating in opening ceremonies, and (5) not feeling ready. Stress starts early, builds gradually and leads to inhibition of performance. Stress management involves a process of learning to lower inhibiting reactions, "gearing down," and increasing the reactions that actually help performance – "pumping up."

Their major focus with superior athletes is the "gearing down" process. Their concept of fine tuning assumes that athletic performance is an integrated psychophysiological process through the use of both internal and external awareness (Figure 11.1). The fine tuning (1) starts with trial and error learning, (2) shifts to feedback information from signifi-

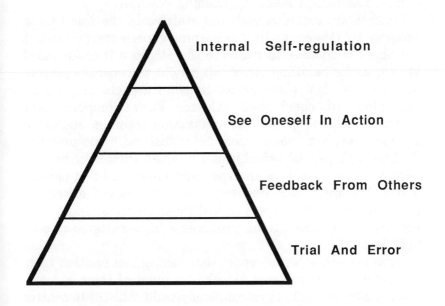

Figure 11.1 A Fine Tuning Model.

From "A Fine Tuning Model for Athletes by D. J. Strong and B. J. Wenz, 1978, unpublished manuscript. Reprinted by permission.

cant others (coaches), (3) proceeds by seeing self in action (video or film), and (4) progresses to awareness and control of psychophysiological functioning.[296] The last stage can be greatly facilitated with EMG and thermal biofeedback and related self-regulation.

They report that: (1) coaches are impressed with the potential of the techniques; (2) successful workshops were taught at the Olympic Training Centers at Squaw Valley, California and Colorado Springs, Colorado; (3) their techniques have been used for eight sport specialties in men and women's track and field, competitive and synchronized swimming, and ice skating; (4) sleep patterns improved the night immediately before competition; and (5) muscle tension decreased and skin temperature increased following training sessions.

Coaches are included with the athletes in the fine tuning program to: (1) de-mystify the learning experience; (2) make it possible for coaches to reinforce the athlete's individualized strategies for handling stress; (3) benefit the coaches personally; and (4) deal with the relationship aspects of joint involvement of coach and athlete. Their comprehensive program includes: progressive relaxation training, autogenic phrases, imaging, biofeedback, individualized home practice, dealing with psychological issues in small groups or in individual discussions with an experienced and qualified person, and follow-ups. They find early and significant effects in performance, and all coaches and most athletes report that the training in fine tuning produces a higher degree of self-regulation.[323]

Even though athletes report that during competition their mental attitudes account for 80% or more of their success, few training programs systematically train athletes to control their mental attitudes.[203] Peper and Schmid[205] developed strategies to enhance peak performance of the United States Rhythmic Gymnastics Team (USRGT). These strategies can be used by any performer such as figure skater, sharp shooter, dancer or musician. Techniques included: electromyographic, electrodermal and temperature biofeedback, progressive relaxation, autogenic training, visualization and breathing exercises, self-monitoring logs during training and competition, energy awareness and other self-awareness and self-assessment tools.[204] The goals are to enhance performance and increase the consistency of the performance. The ability to control thoughts, arousal, and attentional focus seems to be the common denominator in the concentration of winning competitors. Strategies for internal factors that influence concentration include attentional cues and triggers, turning failure into success, and using biofeedback to (1) demonstrate how thoughts affect the body and performance,

(2) monitor physiological relaxation and facilitate shift in arousal at the appropriate time, (3) identify stressful components of the athletic performance during imagery, and (4) facilitate concentration training.[258]

The hand temperature of the 1984 Olympic Rhythmic Gymnasts and Gymnasts at the U.S.A.'s National Competitions was studied just prior and directly after competition with new equipment which does not make contact with the athlete's skin. There appeared to be no correlation between hand temperature and level of competition or cultural background. Often, however, there was a correlation between an extreme drop in hand temperature and a low score.[206,257] In addition to lack of concentration, another variable is lack of self-confidence. Many athletes report they do better in workouts than in competition. It is important that coaches express "similar emotional states in both settings;" the coach's behavior can enhance or hinder performance.[256]

In 1979, Fehmi[85] was invited by the Olympic Development Committee (coaches for developing the athletes who have the potential to be in the Olympics) to do a seven day workshop for middle and long distance runners. He used EMG, GSR and skin temperature, and emphasized EEG biofeedback training. He used biofeedback instrumentation to facilitate a type of attention he developed called Open Focus.[84] Although the 1980 Olympics were subsequently cancelled, athletes' anecdotal reports included an unexpected surge of energy, effortless concentration, and improved performance when they modified the way they paid attention to what they were doing.

More recent anecdotes include Larry Green's "world best" in the half-marathon, who completed the 13.1 miles in 1 hour, 1 minute and 27 seconds in the Citrus Bowl, Florida, December 8, 1984. This still stands as one of the 15 fastest records in history. He wrote to Dr. Fehmi crediting Open Focus training for the way he paid attention, saying, "It was my attentional flexibility that accounted, on that particular day, for my performance more than any other contributing factor."[108]

In 1986 Bob Ward, the conditioning coach of the Dallas Cowboys trained with Open Focus with biofeedback in Fehmi's Princeton clinic. During training he observed that he could reduce the daily 1–2 hour exercise routine he had needed to take care of his own back problem. Instead, with Open Focus he learned to "dissolve" tension in 15 minutes. He reported being able to control his body flexibility by the way he paid attention to it. Fehmi believes that attentional rigidity accounts for illness and "dis-ease" in all cultures. He suggests that the experience of stress is the result, not the cause, of functional (attention) problems.[85]

According to Fehmi and Fritz,[86] "the way we pay attention directly affects our bodies and minds." People who habitually approach new tasks with intense effort and narrowly focused orientation have greater difficulty and progress slowly in biofeedback training. Their performance and health also suffer. Open Focus has as its goal an effortless orientation to the biofeedback task as well as to any wakeful activity. To achieve the open focus attention, one learns to allow awareness to include all perceptible events simultaneously. Exercises include questions like "Can you permit your attention to be equally and simultaneously spread out among body feelings, thoughts, emotions, sounds, while you continue to read?" Attentional flexibility is the goal. Symptom remission and performance enhancement are seen as side effects of the optimization of attentional function.

One of my current hypotheses is that the family's emotional state and behavior (even if not attending the athletic event) affect the athlete's performance. The intervention deals with family processes as well as with the biofeedback and related stress management techniques. Coaches' and families' reactivity are key processes to facilitate an ideal level of reactivity in the athletes.

Biofeedback approaches developed for peak performance are also useful for people with clinical problems: (1) biofeedback techniques and "mental" skills for superior athletes have been worked out in exquisite detail, (2) very ill people are more highly motivated to practice biofeedback when they become aware that this intervention is not only for the unwell or distressed, but also for maximizing the functioning of elite performers, and (3) the focus on performance rather than on "disorders" can be a relief to the unwell.

Space: Pilots, Astronauts

Pilots and astronauts can get motion sickness and pharmacology is not effective. Approximately half of the first human space travellers suffered from "space adaptation syndrome" (SAS) — the zero gravity analogue of ordinary terrestrial motion sickness. Cowings and associates[59] report that work done at NASA's Ames Research Center over the last 12 years shows that biofeedback with related exercises in physiological self-regulation is an alternative to pharmacology. The treatment effect is due to learned self-regulation of autonomic nervous system activity. Apparently, biofeedback training reduces sympathetic tone, thereby preventing the occurrence or likelihood of the parasympathetic rebound.

In 1981 Levy, Jones and Carlson[158] reported the use of biofeedback as non-pharmacological treatment for 20 USAF aviators disabled by motion sickness. The techniques they utilized were developed by Cowings and associates at NASA. Pilots trained with biofeedback-assisted relaxation techniques and physiological monitoring. Motion sickness was provoked in a Barany chair, capable of tilting and rotating. By exercising autonomic regulation they were able to control and abort motion sickness. Of 19 eligible, 16 returned to full flying duties. These pilots had received all available conventional airsickness treatment prior to beginning biofeedback without success. Thus, they are their own "controls." Prior to the use of biofeedback, the USAF School of Aerospace Medicine (SAM) airsickness treatment program employed a treatment program which consisted of learning to adapt in the same rotating/tilting chair and psychological desensitization techniques. The return to flying rate was 45–50%, compared to 84% with the biofeedback program. Again, in 1985 Jones, Levy and associates[133] found that of 53 fliers grounded for chronic, severe motion sickness, 85% returned to flying after biofeedback training. This is an important finding, considering that medication such as dextroamphetamine-scopolmine may be prescribed for airsick U.S. Air Force student pilots, but not for solo pilots because of potentially dangerous side effects. Besides the personal loss, grounding a flier may represent over a half-million dollar loss.

As of June, 1987 of approximately 200 people who trained in NASA laboratory with Cowings[60] and associates, about 85% achieved some degree, which is the same rate of success reported by Levy, Jones and Carlson[158] in 1981. Sixty percent learned to suppress their symptom completely and only 15% did not gain control.

Toscano and Cowings[310] in a carefully controlled study randomly assigned 18 men to three groups: (1) one group was taught to control own autonomic responses with a treatment called autogenic-feedback training (AFT); (2) a second was provided "sham" training in an alternative cognitive task; and (3) the third had no treatment. The amount of feedback presented and the number of responses conditioned were gradually increased. Then the feedback was removed while more distracting environmental conditions were gradually introduced. Results showed that those in the AFT group (1) could withstand the stress of Coriolis (chair) acceleration significantly longer without motion sickness.

Cowings and Toscano[58] have also carefully studied the relationship between susceptibility to motion sickness and biofeedback-learned autonomic control in highly and moderately susceptible men. The highly susceptible showed larger shifts ("augmenters") in autonomic activity in response to Coriolis acceleration than did the moderately susceptible. Differences in adaptation capacity are related, in part, to differences in patterns of autonomic responses to stress. Both groups were able to learn to control motion sickness. Extrapolating from the data it is possible to assume that had the highly susceptible trained longer, they might have achieved the same degree of control as the moderately susceptible. It is important to note that the length of training for these competent, busy individuals was only six hours. The physiological responses measured were heart rate, respiration rate, blood volume pulse, galvanic skin response and muscle activity. Visual feedback was provided simultaneously on all responses.

Cowings and Malmstrom[57] report that both NASA and the Air Force have determined that motion sickness is a problem worth controlling. Their new research with biofeedback includes self-suggestion exercises or mental images which are associated with the body's autonomic responses. Their findings imply that this type of training can be transferred to cope with the symptoms of zero gravity sickness in space.

In 1985 a Space Lab Shuttle experiment took place titled "Autogenic-Feedback Training: A Preventive Treatment Method for Space Adaptation Sickness (SAS)." To complete the study, sixteen people must participate in this experiment in space: eight who have been provided AFT training, and eight controls. Final evaluation of the effectiveness of AFT will be made then. To date, the experiment compared motion sickness of two crewmen with autogenic-feedback training (AFT) with two controls (who had no AFT training). All four people performed the same tasks. They reported how they felt, and were also monitored physiologically. Accurate predictions of motion sickness control were made about the experimental AFT people. The people trained with AFT reported they felt well and their physiological responses showed they were at very low stress levels. Subject A had no vomiting episodes. Subject B had one on mission day zero but did well the rest of the mission. Of the controls, person C had 4

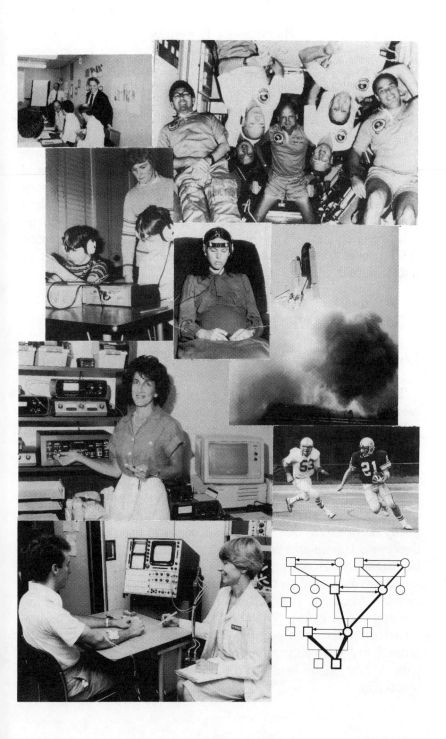

episodes the first day, the first was 7 minutes into orbit insertion (weightlessness). Person D had 2 episodes on the first day. Both experienced astronauts (controls) took more than one type of anti-motion drugs and reported those medications to be useless. Those medications are known to have complex side effects such as on short term memory, visual acuity, and reaction time. Their physiology reflected a very high level of stress for the first 5 days of the mission.[60] When the shuttle program comes back on line, 2–4 people will be studied each time. If at the time the experiment is completed AFT proves to be efficacious, it will become a regular part of astronauts' training.

BIOFEEDBACK FOR THE UNWELL

Diabetes Mellitus

This section is an overview of my clinical work with biofeedback for diabetes and of variations in blood glucose (bg) related to reactivity in the individual, family and in other human systems. The development and course of diabetes appear to be powerfully influenced by arousal-induced endocrine patterns.[286]

During the 1970s, biofeedback was considered potentially dangerous for diabetes mellitus. An unprecedented case study supported the hypothesis that biofeedback training decreases the insulin requirement and stabilizes the glycemic fluctuations. However, the investigators warned that this training could lead to frequent and severe hypoglycemic reactions.[94] About a year after the study the person died of undetermined cause. That biofeedback could produce such a powerful effect as to possibly be contraindicated for diabetes piqued my curiosity about the potential for bg self-regulation. I thought biofeedback could provide a window to study reactivity.

My work with biofeedback for diabetes began in 1976 at a time when emotional stress was not widely believed to have an effect on bg.[229] At that time, the medical community questioned even hypothesizing that stress affects bg, although the literature back to the early 1900s reported effects in animals and later in humans.

In 1935 Bauch[14] pioneered the use of relaxation exercises in diabetes and reported large cuts in insulin dose. In 1969 Luthe's autogenic training was reported to result in reduced insulin dosage.[166] Beginning in 1976, I reported[333,334,229] on the use of family systems therapy with diabetic patients. Stress inoculation[119] training (relaxation therapy and cognitive coping skills) produced a decrease in hemoglobin Alc (HbAlc). Progressive muscle relaxation training by four insulin dependent males produced a significant decrease in bg in two.[151]

The results of few investigators were often contradictory. There are differences in length of intervention time, and in the combination of techniques. Most studies included very few patients. Insulin requirements were reduced with biofeedback but one patient experienced an increased number of hyperglycemic and hypoglycemic episodes and biofeedback was discontinued.[263] EMG biofeedback in the management of diabetes was considered "discouraging at best."[315] No significant differences in the amount of HbAlc decrease were found when comparing four groups, including a control group.[33] Glucose tolerance did not improve in insulin dependent diabetes mellitus (IDDM) after one week of intensive in-hospital biofeedback-assisted progressive relaxation training plus six weeks of practicing relaxation at home.[83] However, glucose tolerance did improve with 6 non-insulin dependent diabetes mellitus (NIDDM).[300] Others found EMG biofeedback and home relaxation exercises resulted in improved bg control.[113] Six patients reduced glycemic excursions, but found no significant relationship between the training and the average bg over a 7-month period.[152]

Periodically a study or an opinion is published suggesting

that psychological stress does not influence diabetes. Recently no effect was found[142] from short-term laboratory induced stressors (such as "delivering" a speech on video). Based on this specific finding, the investigators make the general statement that their study "contradicts the prevailing opinion about the effects of psychological stress on metabolic control in diabetes." But as Templeton[306] elegantly points out, a number of studies and reviews on psychosocial factors and the role of emotion in the course of diabetes have been published. Templeton challenges that study:

> The danger of this conclusion is that it will encourage physicians to manage cases of diabetes with a meager psychosocial data base, to ignore the possible influence of important life crises on the patient's illness, and to omit psychosocial forms of intervention . . .[306]

As people with diabetes know, and clinicians who work with them, stress does play a part in their lives and in their diabetes control.

The mechanism by which biofeedback assisted relaxation works in managing real life stress in persons with diabetes may be associated with a simultaneous decrease in both epinephrine and norepinephrine levels. Under stress both the activity of the sympathetic (SNS) and the parasympathetic nervous systems (PNS) tend to increase. Both epinephrine and norepinephrine increase markedly during stress, especially hypoglycemic stress.[69] These two stress hormone levels may be lowered with biofeedback. In addition, other hormonal levels may be lowered as the interacting components of the endocrine system are decoupled by the quieting effect of biofeedback on sympathetic activity. The pancreatic insulin cells are directly contacted by the SNS which suppresses insulin secretion, and the PNS, which stimulates it. Biofeedback is known to improve the balance of these two systems. Glucose production in the liver may be lowered when norepinephrine decreases. Insulin utilization may rise and corti-sol-associated glucose production may fall with decreased sympathetic activity. However, at this time it is too early to do more than speculate on the mechanisms by which the observed changes take place. Currently, work in collaboration with the Georgetown Division of Endocrinology may provide explanations.

Beginning Biofeedback for Diabetes at Georgetown
    John Canary, M.D., then Director of the Division of Endo-crinology, provided medical supervision to my first diabetes biofeedback research patient in 1976.
    The first report on biofeedback for diabetes that included more than a single case was mine.[228,229,230,233,234,239] Six insulin-treated diabetic patients (four with Type I and two with Type II) who completed a biofeedback program based on family systems theory improved their response to life stressors and none had negative side effects. Four decreased their insulin requirement, one remained stable during two pregnancies and the sixth became stable and discontinued drug abuse. Some follow-ups extend over seven years. Unexpected hypoglyce-mia was partially averted by reducing emotional reactivity in the individual and family. The assumption was that emo-tional processes in the person with diabetes and in the impor-tant relationship systems influence the development and course of diabetes. Unexpected hypoglycemia was avoided by providing information about necessary precautions (See Chapter 6).

Technical Advances Monitor Conceptual Frontiers:
Reflectance Meters
    Reflectance meters provide an immediate (1-2 minutes) measure of bg. They are relatively easy to use and persons with diabetes use them at home to adjust their insulin dos-age. I used the instrument to obtain an indicator of reactivity (variation in bg) before and after biofeedback sessions. The

use of these meters also reduced the risk of unexpected hypoglycemia. Measuring bg with reflectance meters before and after biofeedback sessions showed a reduction in bg level in 18 Type I people who had 1–10 biofeedback sessions. Fifteen of the 18 (83%) had a decrease in mean bg. In sessions in which initial levels were >250mg/dl (mean = 160mg/dl) 14 of 15 (93%) showed an average decrease of 13mg/dl or 8%. In an analysis of 43 sessions in which bg was moderately high (between 125mg/dl and 250mg/dl) bg decreased significantly (p >.001) after a forty five minute session. Some people with an initial bg greater than 250mg/dl showed initial increases in bg, a situation analogous to what is seen in response to physical exercise.[237]

Rosenbaum and Tanenberg[240] concluded from their clinical work that (1) bg monitoring can be used to measure stress-related bg changes, (2) biofeedback can make an immediate difference in bg control when bg is between approximately 125–250mg/dl, and (3) biofeedback with family therapy may improve long-term control of IDDM. These measures were also used as indicators of changes in reactivity in the individual, in the family and work systems.

The use of reflectance meters for self-monitoring of bg levels is itself a form of biofeedback. Patients given feedback on their bg levels improved their discrimination skills and lessened daily bg levels.[110] The best predictor of accuracy in estimating fluctuations in bg levels was awareness of ANS symptomatology and reactivity.[61]

Hemoglobin AlC

This is a single time integrated measure that reflects glucose control over a three month interval. The advent of the now routinely used HbAlc measure made it possible to observe long-term effects of biofeedback. Generally, this clinical work provided a window to study reactivity in the person within a larger system. Specifically, this showed that emotional processes do affect bg and that biofeedback can influence long-term bg level. Questions, however, remained regarding the interaction of insulin, nutrition, exercise and biofeedback.

Computerized Insulin/Dextrose Infusion System

Although I could show clinically that people could stabilize their bg level over a period of time, and that biofeedback could reduce bg level in a single session, there was no way to demonstrate that the change measured with reflectance meters was attributable to biofeedback rather than to other factors, such as meals. The newest breakthrough in demonstrating an effect of biofeedback on bg was accomplished with a computerized insulin/dextrose infusion system or "artificial pancreas" called Biostator Glucose Controller.[5] This medical instrument was developed to keep diabetes under control during surgery or childbirth, or to help a person achieve better diabetic control by having information about the pattern in which the body uses insulin. With this equipment it has been shown that pyschological stress changes bg levels. Direction and degree of bg change were idiosyncratic across subjects but significantly reliable within subjects.[55]

In my work, the Biostator was also used as a form of biofeedback (the patient was periodically told her bg levels). This breakthrough in demonstrating an effect of biofeedback on bg was possible with the collaboration of Robert Tanenberg M.D. and Richard Eastman M.D., Georgetown's Director of Endocrinology. Tanenberg hospitalized an IDDM adolescent patient to diagnose stomach pains and monitor her bg for greater glucose control. She had a 6-year history of IDDM (Sustecal stimulated C-peptide was less than 1.0 ng/ml). She had shown significant clinical improvement with biofeedback and family therapy which had begun 2 years earlier. Prior to biofeedback she had been hospitalized 6 times in 8 months for a total of 43 days for ketoacidosis and severe hyperglycemia. She completed the basic 10 week biofeedback program and had follow-up sessions at least every 2–3 months. During this 2 year period she had only been hospitalized once for 2 days for a bladder infection. She had learned and used biofeedback well.[240]

The patient was connected to the Biostator which kept her from falling below a previously determined (80mg/dl) bg level. The Biostator provides a computerized, continuous record. It automatically samples bg level every 2 seconds and infuses dextrose or insulin intravenously to keep the person's bg at a pre-determined level. While connected to the Biostator, she did 40 minutes of biofeedback self-regulation, relaxed and increased her digital skin temperature by 5 degrees Fahrenheit. She also received verbal feedback on infused insulin level and decreased bg level. As she relaxed, her required insulin dosage decreased by more than 50% from 10 to 4 mU/mn. Her bg decreased from 105mg/dl to 87mg/dl (17%). In addition the computer automatically infused her with a total of 47 mg of dextrose at a rate of 1 to 13 ng/min. At no other time during the 24 hours that she was connected to the Biostator did she show this pattern, which suggests biofeedback had a significant influence.[241] (Figure 11.2).*

Since then, she has continued with intermittent family systems therapy, usually by herself, and biofeedback approximately once very 3–6 months. Her HbAlc shows a trend from 12.4% to 7.1%, which approximates normal and is considered "excellent control." Since the biofeedback training began 4 years ago she has been in the hospital 14 days for diabetes regulation, 11 days for a treatment strategy that highlights diabetes education, and 16 days for gastric pain[236] (medical collaboration with Tanenberg). (Figure 11.3). The longest admission (gastric pain) followed the in-hospital education fo-

---

*With appreciation for Bernard Brown, Ph.D., Rockville, MD., who was instrumental in computer-generated graphs throughout the book and for consulting by the Senior Partners, TeleTypesetting, Boston, MA.

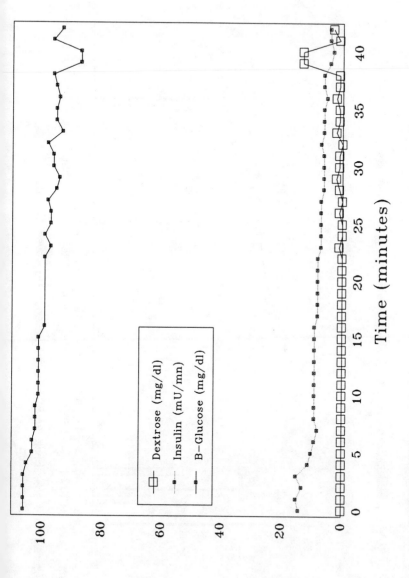

Figure 11.2 Biofeedback on Biostator

159

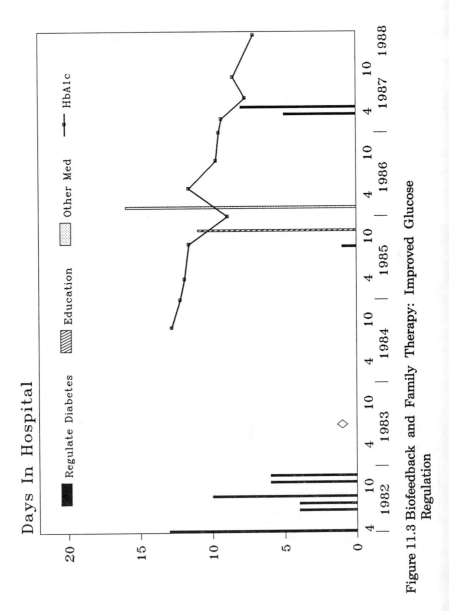

Figure 11.3 Biofeedback and Family Therapy: Improved Glucose Regulation

cused treatment program which exacerbated her own and her family's perception that she was "sick." However, even adding those 16 days to the 14 required for diabetes regulation, she had only 30 hospital days in 4 years (48 months) compared to 43 days in 8 months before biofeedback and family therapy. Before biofeedback 5.4 days hospital/month was average, compared to .6 days hospital/month after biofeedback, or a 88% reduction in hospital days.

Skillful Biostator observation of a nurse aware of systems, showed that the wife's bg was responsive to whether her husband was in the room even before he talked. This motivated the couple to begin biofeedback with family therapy. As the overreactivity in the non-diabetic spouse decreases, the reactivity in the diabetic spouse also decreases and this is associated with decreased bg.

In collaboration with endocrinologists Joanna Zawadzki, Richard Eastman, and Robert Tanenberg, and team assistants[**] a few patients whom I have coached with biofeedback, are being studied on the glucose insulin infusion system to observe if there are differences between baseline, biofeedback, second baseline, stress, and recovery intervals. If there are significant changes in enough people, the long term intent is to study a variety of hormone activity and to explore the mechanisms that account for the changes. Figure 11.4 shows preliminary data on marked differences in blood glucose, dextrose and insulin for one person during two conditions: biofeedback (Figure 11.4.a) and experimental stress (Figure 11.4.b). The experimental stress included talking about personal and family problems. The research protocol is designed to maintain bg near normal within a certain range with the Biostator. Even so, during biofeedback (Figure 11.4.a) her bg

[**]With appreciation to Rosemary McCown, R.N., B.S.N. and Mary Ann Toomey, R.N., B.S.N. Biostator team, and Marjorie Souder, Ph.D. and Bonnie Sobel, R.N., LCSW biofeedback team for their valuable expertise.

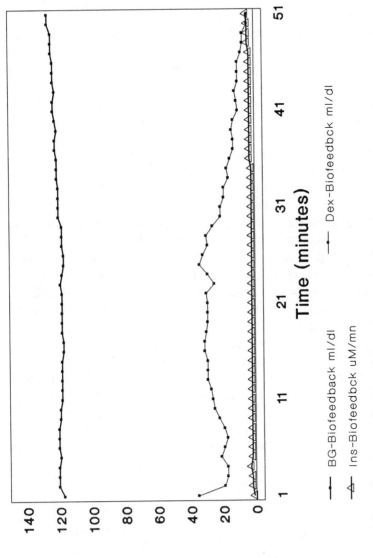

11.4.a Effects of Biofeedback on Dextrose, Insulin and Glucose Levels

162

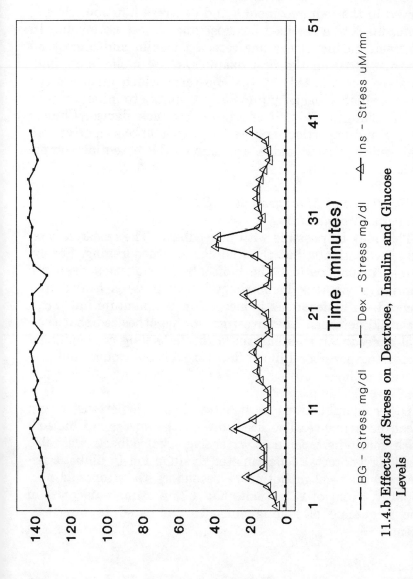

11.4.b Effects of Stress on Dextrose, Insulin and Glucose
Levels

Figure 11.4 Comparison of Stress and Biofeedback Effects (Glucose Controlled on Biostator)

163

decreased slightly, and during stress (Figure 11.4.b) it increased slightly. In addition, significant differences are observed in the required insulin and dextrose infusion. During biofeedback she received dextrose and almost no insulin. In contrast, during stress she received insulin and almost no dextrose.[236] As in the first example, these preliminary findings are not "caused" by the Biostator which monitors the effect of biofeedback by providing a minute to minute record of bg changes. It also can be a feedback device. Clinical theory and expertise, and patient expectations, motivation, and self-regulation skills are among the essential components.

Prevention and Management of Some Diabetic Complications.

This may be possible with biofeedback. The research is on very few patients, but the findings are encouraging. For example, in one patient the biofeedback relaxation exercises aborted a vitreous hemorrhage.[20] Two persons healed foot ulcers with biofeedback induced skin temperature but a calf ulcer did not heal. The investigators hypothesized that thermal biofeedback training can facilitate healing of wounds by increasing peripheral blood flow through the wound and promoting collagen protein synthesis by reducing cortisol levels.[272]

Other complications of diabetes include hypertension and fecal incontinence. The literature on the success of biofeedback for hypertension is extensive. Biofeedback was also used for anorectal sensorimotor dysfunction in diabetic patients with fecal incontinence secondary to autonomic neuropathy. Eight of 11 patients had a 75% or more decrease in the frequency of soiling episodes compared to pre-treatment.[320,321]

Precautions

These are in Chapter 6, but because severe and unexpected insulin reactions can produce brain damage or even death, another note of caution is included here. Some form of sugar must be available to use during or after a biofeedback session if needed. Persons at risk for hypoglycemia are safer not to practice biofeedback or self-regulation techniques while alone. Collaboration between the biofeedback clinician and the primary care physician is essential.

Summarizing, I have observed that everyday disturbances or chronic stress, major life cycle events such as births, deaths, and accidents, and special diabetes related transitions such as receiving the diagnosis, changing from oral agents to insulin, having the first signs of complications such as neuropathy, or beginning laser treatment are stressful and can produce changes in bg level. The potential for biofeedback and related self-regulation techniques as an adjunct for diabetes management has been established clinically, although much research is needed. (1) Biofeedback with appropriate precautions can be used as an adjunct to regulate diabetes mellitus without negative side effects. (2) Biofeedback with family therapy can produce long term clinical improvement. (3) Reflectance meters and HbAlc measures can be used as indicators of reactivity and have reflected long- and short-term benefits from biofeedback. (4) Measurements with the Biostator showed that insulin requirements can drop during biofeedback. And (5) the displays of data from the reflectance meters, HbAlc tests and the computerized insulin/dextrose infusion system can be forms of feedback or adjuncts to biofeedback for glucose control. Clinical work at Georgetown is a base for studies which are being designed to reduce stress effects, to improve glucose control and to understand the mechanisms whereby diabetes bg levels change. It is known from animal research that initial exposure to a new experimental setting produced large elevations in plasma cortisol. In humans (non-diabetic), the novelty of certain test situations increased adrenocortical activity as much as the test stressor.[157] My observation is that the process of being connected to the Biostator is in itself a stressor and probably affects findings.

The complexity of biological processes is emphasized by Pert[208,209] and her associates: insulin is not just a hormone; it is also a neuropeptide which is made and stored in the brain. The brain has insulin receptors. One of the simplest protozoa, like the evolutionary advanced human body, produces insulin. There are many unanswered questions, but the literature suggests that biofeedback and related self-regulation may be useful in diabetes if clinicians and persons with diabetes take proper precautions, and interventions are sufficiently long and comprehensive.

Physical Rehabilitation and Pain

"Learned Nonuse"

Someone you love just had a stroke and one arm is almost useless. Or, a special person in your life had a car accident with a particular kind of injury which will also leave the arm useless. What does the newest research suggest may help recover arm function? Techniques which encourage the person to use primarily the non-functional arm are employed. How was this determined? By innovative research first with monkeys and now humans. Essentially, Taub's[304] research showed that monkeys who were deafferented (certain nerves which bring messages to the brain were surgically cut) could still learn to use the arm with the severed nerves. To be sure, Taub deafferented monkeys at younger and younger ages including the day of birth, and even while still fetuses.

Monkey fetuses were exteriorized at the end of the second trimester of pregnancy and temporarily placed in a temperature-controlled saline bath. Forelimb deafferentation was performed and the fetus was then replaced in utero for the completion of embryonic development. The spinal cord was protected with a vertebral prosthesis, substituting the portions of the vertebrae removed during surgery, forelimb function was similar in almost all respects to the results of deafferentation on the day of birth. Maximal recovery of function had already taken place by the time of birth. The exception was prehension function (which did not emerge spontaneously but which could be developed later by training). The difference between deafferented and intact infants remained constant, being the same in adolescence as it had been in infancy. Monkeys still learned to use the arm with cut nerves. How is this explained? Taub developed the concept of "learned nonuse."

The learned nonuse mechanism prevents use of a limb when only one has been deafferented. Briefly, learned nonuse develops when monkeys with one deafferented limb try to use that limb immediately after surgery, but find they cannot. The monkeys learn *not* to try using the deafferented limb because they have difficulty with incoordination and loss of balance when they try to use the affected limb, and they can get along moderately well by using the unaffected limbs. Unilateral forelimb deafferentation results in a virtually useless extremity. In contrast, following bilateral (both arms) forelimb deafferentation, monkeys in several laboratories make extensive use of their affected extremities.

The "learned nonuse" hypothesis has implications for humans. It suggests that when there is a substantial initial period of loss of motor ability, primarily in one limb (as after stroke and some cases of traumatic brain injury), accompanied by the capacity to carry out many life functions situation with the unaffected extremities, there is a tendency to learn not to try to use the involved limb. This nonuse persists because of learning and reinforcement mechanisms and masks indefinitely the individual's underlying capability for extensive motor activity. Nonuse involves a conditioned suppression of movement; other factors could later contribute to further nonuse. Lack of mobility produces muscle atrophy, and if the limb is held in a fixed position over a prolonged period, spasticity and contracture develop, further limiting the probability of limb use.

The consequences of the experiments are applied in physical medicine. However, I emphasize that the pioneering effort was conceptual. It was necessary to assume that the central nervous systems (CNS) serves as a biofeedback "instrument."

Innovative techniques for overcoming learned nonuse convert a useless extremity into a limb that can be employed for a wide variety of purposes. Taking into account a person's history of failures in this or related matters, the "history of reinforcement" variables, "personality," and motivation, the method provides specific guidelines which include: (1) training to use the affected extremity as soon as possible after injury, (2) using carefully developed shaping (learning) procedures, (3) restraining the uninvolved extremity, (4) keeping motivation high, and (5) practicing.[304]

Based on Taub's learned nonuse findings with monkeys, Wolf[336] began a study for 20 head injury patients ages 20–50 and 40 stroke (20 acute and 20 chronic) patients ages 30–70 to improve an upper extremity function. Presently, 25 stroke and 6 head injured patients are in the follow-up phase of the study. Descriptive data analyses strongly suggest that: (1) forced use does promote faster task-oriented movements; (2) improved movement speed is greater for tasks involving more distal musculatures; and (3) enhanced speed of movement is retained for at least the one-year follow-up period. Taub, a pioneer in thermal biofeedback[302,303] and former president of BSA, is further developing this research.

Dynamic (Active) EMG Evaluation and Treatment for Pain and Rehabilitation

In a variety of post-injury and post-surgery situations maximal effort muscle rehabilitation is contraindicated because the muscles are injured. The goal is to maximally recruit motor unit activity with less than maximal effort. Dynamic (active) biofeedback is being used to study the effect on muscle (EMG) of varying the effort in isokinetic contractions.[72] This important research could improve rehabilitation by optimizing the intensity of the effort.

Middaugh and Kee[181,182,183] made important theory innovations, pioneered EMG recording during movement, and developed specialized techniques to evaluate and treat pain. Without these innovations, about ⅓ of the pain patients found no relief. For this segment of the pain population, there are two important changes: (1) EMG biofeedback evaluation and treatment is done while the person moves (rather than only during rest), and (2) electrode placement is on specific muscles (rather than assuming that one muscle group such as the frontalis provides accurate information about the state of the whole body). The investigators make two major points. First, static evaluation of muscles in an area of pain is not sufficient and can be misleading. Dynamic (active) evaluation tells much more because it is possible to assess the reactivity and over-use of the muscles. Second, there are substantial individual differences in the extent to which muscle factors contribute to a chronic pain problem.

Antalgic means anti-algic or to avoid pain. Antalgic posture is habitual abnormal posture which the patient uses to ease pain. However, over the long run, the poor posture severely strains the muscles and joints and this becomes part of the chronic pain problem. The high incidence of muscle overuse and muscle abuse stems from poor posture and protective bracing.

The method for this type of evaluation consists of placing EMG electrodes over two to four muscle groups in the area of pain. Above-normal EMG levels can be produced by relatively simple postural factors, by muscular bracing and guarding, or by increased muscle irritability. Relaxation of their painful muscles is slow, and often incomplete following voluntary contraction. This muscle irritability is strongly implicated as a major contributor to chronic pain in a high proportion (85%) of patients with chronic cervical/shoulder girdle pain. Back pain patients over-use (hyperactivity) their low back muscles. They involve many more muscles for each activity than are necessary. This habitual, excessive, and almost continuous muscle overactivity keeps the muscles sore, which reinforces the guarding, bracing, and pain. Different treatment strategies are appropriate in each case.

To appreciate the contribution of dynamic evaluation and treatment, it helps to understand previous biofeedback for pain based on a widely held theory that muscle spasm plays a prominent role. Pain, often from an initial trauma, is thought to trigger reflexive muscle contraction or "spasm." The muscle spasm then produces further pain and initiates a pain-spasm-pain cycle. The pain might begin with acute trauma or with gradual musculoskeletal strain. Psychological stress is an important initiating factor. Stress was thought to increase generalized physiological arousal leading to increased muscle tension which triggers episodes of sustained muscle spasm and pain. Once initiated, the pain cycle is further maintained by these very same factors.[181,182] The traditional version of diagnosis relied primarily on a single channel EMG device to electronically record, filter, amplify and integrate the EMG signal. Biofeedback relaxation is then used to reduce or eliminate the muscle contraction and ameliorate the pain.

A new technique with two EMG channels with a TECA clinical electromyograph with an amplifier band-width of 20 Hz to 1000 Hz. and an oscilloscope permits monitoring of the raw (unprocessed) EMG signal and does not miss diagnosing ½ of the patients. It reveals muscle hyperactivity, hypoactivity and asymmetry. Muscle contraction "patterns" can refer to (a) the time course of recruitment and relaxation of an individual target muscle; (b) the continuous variations in muscle contractions occurring during complex movement; or, (c) to the interaction between pairs of muscles with related actions.[181,182,183]

Middaugh's theory[184] differs from the traditional theory regarding pain. Traditional theory emphasizes reflexive, involuntary responses to acute injury. Traditional theory is based on a linear model conceptualization, focused on cause and effect. Middaugh's contemporary theory is based on a systems model which focuses on patterns of over-reaction, over-use or abuse, and irritability of the muscles. Chronic pain is acquired (learned). This theoretical model has different implications for diagnosis, treatment and research. It requires that the whole organism's posture be evaluated during both movement and rest. A systems orientation looks at pain in terms of the body being in a continuum of balance, and in terms of organization and function of pattern.

The importance of over/under reactivity is a theme which emerges in seemingly totally different fields – e.g., in the ANS produces motion sickness, in a caretaker affects reactivity of the young one, and in the immune system has complex consequences. Over or under reactivity of muscles directly affects pain and functioning. The degree of over or under reactivity of the muscles, person, and family system are all connected.

Comprehensive Intervention for Pain

Wilson and Schneider[331] at the Colorado Center for Bio-behavioral Health, developed a comprehensive treatment for fibromyalgia, an extremely painful condition with complex symptoms including sleep problems (Alpha Delta sleep disturbance), multiple trigger points, irritable bowel, breathing difficulties, joint pain, muscle spasms, stiffness, pain, depression, anger, and improvement while on vacation. Fibromyalgia is thought to be in the motor cortex, the gamma motor neurons, and the muscles. Predisposing factors in childhood include physical abuse and/or sexual abuse, injuries to lower extremities, and congenital jaw malformation. Predisposing factors in adulthood include whiplash, knee, ankle, neck and back injuries, and broken legs. People are intense, serious, and display a need to focus intently on tasks and be productive.

Evaluation and treatment is based on a model of interrelated factors in chronic pain syndrome: neurotransmitter dysfunction, psychosocial distress, structural pathology, and functional asymmetry. A personalized method of gaining control of the problem is determined with precise diagnostic techniques including video. Treatment includes especially selected and modified: physical therapy, heat, exercise, movement and posture work, massage, medication, psychotherapy, and relaxation training with EMG biofeedback during movement and resting conditions. Of special interest to me is that hypertone, (another aspect of over reactivity) is basic.[331]

When persistent pain focuses one's attention to a specific body area, a natural reflex increases the muscle tension around, and diminishes the blood flow to, that area. This automatic reaction, called the flexor withdrawal reflex, serves a survival function by "splinting" (immobilizing) the injured area and preventing hemorrhage. This automatic process occurs in the spinal cord and if sustained, constant tension or spasm may lead to additional pain.

Certain chemicals (neurotransmitters) may inhibit or block the spinal reflex. Blocking pain messages is produced by the neurotransmitters serotonin and gamma amino buteric acid (GABA). However, constant overuse may deplete these neurotransmitters which allows pain "messages" to travel more easily. In addition to depletion from overuse because of the pain, extensive use of Valium and other benzodiazepine-type drugs may add further complications. Apparently those drugs compete for the same binding sites as GABA. Biofeedback can reduce the need for these drugs.

Endorphins, naturally occurring brain narcotics, inhibit pain awareness. These substances are depleted by the continuous stimulation of pain, as well as by excessive narcotics use. Pain messages then can make their way to the brain through these depleted spinal cord segments. It is believed that biofeedback can increase endorphins.[330]

Computerized Psychophysiological Brain Scan

The computerized automated psychophysiological scan (Capscan) combines advances in computers, computerized electroencephalography (brain-wave measurements) and bio-feedback.[50] Charles Stroebel,[127] Ph.D., M.D. and colleagues at the Institute of Living in Hartford developed this instrument in 1983 and he continues to develop it now as director of the Institute for Advanced Studies in Behavioral Medicine. Stroebel claims that emotions and thoughts may be represented in specific brain patterns. By becoming aware what these patterns are people may learn to enhance or diminish thoughts or emotions. A person can see the brain patterns in a computer monitor in color and may alter the emotions or thoughts by concentrating on altering the colors and patterns they see of their brain activity on the screen. Sensors attached to a cap are placed on the head. The Capscan displays immediately to the user three variables of his or her own brain activity: brain-wave frequency, brain synchronization, and abnormal brain activity. First, the user can see immediately which areas of the brain are active, the amount of activity, and which hemisphere is dominant at the time. The second variable is harmony – synchronization – of the two hemispheres. When the individual is physically deeply relaxed, calm and mentally alert, synchronization prevails. Lester Fehmi, Ph.D., director of the Princeton Behavioral Medicine and Biofeedback Clinic, also finds that hemispheric synchronization is associated with "rapid healing and normalization of functions." He works with a multichannel EEG that monitors each of the brain hemispheres simultaneously. This anticipated some of the Capscan concepts. The third Capscan displayed variable is abnormal brain activity. The Capscan shows specific brain areas on the right of the screen, and the total image on the left side of the screen. The person can be coached to change the brain processes so that the specific, undesired colors disappear. Essentially, changing the color and pattern of brain waves at will uses biofeedback principles similar to changing skin temperature or blood pressure voluntarily. Capscan complexity and the relative simplicity in using it provide a wide horizon for understanding psychophysiological, emotional, and cognitive changes.[127] Telemetry may be available on Capscan by 1989.[50]

Now available is another comprehensive system which looks at 20 channels of brainwave activity. This system, developed by NeuroMap,[189] provides real time color topograms of brain activity. These color maps add several dimensions to the study of brain function. It is possible to locate the source of brain activity that may be associated with epilepsy, panic, or some psychophysiological disorders. It is then possible to provide very specific feedback for various dysfunctions. The relatively low cost incorporates similar technology to that used in expensive systems that are used in neurodiagnostic medical applications, but is designed to run on a desktop computer. The immediate interaction between patient and instrument described in the Capscan also exists in the Neuro-Map System-20.

This development in psychophysiologic brain scanning and feedback opens a new field of biofeedback treatment of various psychiatric and neurologic disorders for which drug therapy was the standard available alternative. Similar technologies have been used to monitor the effects of psychoactive substances. Steiner[286] is using brain mapping to study the effects of particular drugs on the brain during stressed and relaxed periods without biofeedback. The type of neuroscience equipment used has the same or similar capabilities as the Neuro-Map. His research has frontier implications for topographic brain biofeedback which may help achieve certain arousal states. Brain topography provides a door so that each individual using it may develop ways to enhance brain activity and personal functioning.

Vision Disorders

Vision is an active process. Visual readings, somewhat like blood pressure readings, represent the particular moments in time from which they are taken.[17] These momentary measures do provide an indication of the chronic state of the person, especially if they are obtained under standardized conditions. One basis for using biofeedback for visual retraining is the connection with the autonomic nervous system (ANS). The parasympathetic fibers innervate the contraction of the ciliary muscle of the eye, which increases the convexity of the lens, increases accommodation and thus increases the focusing power. When the parasympathetic fibers are inactive, it causes the focusing muscles of the eye to relax and to decrease the focusing power of the eye.[16]

ANS involvement is only one of several possible mechanisms in visual disorders. Halperin and Yolton[114] published a comprehensive invited review on ophthalmic applications of biofeedback for correction of oculomotor abnormalities including strabismus, nystagmus and amblyopia, refractive error correction, reduction of intraocular pressure (IOP), and blepharospasm suppression. They concluded that biofeedback has proven useful in the treatment of several ophthalmic disorders. Although investigators are still uncertain whether it works for some disorders, they have gone beyond "whether" it works to "how" it works in other disorders including strabismus, nystagmus and refractive error correction. In my opinion, the noteworthy review is required reading for serious consumers and professionals.

An early application of biofeedback was for the treatment of strabismus.[125] This is a condition when people have difficulty keeping their eyes aligned properly. The neuromuscular controls system fails to direct the eyes appropriately. EMG has been used to reduce the level of tension in the muscles surrounding the eyes. In a study by Palmer and Siegel, reviewed by Halperin and Yolton,[114] 26 strabismics (type of strabismus not specified) and 26 controls were given a single 20-minute EMG session to reduce frontalis muscle tension assuming stress contributes to strabismus. The investigators found no correlation between change in frontalis muscle tension and degree of strabismus change. I believe this is a classic example of research and evaluation issue discussed in Chapter 9. To assume that stress may contribute to a disorder is often appropriate. But to assume that one 20-minute biofeedback session can decrease either muscle tension or stress is, in my view, unrealistic. The assumption is an indicator of the understanding of the investigators, but the results are *not* an indicator of whether biofeedback "works."

In contrast to biofeedback-assisted relaxation, the trend is to provide biofeedback by monitoring the eyes directly and feeding back information on ocular position.[114] There are several ways to monitor eye position, including electro-oculography, photoelectro-oculography (PEOG), television systems, and electromagnetic coil monitoring.[114] In PEOG, infrared beams are shone on the front surface of the eye and reflected back to a pair of infrared detectors. As the eye moves, the proportion of light reflected to each of the detectors changes. This change is electronically converted to a tone so that the patient literally hears where the eyes are directed. This type of biofeedback requires "hard work" rather than relaxation.[342]

Detail is included as an example of the complexity of vision and instrumentation in the promising field of biofeedback for vision care. Biofeedback therapy for strabismus usually does not complete the task of restoring functional stereoscopic vision. It does provide approximate ocular alignment, but sensory training (also known as vision therapy or orthoptics) is usually required as a follow-up to biofeedback.

As I understand the literature, vision care specialists provide either specific biofeedback for a specific eye disorder, or in combination with a biofeedback-assisted relaxation approach. Sometimes there are ANS changes such as increased hand temperature and decreased blood pressure associated with changes in eye function. However, the field of biofeedback for vision is still relatively new, and more research is needed to claim that clinically significant eye changes occur with only general biofeedback. Another variable requiring more study is whether biofeedback produces more change provided by itself or as an adjunct to conventional therapy for the treatment of visual disorders.

Retinitis pigmentosa, macular degeneration, and diabetic retinopathy are all retinal disorders that involve the loss of visual fields or acuity frequently to the level of legal blindness. Until recently, traditional vision care specialists could do little to halt the gradual deterioration of vision in these cases, much less reverse the process. Now laser surgery is successfully being used to slow down the visual deterioration in macular degeneration and diabetic retinopathy, and in some cases halt vision losses.[16] Behel,[17] however, reported increases in visual field test scores in 17 people with retinitis pigmentosa, macular degeneration, and diabetic retinopathy who received biofeedback general relaxation training as an adjunct to visual therapies. These visual improvements were accompanied by increases in peripheral skin temperature and decreases in EMG and blood pressure. Although these case reports are intriguing, more systematic research is needed before any hard conclusions are drawn.

In some cases the treatment is designed to activate nerve pathways to the visual cortex area of the brain and can be supported using bi-hemispheric EEG feedback over the occipital cortex. In Behel's case study this treatment was used with a legally blind person who had constricted visual fields as a result of retrolental fibroplasia. Retrolental fibroplasia or retinopathy of prematurity (ROP) is a condition that was common with premature babies who were exposed to excessive amounts of oxygen during incubation. Once the oxygen was withdrawn, an overgrowth of blood vessels (to supply the tissues with the amount of oxygen they became accustomed to) obliterated normal images on the retina. This is known as secondary vasoproliferation. The traditional literature states that once blindness occurs there is no hope for restoration of sight. Three years later she was driving, apparently with an unrestricted license.

Apparently vision and perception are intimately connected to emotion, and habits of emotional response can determine visual characteristics.

> Good vision involves more than 20/20 eyesight. It includes not only the process of accumulating information from the world of light, but also the integration of this information with previous experience, and the organization of this data in a way that initiates meaningful action. Changes in visual acuity are dependent on neural and retinal states, in addition to the focusing characteristics of the eye's optical system . . . Visual training can be viewed as essentially brain training.[16]

Trachtman[331] used a specialized biofeedback instrument called the Accommotrac Vision Trainer ® (AVT) and reported that for people with intraocular pressure (IOP) below 14mm/ Hg, the training had no effect. However, for people with IOP's greater than 14mm/Hg, there was a significant reduction of IOP in both eyes. He notes that the regulation of IOP is by the ANS. He raises several important questions for future research, including whether glaucoma is another stress related disease, whether the (IOP) reductions are long lasting, and whether his work is replicable.

Findings can be statistically significant, yet have no clinical significance (See Chapter 9). Statistically significant changes in intraocular pressure (IOP) may not be clinically significant if the person's IOP is still so elevated as to require medication or if unattended possibly lead to blindness.

Stress may play a part in precipitating acute onset or closed-angle glaucoma (which accounts for about 20% of all glaucoma) because IOP can be affected by the individual emotional state.[271] Stress may also have a role in open-angle glaucoma. Shily reports a study by Ripley and Wolff in 1948 in which during a period of 10 months to 7 years data was collected regarding life history, eye symptoms and IOP in 18 people. Behavior, thought content and feeling states were observed as well as IOP. Severity of eye symptoms and elevation of IOP was apparently related to exacerbation of previous or current psychological states. Research is needed to determine if biofeedback and relaxation, as adjuncts to treatment regimes, can reduce the risk of acute closed-angle glaucoma and lower high IOP in persons with open-angle glaucoma.[271]

EMG feedback and relaxation training were an ancillary treatment for elevated intraocular pressure. EMG biofeedback and taped relaxation instructions were used twice a week for eight weeks with eight experimental subjects. Two people had open angle glaucoma and six had ocular hypertension. The ocular pressure decreases were clinically important. IOP decreased from 21.0 to 19.2, which reduces the possibility of ocular damage.[163] The decreases would not have been as clinically significant if the initial IOP had been higher.

One person lowered his intraocular pressure by 20% in one eye and 12% in the other eye in 30 minutes after 8 sessions of training coupled with a generalization technique which emphasizes tactile recognition, somatosensory integration, and cognitive retrieval. The actual values of change were at least 3 mm. Hg in the left eye, and 1 ½ mm. Hg in the right eye.[18]

Functional myopia (near sightedness) is subject to voluntary control. Randle reported that voluntary control of accommodation is possible with biofeedback training. Accommodation refers to adjustment of the eye for vision at various distances. At NASA Ames Research Center (with six experimental and six control subjects) biofeedback was used to learn to "feel" the accommodative state and alter focus independently of visual stimulus conditions. It had long been thought that myopia was a genetic problem, but recently the importance of environmental factors has been recognized in studies of primates and humans.[312] Pelcyger and Trachtman report that 100 patients used accommodative biofeedback with generalization techniques to reduce myopia. The median refractive error changed from ‾2.37 Diopters to ‾0.75 Diopter with an improvement in unaided distance visual acuity of from 20/200 to 20/30. A diopter is a measure of focusing power and is calculated by finding the reciprocal of the focal length of a lens in meters. Eye examinations determine the focal length of the eye. The power of a lens to change that focal length to optical infinity is defined as the refractive error. The median number of training sessions was eight. Eidetic or vivid mental imagery was a useful adjunct to biofeedback of accommodation to reduce myopia. Biofeedback offers a viable alternative to glasses, contact lens and surgical methods for the reduction of myopia.[201,312]

Trachtman and colleagues developed the AVT ® biofeedback instrument. It measures eye refractive status (refraction is the bending of light by the optics of the eye) 40 times per second with an accuracy of 0.1 diopter. For each refractive measurement auditory feedback is provided. The instrument can be set so that for hyperopes (farsighted) faster feedback of sound pulses indicates an increase in accommodation, and for the myopes (nearsighted) faster feedback indicates a decrease in accommodation. The patient is instructed to make the sound go faster. The goal is to increase accommodative range and flexibility. Parasympathetic nervous system (PNS) activity results in ciliary muscular contraction and the eye lens becoming more convex. This is known as positive accommodation. According to Trachtman and Pelcyger[314] the sympathetic nervous system activity (SNS) inhibits the ciliary muscle making the lens less convex. This is called negative accommodation. The focusing muscle of the eye, the ciliary muscle, is controlled by the ANS and is thus influenced by stress. For myopic patients, relaxing the parasympathetic portion of the muscle, while increasing the sympathetic activity allows a reduction in refractive power of the lens (less myopia). For hyperopic patients, relaxing the sympathetic portion of the muscle, while increasing the parasympathetic activity allows an increase in refractive power of the lens (less hyperopia). For either technique, balancing the ciliary muscle functions seems to lead to an increase of range and flexibility.[314] Research is still under way. The role of the SNS in controlling accommodation is not yet totally understood.[104]

In summary, some findings in biofeedback for visual care generate the kind of excitement that the pioneers on learning of visceral and glandular responses and altering brain waves did two decades ago. Aspects of human physiology previously thought to be out of voluntary control are within voluntary control (See Chapter 1). In biofeedback applications for visual disorders the precautions include collaboration with physicians, optometrists and other vision care specialists (See Chapter 6). More research is important to better understand exactly how and what biofeedback affects vision, and to suggest the best ways to integrate biofeedback and traditional therapy for the treatment of visual system disorders.[114] It is interesting to me that cognition has a significant effect on the level and direction of accommodation. It is also intriguing to note that the theme of over or under reactivity may be applicable to the ciliary muscle and vision as to so many other processes examined in this book.

Twilight Learning

"Twilight learning" refers to the concept of learning during an altered state of arousal. The person is very relaxed and neither fully awake nor fully asleep. This special state is identified by an EEG pattern of predominant theta frequencies (4–7 Hz). Typically people experience dreamlike states which are briefer and more disjointed than the dreams associated with rapid eye movement (REM) sleep. A number of creative people in the fields of science, music, literature and art reported that creative solutions or inspiring thoughts occurred to them in this state.[43]

This learning model relies on the concept of brain lateralization developed by Roger Sperry and others.[43] The dominant hemisphere has the functions of speech, logic, critical judgment, and sequential ordering. The non-dominant appears to mediate the intuitive, emotional, visuospatial processing, pattern recognition, and parallel rather than sequential functions. It is thought that hemispheric functioning and arousal level are related. High cortical arousal or activation helps to prepare for fight-or-flight even when over activation is counterproductive. Critical screening is reduced by procedures that raise or lower cortical arousal outside a certain range. It appears that methods which reduce or eliminate critical screening can permit access to the nondominant hemisphere. When the left or dominant hemisphere lets go of its dominance, the right or nondominant hemisphere becomes available for more direct "re-scripting." The person can more easily learn to give up destructive habits.[43]

Budzynski and associates[45] found clinical changes subsequent to twilight learning with biofeedback theta training and taped "out of awareness messages." These messages are masked with certain sounds so that the person does not "hear" the words consciously. One part of the brain "hears" the words, while the other hears the sounds. This biofeedback method is controversial and raises conceptual questions regarding self-regulation when the individual is not aware of it. This work is included because it is innovative and because it raises questions about just what *is* self-regulation. This process takes place usually with the person's understanding that certain messages will be provided out of awareness during a state of altered arousal. Budzynski pioneered several other important areas and may be developing a new contribution here. His previous contributions include the development of the EMG digital readout and quantification, tri-color visual feedback, variable tone and click audio feedback, variable bandpass, and automatic trial sequencing in 1966. He designed and carried out the first controlled study in biofeedback with tension headache published in 1973, the first biofeedback study in dental applications in 1973, and the first diabetes case study.[44] Twilight learning appeared in *Psychology Today*[41] in 1977; it is still developing and controversial.

Social Disorders: Biofeedback for Prisoners

Biofeedback is for people who function extraordinarily well, for those with psychophysiological, cognitive, emotional or relationship problems, as well as for those with social dysfunctions including committing murder.

In a maximum security institution, in a bare room without furniture, 68 male inmates convicted for a variety of crimes voluntarily participated in temperature biofeedback training, imagery, introspection and self-exploration. The goal was self-mastery. These men were 16 to 42 years old, most were under 25. Six small groups met daily for 5 weeks. Each person participated in 25 hours of group of which 8 hours were in biofeedback and 17 hours were in didactic presentation, group discussion, and selected exercises. What happened? Of the 68 who participated, 62 were released. One to 3 ½ years later, only 12.9% were recidivists—that is, were back in prison. This compares to 35.6% recidivism in that state at that time.[192]

One possible explanation is that the comprehensive program facilitated a more optimum level of reactivity (neither over or under reactive) which allowed a more thoughtful response to life's problems. The thoughtful, broader perspective, and the increased sense of self-mastery could increase functioning and decrease recidivism.

Immunomodulation

Cancer and Other Immune Mediated Disorders

Norris and Garrett Porter[194] report in a deeply personal way Garrett's successful treatment for a right hemisphere brain tumor. An astrocytoma was diagnosed by CAT scan in 1978 when Garrett was nine years old. The diagnosis was confirmed in a second opinion from the Brain Tumor Research Institute in San Francisco, which agreed with the diagnosis and recommendation from physicians in Topeka – the tumor was inoperable and radiation treatment was recommended. When Porter's grandmother died of cancer earlier in the year, she was the third person in the family to die of cancer within 18 months. Garrett's parents, health care professionals, began to look at the cancer literature and concluded that there is a psychological component which needed to be confronted. Garrett was given the maximum medically safe amount of radiation, and simultaneously his parents took him for biofeedback treatment. Nevertheless, his symptoms progressed for a number of months before he began to improve.

Dr. Norris approached the situation with an understanding that "hope has a neuroendocrinological effect on the body – hope affects brain chemistry; beliefs have biological consequences . . . Self-images can either imprison or liberate and help heal." It seemed to her that by combining the best of medical science with the psychoneuroimmunology research the individual's own internal resources could optimize healing. Garrett first worked with biofeedback with Dr. Fahrion at Menninger. Then Dr. Norris worked with him, adding visualization and imagery.

She candidly describes her own personal and professional experiences which she integrated to become who she is including childhood memories of skin temperature self-regulation in freezing Canada and her parents teaching her to "be aware" of the relationship between mind and body. She takes a strong stand on moving away from guilt and denial.[194]

Porter's story of his hard work and the drawings of his visualizations are rewarding reading for a person of any age with personal or professional interest. The photographs of his tumor in 1978 and of the same area of the brain without the tumor in 1980 are facts.

Between 1979–1987 Norris began working with other young people ages 5 to 19 with cancer: four with a brain tumor, three with Stage IVB or IIIB Hodgkins; one age 15 with breast cancer, and one with a naso-laryngeal tumor. Children have definitely been the most "remarkable" patients in terms of recovery for a variety of reasons. All but one are living.[193]

In contrast to this highly individualized work, a fascinating experiment was very carefully designed by Gruber, Hall, Hersh and Dubois[111] to investigate the hypothesis that relaxation and imagery can measurably influence immune responsiveness. The research sample was a group of 10 cancer patients with metastatic disease who were selected from 25 who responded to advertisements in a local newspaper and T.V. station. They had several forms of cancer, and their ages ranged from 34 to 69. A single subject, multiple baseline design was employed with repeated measures. This means each patient was his/her own control. There was also a crossover design for the biofeedback component, which means persons were compared as a group. A double blind procedure was used in which therapists did not know the status of the immune system as measured by the blood tests, and staff involved in the blood bioassays did not know whose blood they were examining.

People were presented with an overview of the immune system and instructed to imagine their immune system acting decisively over the cancer in conjunction with whatever medical treatments they were receiving. They were also instructed to envision themselves becoming healthier. Relaxation exercises were learned with audio cassettes and at the seventh month of the study, six sessions of EMG biofeedback were provided. A group meeting was held each month to do relaxation, imagery, and gather blood samples.

The findings are fascinating and warrant further research. Several measures of immune system function were found to be significantly elevated compared to baseline: PHA mitogen, CON-A Mitogen, Mixed Lymphocyte Response, Interleukin II, Natural Killer Cell Activity, Erythrocyte Rosette Assay, IgG, and IgM. The study is based on the firmly established evidence of bi-directional pathways linking the central nervous and immune systems. It is also known that the channels by which the brain can modulate the lymphoid tissues are regulated in part by limbic structures that also regulate emotions.[111] Elegant thinking, elegant study, and elegant results.

The investigators also noted that patients' involvement with the cancer treatment increased productive "aggressiveness" (not anger or hostility) which may confer some health advantage to the patients. Although these patients were already oriented towards internal control, there is an increase in shift towards more internal control after intervention.[112] Additional research by these investigators has been funded and initiated to further explore active elements of the behavioral intervention.

Peavy, Lawlis and Goven[200] found that biofeedback-assisted relaxation did improve coping skills and phagocytic capacity in high stress subjects. They assessed the level of stress and of phagocytic immune function (nitroblue tetrazolium test) and found that high stress was associated with low immunity. They provided biofeedback-assisted relaxation and found that it affected the quality, rather than the quantity, of phagocytic neutrophils.

Since transient immunosuppression can be produced by heightened and sustained distress, Kiecolt-Glaser and Glaser[146] reasoned that reductions in distress might enhance immune function. They found that geriatric patients who learned relaxation showed a significant enhancement on two different assays of cellular immune function.

Several investigators documented the relationship between stress and frequency and intensity of recurrence of herpes simplex episodes. For instance, stress reduction was used to treat severe recurrent genital herpes virus in 4 subjects (2 in biofeedback training and 2 in relaxation training). While the project has several limitations including the fact that the biofeedback providers were inexperienced graduate students, and that the biofeedback training did not include relaxation techniques, the investigators did find substantial improvement in reported symptoms with both treatments at 6 month follow-up.[318]

In 35 females and 32 males suffering from severe genital herpes frequency, pain, and bother of recurrences were associated with level of emotional dysfunction.[273] The higher frequencies and greater discomfort were also associated with a tendency to use emotion-focused wishful thinking and to avoid using cognitive strategies to cope with stress associated with herpes. They suggested that stress management procedures involving problem-focused coping strategies and provision of social support would be most effective.

Investigators and clinicians in many centers are observing changes in allergies, arthritis, and other immune mediated conditions. Frequently people who come for biofeedback for a difficult problem may not even mention their allergy or herpes at intake, but report its improvement two or three months after beginning biofeedback. Now it is quite common for patients to specifically do biofeedback to enhance immune system function.

AIDS

Acquired Immune Deficiency Syndrome (AIDS) is now a common word even for school children. Browsing through greeting cards I saw " . . . a tisket a tasket, a condom or a casket ..." (Scott Greeting Cards). The cost in emotions, health, life and dollars[115] has been well documented. The implications for public health are a major concern.[129] The necessary agent is a "virus," possibly more than one. The virus mutates so quickly that vaccines are not likely to be available soon.

The HIV cycle is thought to include several stages.[190] After infection there is an increase in the amount of virus present. It takes some time for the immune system to react to the presence of the virus and mount an antibody response. This period of relatively high circulating virus, yet without antibodies has been called the "window." Existing blood tests do not yet detect HIV reactive individuals during this period, which may be months. If these people do not happen to be in so called "high risk" groups their blood, possibly already infected, may be used for transfusions. As part of the infection process, the virus inserts its own genes into the host cells' native DNA. This event is called integration. As a result, the HIV genes are now a permanent part of the cell and thus of the individual. Some time after the infection (2–6 months is an accepted figure) HIV antibodies appear. This is called seroconversion. Concurrently the virus concentration drops dramatically. This stage of the HIV cycle is termed the latent phase. Typically there is a constant level of antibodies to HIV. The virus concentration is very low or non-existent.[190]

Ninety-five percent of hemophiliacs have been exposed to the virus. Approximately 70% of tested persons with hemophilia A and 35% with hemophilia B are seropositive.[56] The ELISA test assays for the presence of specific antibodies that are raised against HIV, not the virus itself. Western Blot involves the identification of antibodies against specific protein molecules. It is believed to be more specific than the ELISA test. One estimate[95] is that the virus will kill up to half of everyone infected.

Yet, there are some intriguing, and less well known facts about AIDS that merit research on a possible intervention:

biofeedback and related self-regulation processes, especially
when conceptualized and utilized in the context of family
systems thinking. The possible relevance of psychoneuroimmunology to AIDS has been addressed.[280] What are the
facts? Dosage and frequency of exposure may affect the individual's chance of becoming infected with the virus. There are
people who have been exposed to HIV and are not infected.
There are also people who are infected and, even after several
years, have not developed either AIDS Related Complex
(ARC) or AIDS. Some investigators have raised the possibility that genetic and/or environmental factors protect these
people. Although the literature addresses the possibility of
"environmental" factors, it does not usually consider the
influence of family processes in psychophysiological functioning or the possible influence of emotional processes in the
development of the conditions which allow the virus to
thrive. It does not even begin to address the possibility that
self-regulation, such as biofeedback, might also be a protective factor which could help delay or possibly even prevent the
next more serious stage in the development of the disease.
The *virus is necessary but not sufficient* for the development
of AIDS.

Melbye and colleagues[178] studied 250 initially healthy homosexual men and concluded that a high proportion of persons infected with HTLV-III will develop measurable
immunologic and clinical abnormalities. The number of T-
helper cells is a strong predictor of the future development of
AIDS among seropositive men; the lower the T-helper cell
count, the higher the risk of development of AIDS. The
investigators report that HTLV-III infection had a detrimen-
tal impact on the number of T-cells in most of those infected.

"Why have some long-infected people not become ill?" Altman[2] reports that scientists in New York are following 13 gay
men who had been infected with the AIDS virus for at least
nine years without any apparent ill effects. Stevens, chief
epidemiologist, states that the immune systems of all 13 look

"perfectly normal." Similarly, Rutheford in San Francisco found that of 155 men infected for 7 years or more, 29 have not developed AIDS. Ten of these have ARC, 10 have swollen lymph nodes throughout the body, and nine are symptom free. These studies of long-term "virus carriers" are possible because frozen blood samples were obtained years ago in Hepatitis B vaccine trials. At the National Institute of Health, Kaslow reported that "very few" people who develop AIDS symptoms later recover, and of 4,955 individuals who developed antibodies against AIDS five no longer had these antibodies at follow-up.[3]

To condense my thinking on psychophysiological and family systems processes in the development and course of AIDS I developed the diagram "Family Therapy and Biofeedback for AIDS: Theoretical and Research Considerations" (Figure 11.5). It reflects a way of thinking about the problem. If psychophysiological and family systems processes can affect the course and development of the disease, it is reasonable to hypothesize that they will also affect the person's quality of life. It is also possible that the same processes affect the length of time before a person proceeds to the next stage of the disease and, possibly, death. The double arrows indicate that the processes in boxes I, II, III, and IV are interdependent. Box I lists the family and other natural systems concepts described in Chapter 5. Box II reflects the idea that an individual's vulnerability to, and subsequent expression of the virus is affected by the processes within the individual, the family and society. A person can carry the virus but the virus may not be expressed in any presently recognizable way. This person may test HIV seropositive even though the virus is not detectable in the blood. A person may be infected and not be sick, or may be mildly sick without progressing to AIDS or death. Box III specifically implies variability in both complications and in the time period before the next state. Box IV lists possible interventions at a variety of levels: cellular, psychoneuroimmunological, individual, and

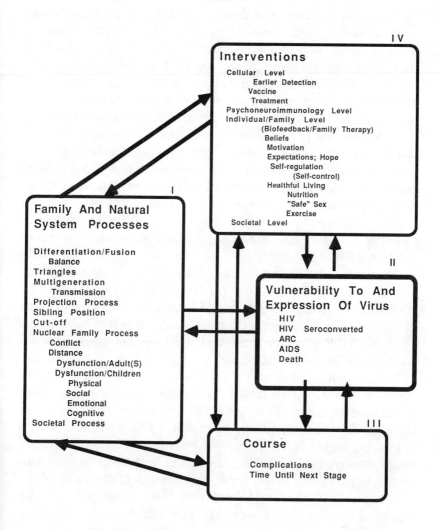

Figure 11.5 Family Therapy and Biofeedback for AIDS: Theoretical and Research Considerations

societal. At the cellular level possibilities include earlier detection (thereby reducing transmission), infection prevention by vaccines, and pharmacological treatments, all under intensive research. At the level of the psychoneuroimmunological (PNI) system, it is possible that individuals can strengthen their immune system. (More on PNI in Chapter 2.) This might be facilitated by family systems therapy, other forms of psychotherapy, and/or a variety of self-regulation techniques including biofeedback. At this level, motivation, beliefs, hopes, and expectations are essential considerations. So too is the role of healthful living practices including "safe sex," nutrition, and exercise. Processes at the societal level center on influencing the population's views on viral exposure, infection and intervention. Anthropologists, sociologists, economists, epidemiologists, politicians, natural systems thinkers and other experts are necessary for intervention at this level.

Ferguson[87] shows the course of one of her biofeedback patients who tested HIV positive for antibodies (Figure 11.6). He was identified in the Johns Hopkins University Study to Help the Aids Research Effort (SHARE) program in August, 1984 as "HIV positive" and had a T4 (helper cells) and T8 (suppressor cells) count of 600 with a ratio of one. In June, 1985 his blood converted to "HIV positive, which meant that there were antibodies to HIV virus in the blood. This was confirmed by growing the HIV virus from his blood." At that time his T8-cell count dropped to 400. In September 1985 he began biofeedback training. By February, 1987, his T8-cell count was up to 1200. The change is best seen in absolute count, both T8-cell and T4-cell, rather than in the ratio of T8 to T4. In 1986 three HIV cultures were attempted at the National Institute of Health. The first and second were negative. Only the third, with a tetanus bolus to purposely stimulate the immune system, was positive.[87] Is this simply a function of the attempt to isolate a virus which is not always possible? Is this a random, accidental single case finding? Or

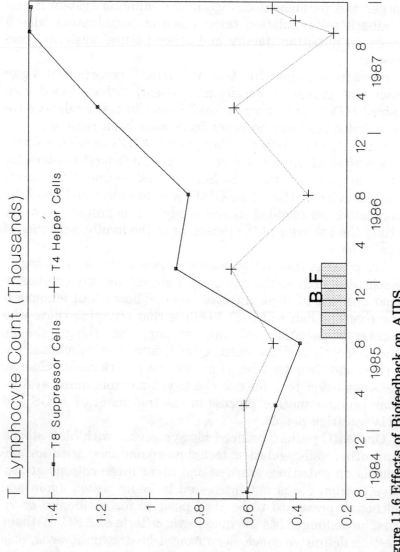

Figure 11.6 Effects of Biofeedback on AIDS

193

is this one of the very few documented cases which suggests further research? Research questions abound. One crucial question can be posed – is there more likely to be a faster, larger and permanent change in the immune system if biofeedback self-regulation takes place in combination with a focus on nutrition, family and other natural systems processes?

Recently the *John Hopkins Magazine*[132] reports that 3 gay men (not including Ferguson's patient) "whose blood contained HIV now test virus free." Errors in test analysis have been ruled out, but no other facts have been released.

Some characteristics of "long-term" AIDS survivors (three years after diagnosis) are studied at the federal Centers for Disease Control[56] with the hope of discovering clues about the behavior of the virus. Of 99 who are alive and could be contacted, 26 enrolled in the study.[29] The project does not study the behavior of the person or of the family, only that of the virus.

My point is that AIDS may *not* necessarily lead to death. Estimates such as the one quoted above[95] usually emphasize that one half of those infected will die; how about emphasizing that one half will live? I believe that studying those who recover is essential. This may, among other things, change the perception of the disease by health care providers, patients, and their families. If perception and thoughts change, self-regulation to influence the psychoneuroimmune system may become another process in the treatment of AIDS and HIV positive people.

One ARC patient reduced his symptoms with biofeedback and other self-regulation techniques combined with an emphasis on nutrition, exercise and other interventions attractive to him. He is not interested in being tested again and although presumed to be HIV positive for antibodies or virus, he no longer fits the diagnostic criteria of ARC. Without testing definitive conclusions cannot be drawn; however, it is common for infected people who feel well not to want to be tested again. On follow-up one year later he remained symptom free.[4]

Skeates[276] has been director of a facility which screened approximately 2700 people for HIV positive antibodies during a two year period. About 33% tested positive. He had direct, rather than only administrative, contact with most of them and was able to formulate clinical impressions and hypotheses. Beginning in 1986, he provided stress management, guided imagery and biofeedback to approximately 150 of those who tested positive. His clinical impression is that biofeedback and other self-regulation techniques prevent or slow down to some extent patients moving into the more serious stages of ARC and AIDS. He is presently analyzing the data of 100 people who were in one of 3 groups: placebo biofeedback, genuine biofeedback, and control. His preliminary impressions are that stress plays an important role in the course of the HIV virus, and that biofeedback can be helpful in managing stress and possibly altering the course of the virus. The time to start working is when people are told they are positive and are most open to the possibilities of self-regulation.[276]

His impression is that people, rather than waiting to see how soon ARC or AIDS follows, did learn biofeedback skills which are helpful in dealing with life issues. In the process, several secondary, common problems were identified such as migraine and Raynaud's. Biofeedback was helpful and strengthened the peoples' sense that they had more skills for effective living. With a very few people who already had ARC or AIDS, biofeedback made the persons more comfortable and enhanced the management of specific symptoms such as respiratory problems.[276]

At Georgetown, Maloney-Schara[172] is using biofeedback and family systems therapy with both members of a homosexual couple in which one person has AIDS and the other is well. The focus is determining if biofeedback with family systems therapy directed towards reducing the emotional cut-off between the infected person and his family can ameliorate AIDS symptoms. Reducing the emotional distance requires strong motivation by the couple and each family. Mr. X was on AZT treatment. Beginning 1–10/88 he has been on DHPG (ganciclovir), an experimental drug which appears to stop the progression of cytomegalovirus (CMV) in the eye. This is an infection of the retina which destroys vision and destroys white blood cells (WBC). His WBC count was under 1200 when he began biofeedback. To take CMV, his WBC count had to be a minimum of 1200. In early February 1988, his WBC was 1300. In February 10 it was 1900, and by March 8, 1988 it was 2400. He has had 11 biofeedback sessions and has learned to warm his skin temperature from 72 F to 90 F. Research could determine to what extent if any biofeedback facilitated an increase in WBC.

A homosexual's sister had been consulting with me about personal and family processes two years before her brother was diagnosed with AIDS. Their mother believes that God is punishing him and does not have communication. The rest of the family has frequent and meaningful personal contact with him, even the sibling living in Asia. As soon as he was diagnosed with AIDS, treatment with AZT was started. He is relatively symptom free. Is the AZT entirely responsible for his wellbeing; is his family's effort to re-connect with him part of the process?

Norris[193] uses the same techniques and concepts as for cancer with a few AIDS and ARC patients: reduce anxiety, ameliorate symptoms and distress, and help the terminally ill to die peacefully.

Exceptions sometimes teach more than the common events. I have a special interest in understanding what processes operate in people (and their families) who are exposed but not infected, who are infected but not sick, who were sick but are now symptom free, who were positive for HIV virus and now no longer test positive, and whose T4 and T8 cells count was low and now is high.[235] The following are self-reports of two people who tested positive (one became very ill) and now test HIV negative. Both encouraged me to tell their experience in the hope it will help others (I can forward mail to Mr. E. who would like to hear from others with AIDS).

Mr. Y. age 24 years lives in a midwestern urban area and was born with leukemia to a mother with cancer. He remembers being told that it was expected he would die at birth or soon thereafter. Since he did not die and his mother was very ill, she tried to kill him and herself. They both survived the attempt and she decided that she and her son (the youngest of several) were intended to live. She and her husband raised their son and she is alive and well. One of her basic themes became that if someone is sick, "you don't lay down to it." Years passed, and when he first told his mother he was gay, she did not talk to him for two days. However, they "worked it out," and family contact continued with his parents, grandparents, and large number of siblings and their spouses and children even though he is now in another city. When he was diagnosed HIV seropositive and confirmed with the Western Blot, he cried and literally "lay down for a couple of days." His mother went to see him and said, "Don't lay down to it." He proceeded "the best way he could" with his life. Two years later he decided to be tested again. He tests HIV negative. He has been living one year with a man who also is HIV negative and is now his lover. This man, Mr. X., reports he and his small family have very good contact with each other. Mr. X. was formerly lover for several years to another man, Mr. K. who died of AIDS about a year ago. It is reported that Mr. K. felt "too close" to his family, and that "they kept him in bed and would not let him do anything for himself."

The second person HIV seropositive in 1985, was tested and confirmed (by ELISA and Western Blot) in a major university medical center, but no longer tests positive (by culture). He, Mr. E., is a mental health professional who once lived in a large mid-Atantic metropolitan area. Shortly after he was diagnosed HIV seropositive, his T4 cell count began to drop rapidly to 225, 210, and 190. By the time he decided to move, his T4 cell count was 90. He found a small southern town where he thought he would go to die. A recovered alcoholic, he began drinking again after 11 years of sobriety. Somehow in the dying process, he began making major changes and taking large amounts of vitamin E and zinc. To regain sobriety he took antabuse, which is now considered to be very similar to the drug diethyldithiocarbamate (DTC). DTC is currently under study for its immune modulating action in restoring T4 cell function but he did not know that at the time he took antabuse. He has what he describes as "real" contact with his family of origin. Two years later, now totally symptom free, his T4 cell count has been 500–600 (most recent 560) and by culture test, is not longer HIV positive. A single negative result is not necessarily significant in research. However, he feels well and trusts the tests results from a major university medical center.

Three points are important: (1) because these are self reports, it is not definitive whether "positive" and "negative" refers to virus or antibodies; (2) according to family systems theory, no contact or too intense contact are both dysfunctional (See Chapter 5) which would help explain these accounts and suggests research; and (3) the fact is, regardless of the unknowns, that these two men are healthy.

What strengthened these two men's immune systems? Their beliefs? Their physiological and genetic predisposition? Their family history and processes? Nutrition? Exercise? Other factors? All, some, or none? Did they do a form of "self-regulation," and increased their differentiation? Neither seeks religious explanations. They believe, among other things, that how they see themselves is essential.

Badgley's[9] focus is on the importance of strengthening the immune system and not accepting the idea that AIDS/ARC is necessarily fatal. He cites the histories of eight "survivors" and the "natural therapies" such as relaxation and especially nutrition which they worked out for themselves. "The key was that all the therapies worked synergistically to balance the body and the net result was increased vitality." All became ill between 1980 and 1985 with a variety of symptoms: (Mr. A) bedridden for two years, three years of diarrhea, Kaposi's sarcoma-like skin lesions (not biopsied), night sweat, Candida, fungi, lymph gland swelling, Cytomegalovirus and herpes infections, shingles, amoeba parasites in the intestine and pneumonia three times; (Mr. B) Kaposi's sarcoma (biopsied), positive HIV, 14 episodes of gonorrhea, lymph node syndrome, Candida of the tongue, weight loss, depression; (Mr. C) Kaposi's lesion, depressed T4/T8 cell ratio and depressed absolute helper cell count, interferon treatment which did not help; (Mr. D) biopsy-positive Kaposi's lesion, HIV positive, lymph node swelling; (Mr. E) swollen lymph nodes, unexamined Kaposi's sarcoma, over 100 warts, parasites, and bedridden two months; (Mr. F) hepatitis, pancreatitis, herpes, pneumonia, parasites, Candida, swollen lymph nodes, HIV positive, T-4/T-8 ratio of 0.6; (Mr. G) 35 Kaposi lesions, lymph node swelling, diarrhea; and, (Mr. H) positive HIV antibody, swollen lymph nodes, parasites, diarrhea, mouth ulcers. All were alive and well in 1987.[9]

A health educator who counsels people about the results of their HIV antibody blood tests told me she has observed that at least 70% of the people who test antibody positive appear to have emotionally distant relationships with their families. No formal study has been done. As more biofeedback clinicians work with individuals who are HIV positive, seropositive, or who have ARC or AIDS, it will be intriguing to study if biofeedback and other self-regulation techniques "work" better in people who are in family of origin systems with quality contact.

BIOFEEDBACK FOR CHILDREN

Introduction: Stress and IQ

Biofeedback with children is used in public schools and in clinical situations. It is well known that stress affects children's physical, emotional and social performance.

Brown and Rosenbaum[35,36] in a study of over 4,000 seven-year-old children found that the higher the stress, the lower the IQ as measured by the Wechsler Intelligence Scale for Children (WISC). We devised an index based on 74 stress variables and found that the number of stressors, rather than particular ones, produces the negative effect. I developed the hypothesis that stress affects IQ, from family systems theory (See Chapter 5) which proposes that level of functioning is determined by two main variables: the degree of differentiation (autonomy, coping ability, integrity) of the individual, and the degree of stress or reactivity in the family emotional field. The dysfunction can be physical, emotional, or social. I added cognitive functioning explicitly. The stress index is based on data collected in the 1960s in the Collaborative Perinatal Project files by the National Institute of Health. The findings confirmed the hypothesis that stress affects intelligence in the immediate testing situation and developmentally; and, they have implications for improving functioning and possibly intelligence. In her BSA presidential address Dr. Norris referred to this study stating,

> It seems obvious that all school children could benefit from stress management training, as well as learning to use biofeedback and visualization for voluntary control of internal states, demonstrating increased performance.[191]

Biofeedback in Public Schools

Children who are over or under reactive in schools function less well than their potential. Biofeedback can facilitate appropriate levels of reactivity and thereby maximize functioning. Engelhardt's program in the public schools did exactly that.

Engelhardt[75,76,77,78] is a creative pioneer. In 1975-78 she developed a program which has become eminently successful in South Dakota. Under the Elementary and Secondary Education Act, P.L. 89-10, Title III, now Title IV-C funding was awarded over a three-year period to the Spearfish School District for the implementation of the Awareness and Relaxation Through Biofeedback Program. This sort of biofeedback project could be done again in states that have block grant money available.

It was the intent of the program that the participating students and/or educators acquire muscle relaxation skills, decrease their general anxiety level and improve their self-concept. Approximately 1,515 students and 80 instructors, predominantly of a Caucasian middle class background were involved in each of two elementary, junior and senior high schools.

Total instrument practice time per participant involved 5 to 15 minutes two times a week for six weeks. The program was implemented as curriculum components in a variety of educational areas and grade levels in Spearfish. Title IV-C projects in Colorado, Oklahoma and Indiana also implemented this approach to learn self-regulation and reported gains in reading and mathematical skills.

In summary, Engelhardt[76,77] found that muscle-relaxation skills can be acquired as a health habit by both students and educators as part of their educational curricula. Forty-two educators first acquired the skills themselves and 95% reached criterion level. They then implemented the awareness activities, progressive relaxation, passive exercises and biofeedback training with electromyograph and temperature trainers. Using biofeedback instruments, 194 students learned relaxation skills. Analysis of pre- and post-measurements showed that participants decreased their anxiety level significantly and increased their self concept scores. Biofeedback instruments demonstrated that students can decrease the frontalis muscle-tension level and/or increase hand temperature during the public school classroom routine. The program was so well received and integrated into the school system that although Dr, Engelhardt's project ended in 1979, it is still used. One important component is the fact that to change children's functioning, adults' functioning was improved first. This happens to be consistent with family systems theory regarding the importance of decreasing over reactivity and increasing the adult's functioning to affect a change in the child. It would be interesting to replicate the Engelhardt design without providing biofeedback to the children and observing what percent of children change as a consequence of changes in the teacher.

Relaxation without biofeedback has been taught in the Swedish public schools since 1975 with physical education. Positive results are reported for the "development of seven capacities, the 7-C's, (self-) confidence, commitment, calmness, creativity, cheerfulness (positiveness), concentration, and (self-) control." Relaxation is viewed as "nature's own medicine," used with imagery and practiced at home 5 times per week. There was a difference in anxiety level, and over half of the students said they managed their school work better.[265]

Fisher and Peper[92] reported a successful program in Idaho using biofeedback, individualized imagery and an adapted version of Kiddie QR[295] to enhance positive self-awareness in 275 children ages 6 to 9 in public school. Over a three year period, all children and their 6 teachers practiced 15 minutes, three times a week, for 6 weeks. The program included strategies by which the child practiced the skills on his/her own, thereby learning more autonomy and generalization. The biofeedback component, used in groups, included hand warming, muscle awareness, and skin reactivity. The program was assessed by the responses of children, teachers and parents. Children learned the coping skills more quickly than their teachers. The six teachers and 88% of parents wanted to be continue and expand the program.

Yeager[341] combines age appropriate stress theory, general relaxation, biofeedback demonstrations, and the use of skin thermometers to work with students in kindergarten through 12th grades in private and public schools. He also lectured or demonstrated to 2,500 parents, 2,000 teachers, and 500 administrators. Of 7,500 students who received a one time demonstration, approximately 1,500 were in schools which provided an ongoing biofeedback-relaxation program of 3–4 weeks or of one semester duration. Empirical findings about the effects have not been collected, but clearly a 4th "r," "relaxation and biofeedback" is received enthusiastically in some schools.

Learning or Clinical Problems

Children's psychophysiological disorders are almost as many as those of adults. Here focus is on some of the most important work with learning disabilities and other clinical school-related problems.

Green[107] describes the use of biofeedback training and adjunctive techniques in the treatment of stress related illnesses, behavioral disorders, and learning disabilities in children in a clinical setting. The treatment goal is psychophysiological self-regulation through relaxation and stress management, and self-image and cognitive changes. She provides a bridge between education and treatment. In a sense, treatment is a learning process. She clearly describes how self-regulation through biofeedback training is based on principles common to all learning. The crucial link in the stress response and in the development of psychosomatic illness seems to be the connection of limbic system and emotional/mental events, whether those originate from external or internal stimuli. That same link is used to promote psychophysiological health through biofeedback training and therapeutic techniques which promote a homeostatic interaction of mind and body. Intervening variables which affect this learning process include attitudes, beliefs, expectations, commitment to change and a sense of self-responsibility.

Even when the biofeedback is for treatment, she introduces herself to children as a "biofeedback teacher." She explains that she teaches ideas and skills, that she likes to ask and be asked questions. She has each family member attach the thermistor of a temperature feedback unit to the middle finger of the dominant hand, and then goes on to demonstrate the body/mind link. When appropriate the child brings school work to the session. She also "plays" a variety of games with the children to clarify that link further as well as to heighten their interest in learning biofeedback and adjunctive techniques. Clinical results are often dramatic.[107]

Carter, Lax and Russell[54] found that a combination of electromyographic (EMG) forearm muscle relaxation and prerecorded relaxation home exercises resulted in highly significant gains in basic academic skills as well as in handwriting quality. Parents and teachers observed behavioral changes in greater self-control in these children. Spelling, arithmetic, and writing legibility also changed significantly without academic remediation. Learning disabled boys showed significant improvement over controls on measures of reading, spelling, verbal IQ, eye-hand coordination, auditory memory, and handwriting legibility. Children from poor families did not have cassette tape players to practice relaxation at home. Practicing biofeedback at school 10 minutes, 3 times/week for 6 weeks produced remarkable results. The investigators hypothesize that as children become more relaxed they have more efficient access to previously learned material and can attend more effectively to the schoolwork.[53]

They hypothesized[52] that attending school daily while performing poorly is a source of considerable stress which even further limits school performance. It had been shown that learning disabled children show much more autonomic lability and inability to focus attention than do normal controls. Chronic poor school performance results in a sustained fight or flight pattern of arousal.

The children who received biofeedback and heard the tapes showed significant change in 10 of 11 measures; the change was maintained or improved over time (10 month follow-up). Children who did not receive the treatments showed improvement on only 1 of 11 variables and the follow-up scores tended to decrease slightly if not significantly. Significant improvements were obtained in verbal IQ, reading, spelling, arithmetic computation, auditory memory, eye-hand coordination and written expression.

Trained biofeedback clinicians were able to bring about greater gains than were teachers who had little clinical biofeedback training. The children who made the greatest changes were those trained by an experienced biofeedback clinician and in the treatment group which used a combination of EMG biofeedback and prerecorded relaxation tapes.

Carter and Russell demonstrated with 650 learning disabled children and 82 teachers in 24 different schools that a kit of prerecorded relaxation tapes and a handwriting workbook with instructions could be used effectively by teachers. The improvements in cognitive, achievement, and psychomotor abilities were practical and highly statistically significant. A small group of underachieving gifted elementary age children and 79 secondary age emotionally disturbed students made significant gains. The investigators conclude that the intervention (with a total 801 students) is appropriate for a variety of handicapped children including learning disabled, educable mentally retarded, emotionally disturbed and non-diagnosed students with academic learning problems.[52,53]

Biofeedback is also used in highly individualized clinical situations. Lubar and Lubar[165] reported successful treatment of 6 students ages 10–19 with electroencephalographic bio-feedback of sensorimotor rhythm SMR and beta for attention deficit disorders in a clinical setting. The training consisted of two sessions per week, for 40 minutes, for 10 to 27 months. Feedback was provided for either increasing 12 to 15-Hz SMR or 16- to 20-Hz beta activity. Treatment included academic training in reading, arithmetic and spatial tasks to improve attention. All students increased SMR or beta and decreased slow EEG and EMG activity. Changes could be seen in their power spectra, in improvement in schoolwork, and in discontinuing use of medications for hyperkinetic behavior.

Lubar and Deering[164] emphasize the importance of accurate categorization of learning disabilities and of determining which is the primary, secondary or tertiary problem before providing biofeedback, family therapy, and other treatment components. They critically review the literature and caution that positive results obtained with EMG biofeedback may not be stable over time and may not work with all children. They conclude that SMR training combined with training for inhibition of excessive EMG activity and slow activity between 4 and 7 Hz is the most potent biofeedback paradigm for long-term training of low-arousal hyperkinesis or hyperkinesis which responds to stimulant medication. The use of EEG biofeedback paradigms will produce stronger and longer lasting effects than EMG training by itself.

Estrada, Kelso and Gladman[80] treat attention deficit disorder with a "multimodal" approach of biofeedback, behavior therapy, and supportive psychotherapeutic counselling taking into account the family, peers and school. Biofeedback includes training for hand warming, muscle relaxation (inhibiting motor movement improves cognitive performance), and bilateral EEG training. They report greater self-regulation and reduction of medication by the third visit. Overactivity, restlessness, distractibility, and short attention span are significantly diminished. Sleep patterns improve, as well as self-concept, self- and inner-awareness, and parental and peer relationships.***

In my practice, biofeedback for children is provided in the context of family systems therapy. This implies that in addition to working with the child on specific skills, work with parent(s) or other responsible adult is essential. Biofeedback training is encouraged for teachers and administrators. The main goals with the adults (teachers, parents, etc.) are to facilitate a decrease in their overreactivity, and to provide a broader perspective with which to understand the symptoms, problems, or life process of specific child(ren). The single most important variable in predicting the level, intensity, and duration of reactivity in rhesus monkeys is the reactivity of the caretaker monkey.[299] This finding parallels clinical experience in my program – decreasing overactivity in the important adults in a child's system, decreases the reactivity and increases the functioning in the child.

Werner and Smith[324] concluded that some children and youth who were vulnerable were "invincible." Almost 700 multiracial youth exposed to poverty, perinatal stress, family instability and serious mental health problems were studied from birth to age 20. One of every five developed serious behavior or learning problems. As family systems theory

---

***As this book goes to press, a promising new treatment for attention deficit hyperactivity disorder (ADHD) combines EEG beta activity training with cognitive skills rehabilitation training. Youngsters learn to increase the amplitude of EEG in the 13 to 25-Hz range using biofeedback. The "reward" for learning is time spent playing a cognitive rehabilitation computer game designed to increase specific areas such as visual/spatial relations, and attention, mathematical, and integrative skills. This approach extends the concept of ADHD from "dysfunction" to "dysregulation" (Amar, Director, Ambler Psychological Services, Ambler, PA).

might have predicted, a second or third adult in the household (reduced intensity of interaction), sibling position, seeking and obtaining help from informal sources of support including extended family, teachers, clergy, "family closeness and respect for individuality," "cohesiveness of the family," and the "presence of an informal multigenerational network of kin and friends" were among the "protective factors."[324]

The balance between the "risk factors, stressful life events" and "protective factors" within the child and the environment account for the differences in resilience and health in the invincible ones.[324] One implication is that interventions can either decrease the exposure to risk, or increase the number of "protective factors." I believe biofeedback with family systems therapy to increase coping can be a powerful combination to increase "protective factors" in children and youth. More intriguing, since children normally have greater flexibility and growth potential than adults there are greater possibilities of health, performance and cognitive enhancement. Biofeedback may open frontiers to increased functioning and self-regulation of body/mind in young people.

12

CONCEPTUAL FRONTIERS: APPLIED TO THE PHYSIOLOGY OF RELATIONSHIPS

Biofeedback frontiers develop in two broad but related areas: practical uses (See Chapter 11) and conceptual advances. This chapter describes a conceptual frontier and its applications: family systems theory with biofeedback which is not simply combining two techniques but conceptualizing individual physiology as an indicator of the functioning of family and other relationship systems. The individual is seen as a part of relationship systems and the biofeedback "numbers" can represent much more than the specific muscle activity, skin temperature or blood pressure of one person.

In natural systems thinking, the individual within the larger emotional unit is analogous to the heart within the human body. Though it is possible to measure the heart and observe how it responds, it is impossible to understand the complete functioning of the heart unless it is viewed in relation to the entire body. A symptom that occurs in the heart may be the lungs compensating for a problem that exists elsewhere in the body. So too, an exclusive focus on the symptoms in one family member can miss the process in the family unit. Biofeedback training from a family systems perspective considers the processes of the larger emotional units (family, organization) and tries to understand the part the individual and the symptom play in the larger unit. The goal is to assist the change of a person's functioning within the larger unit. The ability to challenge and cope with emotional processes in the most important relationships, rather than to run from them, allows improved management of physiological responses such as blood pressure. For example,[98] the individual learns to self-regulate blood pressure while quiet and relaxing, then while talking about a difficult relationship and later even in the presence of the person with whom there is an intense relationship.

Chronology: Theoretical, Clinical, Research and Administrative Issues in Combining Family Systems Theory and Biofeedback

My interest in biofeedback grew out of my participation in one of Bowen's early research projects – observing change and reactivity. In 1968, he asked me to participate in a research project conducted in the context of multiple family therapy sessions he had been holding weekly since 1966. The goal was deceptively simple: to devise some way to observe change in people who were working to improve their functioning. I decided to record the types of pronouns people used as an indicator of change and reactivity. I used content analysis of recorded interviews and developed a "change ratio" called the "qualified pronoun count."[332] However, I kept wondering how to obtain a more solid, biologically based indicator of change.

A few years later, in 1973, I became aware of the then new development called biofeedback. Initial questions were: how information via a machine could accomplish any solid change and how to "treat" the symptom and not get focused on it, an important aspect of family systems theory. Then I saw that in addition to facilitating physiological change and symptom reduction, the instrumentation might be useful to (1) monitor changes in *reactivity* in relationship processes, (2) observe changes in reactivity in more than one person in the emotional system, even if only one person was working with biofeedback, and (3) enable changes in overall reactivity and in differentiation. Family systems theory was then unknown to biofeedback investigators and clinicians.

After much consideration I decided to set up a biofeedback laboratory either in my private practice or at the Georgetown University Family Center. Dr. Bowen encouraged me to do it up at Georgetown. He had been interested in the notion of biofeedback for many years and thought that it might bridge psychological and physical functioning. In fact, I think one of the important contributions of biofeedback is that it eliminates a conceptual dichotomy between the mind and body or between emotional and physical phenomena.

Based on theoretical considerations I made a number of administrative decisions regarding purchasing instrumentation and operating the laboratory. I wanted to (1) continue to observe, monitor and understand reactivity; (2) develop family systems theory; (3) make contact with medicine regarding another way of thinking about health and illness by using biofeedback as a bridge; (4) provide a new and valuable clinical service; and, (5) establish a laboratory for research, clinical service, professional training and consultation which would be respected for its excellence locally and nationally. In 1975 I decided to start the clinic by encouraging a few people whom I was seeing for psychotherapy in my private practice to try biofeedback in the program I established at Georgetown and to have them pay Georgetown rather than me. Soon I also began a biofeedback professional training program.[238] One guiding principle was that clinical practice, professional training, and research would use biofeedback in the context of family systems theory. By 1987 almost 3,000 people had clinical biofeedback at Georgetown. The professional program also quickly expanded to include postgraduate, professionals, fellows, interns, and medical students (See Chapter 8).

A number of study proposals emerged. For instance, in 1975 I proposed a study "Individuation and Biofeedback" to: (1) examine whether patterns of physiological functioning as reflected in biofeedback indicators (EEG, EMG, GSR, skin temperature) are associated with degree of differentiation, (2) examine if when any of the patterns of physiological indicators changed with biofeedback, there would also be a change in differentiation. Another of my earliest proposals, "Biofeedback and Family Therapy for Marital Conflict," was to study changes in reactivity in the marital relationship. The plan was to provide biofeedback training with family therapy for either spouse, and look for changes in the family system. Another proposal[333] was to study mothers and schizophrenic offspring to determine (1) if there is a characteristic EEG pattern between them, and (2) if altering (through biofeedback) the EEG pattern between them alters the intensity of the schizophrenic behavior. These ideas were great for advancing family systems thinking, terrible for making a bridge with the medical community and for establishing a biofeedback clinical program. I put the proposals on hold, not the thinking.

Initially, I also thought of connecting simultaneously more than one person to biofeedback instrumentation to study reactivity as a phenomenon that occurs not only within each person but also between people. Some instrumentation was marketed for "group process" to have all people in the group work together and be responsible for the physiology of all other persons. For instance, the skin temperature readings were a composite of all the temperatures of the people in the group. This, I thought, could not advance differentiation.

There was a range of models, based on theories of individual functioning, to provide biofeedback to one patient at a time, or several at a time as a group, or several at a time individually. Thinking systems I saw possibilities to work with an individual, couple, or family and to connect them to the instrumentation at the same or at different times. I decided that the conceptualizations about the presenting problem and the change processes were crucial, rather than which family members were in the biofeedback laboratory. I decided to set up the biofeedback laboratory in such a way that each person worked individually with a coach on self-regulation of reactivity. This meant delaying (See Chapters 4 and 9) some aspects of explicit studies of reactivity in relationships. But, it still allowed conceptualizing family systems theory while using biofeedback for psychophysiological symptoms.

The primary focus was on increasing regulation of overreactivity and thereby on facilitating a decrease in a variety of psychophysiological symptoms, pain, and the intake of prescribed drugs. Persons used the biofeedback instrumentation to observe physiological and emotional responses in self, to monitor reactivity in the laboratory and in their relationship systems, and to learn to self-regulate it. Changes in physiological responsiveness were observed in connection with events, feelings and thoughts about important systems (family, school, work). It quickly became apparent that given certain situations and emotional processes, even thinking about another person can produce measurable physiological changes.

Early Observations of Reactivity in Relationships

While the clinical service focused on biofeedback for psychophysiological symptoms, the study of reactivity in family systems continued to be essential. Beginning in 1978, the cooperation of faculty and staff made it possible to do a small, preliminary observation of mothers and their young.

The goals were (1) to study relationships in parent/child bio-feedback baselines pairs, (2) to develop laboratory stressors for infants and children, and (3) to observe physiological reaction children when mother left the room.

Suomi[298] (See Chapter 2) found that individual differences in response to stress and challenge can be detected early in life and that these differences are remarkably stable over time. Currently he studies the extent and the degree of reactivity in rhesus infants raised by foster mothers. That is, if a "high-reactive" infant is given a "low-reactive" foster mother, will the infant respond with less extensive and intensive reactivity during stress? His research points in that direction. One implication for human mothers is the potential of bio-feedback training for decreasing their own reactivity and thus influencing the reactivity of their infants.

Georgetown biofeedback clinicians* also did baselines on parents and adult offspring, including pairs where a mother was 70 years old. Some baseline sets included three generations, or other combinations of interested family members. Lack of interest or of geographical availability of some family members, resulted in incomplete data. Computerized data collection was not technically possible at the time. Nevertheless, these clinical explorations in 1979–1980 produced some interesting observations and raised a variety of research questions for future study.

Table 12.1 shows data on a mother with migraines. The relatively low skin temperature is typical of vascular disorders including migraines. The son had behavioral, not physical, symptoms. Can differences in baseline patterns be expected if the presenting symptom is physiological rather than behavioral?

*These people collaborated with me in doing baselines or organizing data: Ames, M.A., Brown, B., Cordts, G., Friesen, P., Greco, P., Harrison, V., Kelley, L., Martin, P., Muszinski, K., Rauseo, L., and Trogdon, E.

TABLE 12.1 / Family Baselines (1979): Mother and Son

Age	Occupation Relationship	Presenting Problem	Baselines RX	S	RE
40	Homemaker Mother	Migraines	5.85 74.3 .09	7.49 76.3 .12	7.78 79.4 .09
17	Student Son	Behavior (Marijuana)	4.40 88.8 .33	4.54 88.8 .31	3.78 89.3 .31

In another family (Table 12.2) the mother had migraine and tension headaches. Notice the relatively elevated muscle tension (EMG) and relatively low skin temperature. The father had hypertension and back pain. The paternal grandmother had no symptoms. Her baseline indicates a flexible EMG recovery pattern, but low skin temperature. Even though she is symptom free, could this indicator of reactivity in the baseline be a precursor to symptoms in the next generation? The grandson had somewhat elevated EMG and headaches. The granddaughter did not have a baseline done. The grandson's EMG decreased (instead of the more common increase) during the stress part of the baseline, but his hand temperature stayed above 93°F. Husband, wife and son learned important biofeedback skills well enough to decrease reactivity and symptoms. How much less success does a family have in learning to decrease reactivity if the previous generation is severely symptomatic?

Recent research shows that cognitively enriched environment of pregnant rats alters the brains of unborn rats. Although the mechanism for such apparent transfer of effects is unknown, the effects (increasingly thicker cortices) transfer to each succeeding generation.[66] In human families the functioning of previous generations affects the functioning of present generations. Do conditions which affected the symptomatic person's mother at the time she was pregnant play a role not

TABLE 12.2 / Family Baselines (1979): Three Generations

Age	Occupation Relationship	Presenting Problem	RX	Baselines S	RE
70	Homemaker Paternal Grandmother		5.33 71.6 .13	11.40 71.8 .16	4.0 72.0 .18
39	Homemaker Wife/Mother	Headaches	13.09 73.7 .10	14.67 73.2 .10	14.42 73.0 .06
40	Physician Husband/Father	Back pain Hypertension	12.15 88.5 .67	7.89 89.16 1.58	6.82 85.6 1.02
12	Student/Son	Headaches	12.49 92.3 .57	9.18 93.2 .61	12.54 93.2 .61

only in the symptomatic person's functioning, but also in learning biofeedback self-regulation?

One last baseline set is about a mother with migraines, Raynaud's disease and insomnia and her three daughters of whom two came for a baseline (one was in Europe). Table 12.3 shows her relatively low skin temperature. Neither daughter was symptomatic and their baselines are similar. Both respond with EMG elevation during stress, flexible EMG responses and recover to lower levels than their initial EMG. What family processes contain the symptoms in the mother and leave the daughters symptom free?

Over the years of developing a biofeedback clinical practice, I have intermittently tried different strategies to study reactivity.[232] Figure 12.1 shows the skin temperature of an adolescent girl in an emotional triangle during a session with her parents. She was estimating her parents had spent about $40,000 on beer, cigarettes and drugs, in 20 years. The skin temperature dropped steadily, one indicator of reactivity. She listened without participating during the next few minutes

TABLE 12.3 / Family Baselines (1979): Mother and Two Daughters

Age	Occupation Relationship	Presenting Problem	Baselines		
			RX	S	RE
48	Home; Free-Lance Research And writing Mother	Migraines	3.22	5.05	3.79
		Raynaud's	76.3	74.8	74.1
		Insomnia	.10	.12	.12
20	Student Daughter	Headaches	4.82	10.27	3.31
		Anorexia	87.6	87.6	87.1
			.95	.18	.09
17	Student Daughter	—	4.68	5.24	3.68
			88.0	88.1	87.9
			.33	.26	.26

while her parents focused on their problems but she was still in the emotional triangle. Her reactivity increased and her skin temperature decreased at a rapid rate. At the end of the session she said she was frustrated because she could not "help" her parents. This reflects the intensity of the parent/child triangle.

Figure 12.2 shows a husband and wife, both highly recognized in their own professions, talking about their adolescent and adult offspring, all highly competent individuals who were not in the session. Both had finger temperature thermistors. The wife was talking with concern about the son who was actually functioning very well in medical school. The husband listened, uninvolved. Her skin temperature dropped, his remained stable. I then decided to see what would happen to the skin temperature if I tried to refocus the parents on themselves and where they would live (potential two-city marriage). Her skin temperature increased (indicator of decreased anxiety) as the focus changed away from the son. As each parent focused on self, career, two cities, and their already conflictual marriage, the mother's anxiety about the son decreased, and her skin temperature increased. In that

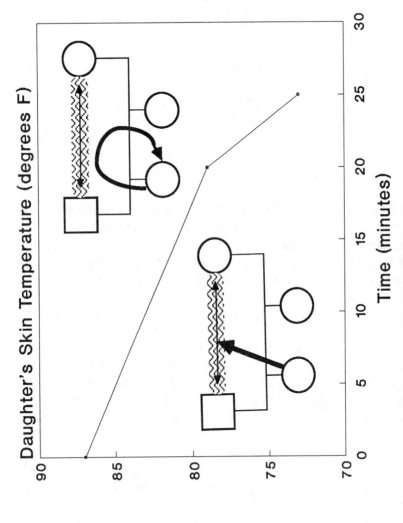

Figure 12.1 Emotional Triangles and Psychophysiology

218

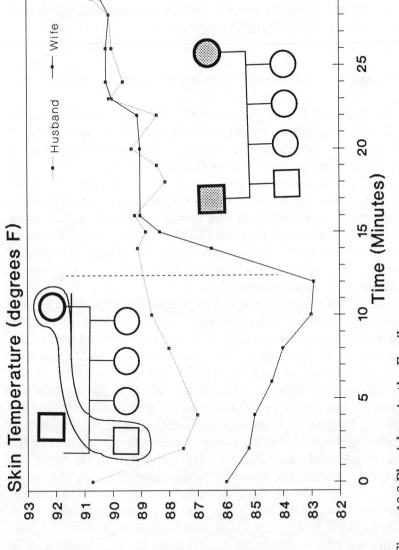

Figure 12.2 Physiology in the Family

session, the father was able to "stay on course" regarding the marital problems, which the mother experienced as "distance" but which later facilitated de-focusing their offspring and attending to the more basic issues in their marriage. Physiology reflects family systems processes.

Biofeedback and Family Systems Concepts

Biofeedback based on theory of individual functioning, regards the symptom as an entity in itself. For instance, to help a child with fecal incontinence, biofeedback is provided to strengthen or relax the anal sphincter. Only as an afterthought is the parents' reaction and behavior to the child's symptom considered relevant to the treatment outcome. The fact that a mother views one bowel movement a day as an indicator of constipation, and that a father is indifferent to the mother, influences the processes which keep the youngster with diarrhea. Systems thinking provides a guide to understand larger process.

What basic family systems concepts are important to biofeedback training? Arousal (reactivity) can be evaluated in terms of the frequency, intensity, and recovery pattern of the specific responses and of the organism. How well a function recovers is determined in part by the (1) flexibility of the function in question, and the (2) flexibility of the organism in general. Other factors which affect the specific function are the (1) level of differentiation (functioning of the individual and family over time), (2) the level of reactivity present in the individual and the family at the time of the onset of the symptom and at the time the person is working to change it, and (3) the role of the symptom in the multigenerational transmission process (e.g., family and work systems).

Biofeedback training (1) produces changes in clinical symptoms, in pain management, in stress management, and in performance enhancement; (2) communicates systems thinking to the medical and other health care professions. (In my experience, the most productive way to communicate theory is to practice well and to make theory explicit at the appropriate time.) (3) contributes to optimum performance by facilitating the unlearning of, or the cortical overriding of, ancestrally determined (reptilian or limbic) responses in appropriate situations; and, (4) contributes to the development of natural systems theory by encouraging questions and development of technology to think about, observe and change reactivity within and between individuals.

Natural systems thinking provides a way of conceptualizing the phenomena observed in biofeedback training and an action blueprint. Three systems concepts illustrate symptom formation and symptom management: (1) forces of individuality and togetherness; (2) the notion that human functioning, even though unique in some aspects, has much in common with other living systems and is part of the evolutionary process; and, (3) multigenerational transmission process (See Chapter 5).

First, individuality and togetherness forces are instinctual and automatic. A symptom (physical, emotional, social or cognitive) may be an indicator how the system functions and of the pull between these forces within an individual and within a relationship system. When a symptom is acute and originates outside the individual (e.g. pain following a car accident injury), the life forces of individuality and togetherness still play a part in determining management and recovery.

Second, human functioning, even though unique in some aspects, has potentials and determinants within the evolutionary process. Biofeedback can, within limits, maximize functioning and enhance performance.

Third, multigenerational transmission processes may influence symptom management. While research is needed to understand exactly how and what is transmitted, clinical observation over twenty five years by dozens of clinicians suggests that, emotional processes, behavioral patterns, physiological susceptibilities and patterns of adaptability are transmitted from one generation to another. Biofeedback for the improvement of a specific function may be intervening in processes determined by more than one generation. The past and anticipated future of the person and of the family are taken into account as well as the present state of functioning at the time of biofeedback training.

Evolution and Biofeedback

Biofeedback training may also enhance human potential (and possibly over a very long time also evolution) by increasing the human's ability to self-regulate – to use its brain in new ways. Brown[39] examines "super-mind as the ultimate energy," learning and the evolution of behavior. One of the amazing abilities of nerve tissue, however primitive, is its ability to "learn." The simple neural tube of the earthworm can store in memory enough information to "learn" how to distinguish one signal from another. The barely differentiated cells of minute marine animals can "learn" not to react with their usual body contractions to pressure stimuli after the stimuli are repeated at frequent intervals. The opposite kind of "learned behavior," where the organism increases innate reactions to environmental changes (by rate or magnitude of response) emerges at a later evolutionary level.

Restak[221] considers the brain the last "frontier" and uses MacLean's and E.O. Wilson's work as a basis for posing possibilities for society's future. To what extent are humans able to free themselves from the influence of ancient animal forebears? How can we retain what is useful and eliminate or control the destructive consequences that may result from the unchecked expression of older structures such as the limbic system?[221]

Biofeedback with family therapy can be powerful to facilitate increased cortical control. Possibly an important biofeed-back function is that it facilitates awareness of automaticity and unlearning automatic physiological, emotional, and social responses associated with evolutionary older brain areas. This may free newer parts of the brain to learn new responses, to have a wider range of choices, and to have more flexibility in responsiveness (See Chapter 3).

Transmission of Reactivity: Examples from Animal Research

Bowen theory predicts that important human family processes are non-genetically transmitted. Nongenetic transmission affects the behavior of stressed infant rats. The experience of their grandmothers as infants, even if these grandmothers are *foster-grandmothers*, influenced infant rats.[64] One-generational transfer of experiential effects has also been shown for both behavioral and physiological characteristics.[65] The behavior of rats was modified by the experiences their *mothers* had as *infants*. A non-genetic "vertical" transmission of acquired ulcer susceptibility in the rat has been described.[277] The altered susceptibility is acquired by environmental manipulation (premature separation) during postnatal development in one generation and the susceptibility to ulcers is transmitted to the offspring of the next generation (See Chapter 5). This "raises the clear specter of familial effects in certain disease conditions that may *not* be genetic in origin."[147] There is a non-genetic transmission of family processes, at least in rats, which affects both behavior and physiology and merits thinking about the multigenerational transmission processes in human families.

Baboons studied in Kenya have different physiological stress responses according to their place in the social hierarchy.[255] The top male in a baboon society, who fathers 40 percent of the babies born each year, has lower blood glucocorticoid levels than the other male baboons. (The fight-or-flight response triggered by stress causes the release of glucocorticoids which signal the body to increase blood pressure, heart rate, blood sugar and the flow of blood to the muscles. Continuously high levels can harm brain cells and make them prone to seizure or stroke damage). The leader's glucocorticoid levels in response to threat rise rapidly but also fall more quickly once the danger has passed.

Biofeedback with humans facilitates rapid, flexible recovery which is associated with symptom reduction and with increased performance. It is intriguing that in nature physiological recovery time is shorter for baboon leaders than nonleaders and suggests similar research with humans.

The physiology of golden hamsters is also responsive to social dominance.[89] Immunological responsivity of adult mice was modified by their experience during infancy.[281] Research shows that social rank, handling, and early experience are among the "social" factors that affect immunity. In humans, acute life stress and chronic family disorganization significantly contributes to immune system function (See Chapter 2). The phenomenon that the physiology of one person is responsive to the physiology of important others in the relationship system has been frequently observed in my clinical work.

Recent Examples at Georgetown

Theory determines what a biofeedback "coach" does (See Chapter 8), biofeedback instrumentation use, and seeing new possibilities such as using medical instrumentation to monitor reactivity in people with diabetes (See Chapter 11). Other examples of theory guiding practice follow. Although an 11-year-old child with a gastrointestinal disorder was the referred "patient," baselines were done for mother and child. The son's reactivity is responsive to the reactivity and emo-

TABLE 12.4 / Mother's Reactivity and Focus Affect Son's Reactivity as He Listens and Does Biofeedback

(a) Fourth Session: Son using biofeedback instruments and listening to mother

EMG	DST	EDR	
14.00	94.8	1.80	Work stress in her office; describing her
6.00	97.0	1.80	level of exhaustion.
13.00	95.9	1.80	
5.00	95.9	2.80	
6.00	97.3	2.50	Shift to extended family & their function-
8.00	97.9	3.10	ing. Mother's worries about son's injury,
10.00	94.8	2.80	danger in the world. Death of mother's
16.00	95.1	3.10	youngest brother from drowning. Her posi-
6.00	94.8	2.80	tion as eldest responsible.
4.40	94.7	2.00	
4.00	94.6	2.00	

(b) Follow-up Session, three months later. Son's reactivity is lower when mother not focused on him.

EMG	DST	EDR	
6.10	92.9	1.12	Mother describing her practice at home
4.00	92.5	1.00	2–3 times a week regularly.
4.00	92.7	1.00	
4.00	93.1	1.00	
4.00	92.6	1.00	
8.00	92.3	1.70	Mother describing family events: Grandfa-
8.00	91.3	1.70	ther's stroke, Grandmother's breast cancer
8.00	90.9	1.10	and surgery.
3.20	92.5	1.50	
3.00	93.3	1.18	
3.50	93.5	1.00	Family reunion for those above which mother planned and executed with more cooperation from her mother and estranged aunt. Described how this experience shifted her sense of aggravation with the family & her sense of being unappreciated for her efforts.

tional focus of the mother (Table 12.4). In the fourth session (Table 12.4.a) mother is focused on child. In the follow-up session 3 months later (Table 12.4.b) she reports important work with her family, is calmer, and is not focused on the son. Biofeedback monitoring provided an opportunity to observe the responsiveness between mother and child. When the mother talked about her worries about her son, his levels of tension (and symptoms) increased. In contrast, as she shifted her thinking and conversation to facts in the family history and her own experiences as the eldest sibling responsible for others, the boy's physiology settled down. The mother understood the theoretical implications of calming herself and practiced biofeedback at home. The boy did not practice at home. At follow-up three months later (Table 12.4.b) the mother, who was still using her relaxation skills, described a family reunion in which she was able to relate in a different way to her aunts and mother. The son, symptom free, demonstrated lower levels of reactivity in this session while the mother talked about her efforts to focus her anxiety back into her family of origin and managing it differently there. At the 4th year follow-up, the son was still symptom free.[16]

Biofeedback can facilitate awareness and understanding of these instinctual togetherness/individuality forces. Changes in reactivity can be indicators.[217] One goal of biofeedback is restoring their natural balance. This type of biofeedback training goes beyond substituting biofeedback for medication. It deals with the symptom, but also with balances within the organism and in the larger system.

Observation of some clinical cases of successful asthma management with biofeedback suggests that when deep facial muscle relaxation is accompanied by handwarming of more than 3° F. per session, sympton relief occurs. When deep muscle relaxation is not accompanied by hand warming, symptoms are generally unrelieved and may worsen in the session.[218] There seem to be parallels in the overreactivity of the ergotropic or trophotropic tuning of the autonomic ner-

vous system and the overeactivity in family processes. High
levels of emotional reactivity were observed in the multigenerational history and in the nuclear family. The person
who develops asthma seems to make efforts to remain "calm"
by inhibiting muscular expression of emotion at a time of
high reactivity in self and in the family system.[216]

Pain can function either as part of the forces of togetherness or as part of the forces of emotional distance.[97] This
understanding of chronic pain management goes beyond dealing with certain muscle groups and reducing general level of
arousal. Three factors affect the degree of flexibility in pain
management: (1) the level of functioning of the individual and
family over time; (2) the level of anxiety present in the family
at the onset of the symptom; and (3) how pain functions in
the relationship system.

An educator who participated in the Georgetown biofeedback professional training program reported her own successful experience regulating arthritis (Figure 12.3).[305] In 1986 her
physical functioning was seriously limited. Her sedimenta-
tion (sed) rate was 46 for six months. Walking was extremely
difficult and she needed a cane. Brushing her teeth or taking
a shower involved a great deal of pain and effort. Daily
nursing services and a physical therapist several times a
week were necessary. Very reluctantly she had to give up
teaching.

After seeing a psychologist to deal with loss, she learned
self-regulation through biofeedback with Dr. Fehmi in Princeton. She was so impressed by how much better she started to
feel that she decided to pursue biofeedback training as a new
career, chose Georgetown, and became more proficient in self-
regulation. She also began to learn and use family systems
theory in her own life. Her sed rate dropped to a normal level
of 19, and she had a negative C-reactive protein test. She was
still taking anti-inflammatory medication, but in July, 1987
she developed a stomach problem and had to discontinue it.
Her sed rate began to rise. Now her sed rate is 22, still

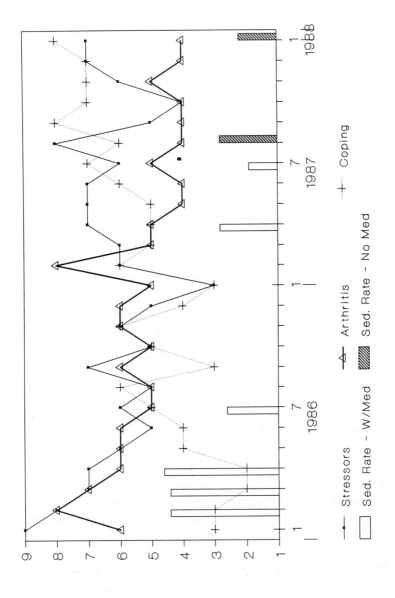

Figure 12.3 Arthritis, Stress, and Coping

without medication, she can shovel some snow, and is medically allowed part time work. In addition to rigorous physical therapy, she continued self-regulation and extensive family systems work. She decreased her over-responsibility and over-responsiveness to important relationships, and changed some aspects of her part in the family process. She is able to recognize and lower her stress, increase her psychophysiological functioning and increase her control of arthritis.[305]

Preparation for childbirth includes 8–10 weeks of biofeedback assisted relaxation training, detailed personal and family histories, and conversations focused on the emotional process in the family and the expected birth.[8,117] Visualization, breathing techniques, and simulated labor practice are included closer to the delivery date. Specific skills are designed and practiced according to circumstances and particular anxieties of each woman.[117] Physiological monitoring and discussion of the history and experiences of the family over generations helps identify (a) levels of anxiety in the person and in the family, (b) intensity of relationships, and (c) physiological patterns of managing anxiety which can disturb the functioning of the individual and render reproduction and birth difficult.

Of eleven women, seven had ongoing physical symptoms that complicated pregnancy and childbirth. The problems included high blood pressure, phobic panic attacks, and gastrointestinal disturbances requiring medication which could not be continued during pregnancy. However, all were anxious about the expected births. All eleven proceeded through the pregnancy with decreased symptoms and improved functioning. Minimal intervention was required in nine vaginal births. Two Caesarians were performed when fetal distress occurred. There were differences in: (a) the extent to which individuals could think about the influences of the emotional system and about their own reactivity; (b) activities in the emotional system around birth; and (c) relationship responsiveness. Future studies may investigate the ways in which anxiety is transmitted across generations and the extent to which the transmission can be modified with biofeedback and family work during pregnancy and childbirth.[117]

Non-Georgetown Studies Suggest Relationship Systems

The idea that physical health depends in part on social relations and that sickness follows social disruption is believed in so-called primitive societies. The patterns of adult mortality in modern society also support this view.[286]

If patients about to have coronary-bypass surgery were assigned hospital roommates who already had their surgery (post-operative), regardless of type of surgery (pulmonary or cancer), they were less anxious preoperatively, were more ambulatory postoperatively, and were released more quickly from the hospital than patients who had preoperative roommates.[149] The investigators do not consider reactivity as an explanation, but it seems to me that it is an important variable. Possibly postoperative roommates were less reactive, which calmed the preoperative patients.

The system can be a team and coach. In a study of a Harvard boat race eosinophil count declined (a type of white blood cell which is an indicator of immune system activity) in the crew four hours after the race and in the coxswains and coaches even though they did not participate in the physical activity.[220]

Monitoring skin sweat gland activity continuously during dynamic psychotherapy sessions can more clearly and immediately establish the body-mind connection. People differ in emotional responsivity and are "over-reactors, under-reactors or variable reactors." Direct training of the dysfunctional SNS and a different use of the therapeutic relationship is possible.[309]

In a study of 148 fathers with 2-3 day
blood pressure and heart rate of each father an
affected by each other. Fathers are aroused by h
infants, particularly crying ones. Infants' measures
during holding.[134]

There are differences in electrodermal responsivity of
dren of schizophrenic mothers when compared to children
normal parents. High risk children who were later classifie
as "sick," showed this pattern of responsivity five years earlier, whereas children who were classified as "well" did not.[79]

Type A behavior "may be moderated by spouse characteristics." Of 130 men, 55 developed coronary heart disease over
an 8.5 year period. Their wives, when compared to wives of
healthy Type A's, "were significantly more dominant and active."[253]

Levenson and Gottman[156] who began their research in 1980
unexpectedly found that the more physiologically aroused
the couple was in the 1980 interactions, the greater the marital dissatisfaction was in 1983. Four physiological measures
were obtained from each spouse during the first baseline and
interactions: heart rate, measured by the interbeat interval,
pulse transmission time to the finger, skin conductance level,
and general somatic activity (muscle activity). A second important unexpected finding is that although there was no
interaction between the couple during the physiological baseline, the period of *expectation* of interaction had an impact on
the physiology of each spouse.

These types of studies document the functional connectedness of humans to each other. As more investigators and
clinicians "discover" what is obvious with a natural systems
orientation, biofeedback with family systems theory may often be the "treatment of choice."

Kamiya, pioneer of brain wave biofeedback over 20 years
ago, and former President of the BSA, listening to my concept that thoughts affect physiology and that the physiology
of one person affects the physiology of others in the system

mmented that an important frontier in biofeedback is the awareness that the study of physiology is not just the study of metabolism.[135] It is also the study of life, death, and relationship processes.[136] The social and emotional aspects of humans are deeply ingrained in physiology and evolution.

From the work I began in 1975, challenging and important observations have emerged from the Georgetown Biofeedback Program. Biofeedback with family systems theory in a natural systems framework is making a unique contribution to the biofeedback field.

CONCLUSION

Socrates, 500 B.C.: "There is no illness of the body apart from the mind."

In twenty years of clinical experience, I observed that most people initially want to change a symptom without changing other aspects of their lives. They want it immediately, without effort or practice, easily, and permanently without responsibility to maintain it. That is not possible, with or without biofeedback. Biofeedback self-regulation can, however, facilitate improved emotional, physical, social and cognitive functioning. Processes which augment the opportunity to increase the brain's control over itself increase differentiation, maturity, and functioning. Biofeedback is one such process. Motivated, responsible people usually find unexpected rewards: ability to control one (sometimes very small) function increases the possibility of extending self-regulation to other functions; reduced symptoms in unexpected fields; reduced health care expenses; improved thoughtfulness, predictability of own and others' responses, stability of self and improved recovery from problems without loss of spontaneity.

This volume provides introductory questions and answers. The history of biofeedback is reviewed, basic physiology of the stress response is introduced and advanced, new physiological concepts such as psychoneuroimmunology are explored. Routine and innovative instrumentation is delineated. Basic biofeedback training and related self-regulation techniques are described. The importance of theory and professional training, keys to effective biofeedback implementation, are highlighted. My biofeedback program is described. An array of concepts such as voluntary self-regulation, responsibility for self, homeostatic balance, reactivity, family systems theory, systems view of illness and dysfunction, natural systems, evolution, and body/mind is integrated. Biofeedback is now the treatment of choice for a variety of conditions. Research and evaluation issues, and national implications of biofeedback cost-effectiveness are addressed. Enduring as well as relatively unexplored biofeedback frontiers are presented.

Biofeedback is a special frontier. It helps to "conquer" external processes and space, by controlling internal processes and space. It succeeds by "moving" with nature rather than attempting to overcome it. Frontiers described include the use of biofeedback to enhance superior performance such as that of athletes and astronauts; to assist education and improve learning disabilities; to treat acute injuries, visual and stress-related dental disorders, and pain; to improve physical rehabilitation; to prevent, manage or ameliorate chronic diseases including diabetes, cancer and AIDS; to facilitate psychophysiological recovery; and to maximize personal relationships and growth.

One issue which frequently emerges in biofeedback training is the person's struggle with the polarity of no control versus almost complete control of self. A significant influence in my life is the view in the Judaic tradition that a person's life proceeds "from dust to dust" and yet the human is "but little lower than the angels." For me, striving for balance between "being dust" and "being master" is part of what promotes a perspective of life that has meaning, plan and purpose. It also promotes responsible biofeedback self-regulation with a perspective that recognizes a continuum between what is and is not possible to self-regulate.

Homeostasis is the tendency of an organism to maintain internal stability by coordinated responses that automatically compensate for external changes. The organism strives for homeostatic balance. According to Claude Bernard the degree of an organism's independence from its environment is proportional to its ability to maintain constant its internal environment in the face of fluctuating external conditions. This relative autonomy from one's own inner and outer "environment," I believe, increases with voluntary biofeedback self-regulation and affects both physiological and social relationship processes. Biofeedback provides, among other benefits, a vital process to regulate responsiveness. Reactivity, an essential component of life can be self-regulated – which allows the person to be more clearly defined and become more him/her self.

The compensatory forces within and among all living systems – cells, neurotransmitters and receptors, permeable and non-permeable cell membranes, organs, people, families, social and work organizations – are infinite. Homeostatic balance exists within and among species. The tetrahymena (single-cell organism), corals, fishes, reptiles, birds, and mammals strive for survival and stability. Balance, at least for very long periods of time, also prevails among the earth and other planets, the sun, among the stars of the Milky Way and other galaxies. The human species evolved the prefrontal cortex which makes it possible to look inside self and to plan ahead. This can enhance stability between past, present and future and facilitate personal growth.

I believe that the intricate and infinite balancing forces in natural systems are not random or purposeless. One of the organizing forces in natural systems is evolution. What other forces or processes provide unity in diversity?

I hope I have communicated my respect for the unknown and sparked some questions about biofeedback's potential for the future. What other enhanced functioning is possible? How will biofeedback continue to modify disease prevention and treatment, health care services, education and superior performance? Can biofeedback continue to be a bridge between disciplines, between theories? Does biofeedback advance the functioning of the prefrontal cortex? Will biofeedback be considered a technique, or a process which nurtures a vision of new evolutionary possibilities of human self-regulation? How will increased self-regulation affect the evolution of the individual, family, and society? As time changes, so will biofeedback. I believe the real value of bio-feedback is that it is a *process,* not a product, which can maximize one's potential for self-regulation, and thereby enhance health, performance, and thinking.

REFERENCES

1. Ader, R. & Cohen, N. (1985). Behaviorally conditioned immunosuppression. In S. Locke, R. Ader, H. Besedovsky, N. Hall, G. Solomon, & T. Strom (Eds.), *Foundations of Psychoneuroimmunology* (pp. 279–285). New York: Aldine Publishing Co.

2. Altman, L.K. (1987a, June 30). AIDS: why do some infected men stay healthy? *New York Times,* Section C.

3. Altman, L.K. (1987b, May 26). Does the AIDS virus work alone? *New York Times,* Section C.

4. Amar, P. & Ladd, P. (1987, March). A biobehavioral approach to stress and the immune system. Short course presented at the Eighteenth Annual Meeting of the Biofeedback Society of America. Wheat Ridge, CO.: Biofeedback Society of America.

5. Ames Life Science Instrument Division (1988). Miles Laboratory, Elkhart, Indiana.

6. Asterita, M.F. (1985). *The Physiology of Stress: With Special Reference to the Neuroendocrine System.* New York: Human Sciences Press.

7. Asterita, M. (1987). Personal communication.

8. Atlas, S.J., Harrison, V. & Rosenbaum, L. (1985). Stress, Fertility, and Conception. *National Women's Health Report, 3,* 5.

9. Badgley, L. (1987). *Healing AIDS Naturally.* San Bruno, California: Human Energy Press.

10. Barlow, D.H., Blanchard, E.B., Hayes, S.C. & Epstein, L.H. (1977). Single-case designs and clinical biofeedback experimentation. *Biofeedback and Self-Regulation, 2,* 221–339.

11. Bartrop, R.W., Lazarus, L., Luckhurst, E., Kiloh, L.G., & Penny, R. (1985). Depressed lymphocyte function after bereavement. In S. Locke, R. Ader, H. Besedovsky, N. Hall, G. Solomon, & T. Strom (Eds.), *Foundations of Psychoneuroimmunology* (pp. 337–340). New York: Aldine Publishing Co.

12. Basmajian, J.V. (1963). Control and training of individual motor units. *Science, 20,* 662–664.

13. Basmajian, J.V. (Ed.). (1983). *Biofeedback: Principles and Practice for Clinicians*. Baltimore: Williams & Wilkins.

14. Bauch, M. (1935-1936). Beeinflussung des Diabetes Mellitus durch psychophysische Entspannungsubungen. *Deutches Arch. fur Klinische Medizing, 178:* 149-66. Berlin: Verglag von F.C.W. Vogel.

15. Beal, E. (in press). Family therapy treatment of adjustment disorders. In T.B. Karasu (Ed.), *Treatments of Psychiatric Disorders*. Washington, D.C.: American Psychiatric Association.

16. Behel, P. (1985, April). The use of biofeedback in the retraining of visual disorders. A short course presented at the Sixteenth Annual Meeting of the Biofeedback Society of America. Wheat Ridge, CO.: Biofeedback Society of America.

17. Behel, P. (1985-86). Developing eyesight: new techniques that improve visual skills. *Somatics, 5,* 36-41.

18. Behel, P. (1987). Muscle awareness: a streamlined approach to tension reduction. *California Biofeedback, 3,* 4.

19. Benson, H. (1975). *The Relaxation Response*. New York: Morrow.

20. Berent, J. & Sacker, I.M. (1980, March). Biofeedback treatment and hemorrhagic diabetec retinopathy, a case study. Poster paper presented at the Eleventh Annual Meeting of the Biofeedback Society of America. Wheat Ridge, CO.: Biofeedback Society of America.

21. Bernard, C. (1865). *An Introduction to the Study of Experimental Medicine*. New York: Dover Publications, 1957.

22. Besedovsky, H., del Rey, A., Sorkin, E., Da Prada, M., & Keller, H.H. (1985). Immunoregulation mediated by the sympathetic nervous system. In S. Locke, R. Ader, H. Besedovsky, N. Hall, G. Solomon, & T. Strom (Eds.), *Foundations of Psychoneuroimmunology* (pp. 55-64). New York: Aldine Publishing Co.

23. Besedovsky, H., Sorkin, E., Felix, D., & Haas, H. (1985). Hypothalamic changes during the immune response. In S. Locke, R. Ader, H. Besedovsky, N. Hall, G. Solomon, & T. Strom, (Eds.), *Foundations of Psychoneuroimmunology* (pp. 51-53). New York: Aldine Publishing Co.

24. Birk, L. (Ed.). (1973). *Behavioral Medicine: The Clinical Uses of Biofeedback*. New York: Grune and Stratton.

25. Blalock, J.E. (1984). The immune system as a sensory organ.

The Journal of Immunology, 132, 1067-70.

26. Blalock, J.E. & Smith, E.M. (1985). A complete regulatory loop between the immune and neuroendocrine systems. *Federation Proceedings, 44,* 108-111.

27. Blanchard E.B. (1982). Behavioral medicine: past, present, and future. *Journal of Consulting and Clinical Psychology, 50,* 795-796.

28. Bonner, J.T. (1969). *The Scale of Nature.* New York: Harper & Row, Publishers.

29. Boodman, S.G. (1988, February 8). AIDS survivors: Beating the odds. *Washington Post.* pp. A1, A7.

30. Borysenko, J. (1987). *Minding the Body, Mending the Mind.* Reading, MA.: Addison-Wesley Publishing Co., Inc.

31. Bowen, M. (1978). *Family Therapy in Clinical Practice.* New York: Jason Aronson.

32. Bowen, M. (1988). Personal communication.

33. Bradley, C., Moses, J.L., Gamsu, D.S. & Ward, J.D. (1985). The effects of relaxation on metabolic control in type I diabetes: a matched controlled study. *Diabetes, 34,* Supplement:1 Abstract #66.

34. Bridgwater, W. & Sherwood, E.J. (1956). *The Columbia Encyclopedia.* New York: Columbia University Press.

35. Brown, B. & Rosenbaum, L. (1983, May). Stress affects IQ. Paper presented at the American Association for the Advancement of Science. Detroit, MI.

36. Brown, B. & Rosenbaum, L. (1984). Stress and competence. In J.H. Humphrey (Ed.), *Stress in Childhood* (pp. 127-154). New York: AMS Press.

37. Brown, B. (1988). Personal communication.

38. Brown, B.B. (1966). Specificity of EEG photic flicker responses to color as related to visual imagery ability. *Psychophysiology, 2,* 197-207.

39. Brown, B.B. (1980). *Supermind: the Ultimate Energy.* New York: Harper & Row, Publishers.

40. Budzynski, T. & Stoyva, J. (1969). An instrument for producing deep muscle relaxation by means of analog information feedback. *Journal of Applied Behavior Analysis, 2,* 231-237.

41. Budzynski, T.H. (1977). *Psychology Today, 11,* 38.

42. Budzynski, T.H. (1978). Biofeedback in the treatment of muscle-contraction (tension) headache. *Biofeedback and Self-Regulation, 3,* 409–34.

43. Budzynski, T.H. (1986). Clinical applications of non-drug-induced states. In B. Wolman & M. Ullman (Eds.), *Handbook of States of Consciousness* (pp. 428–460). New York: Van Nostrand-Reinhold.

44. Budzynski, T.H. (1987). Personal communication.

45. Budzynski, T.H., & Doche-Budzynski, L. (1985). Douze ans d'experience de bio-feedback dans une clinique privee aux U.S.A. *Psychologie Medicale, 17,* 1545–1550.

46. Butler, F. (1978). *A Survey of the Literature.* New York: Plenum Press.

47. Calhoun, J.B. (1986, April). Universal autism: extinction resulting from failure to develop relationships. Paper presented at the Georgetown University Family Center, Washington, D.C.

48. Campbell, D.T. & Stanley, J.C. (1963). *Experimental and Quasi-Experimental Designs for Research.* Chicago: Rand McNally College Publishing Co.

49. Cannon, W.B. (1932). *The Wisdom of the Body* (revised ed. 1967). New York: W.W. Norton & Co.

50. Capscan Corporation (1988). Ossining, N.Y.

51. Carlson, J.G. (1978). Biofeedback as a research tool: task force study section report. Wheat Ridge, CO.: Biofeedback Society of America.

52. Carter, J.L. & Russell, H.L. (1984). Application of Biofeedback Relaxation Procedures to Handicapped Children: Final Report. Project No. 443CH00207. Washington, D.C.: U.S. Dept. of Education, Bureau of Education for the Handicapped.

53. Carter, J.L. & Russell, H.L. (1985). Use of EMG biofeedback procedures with learning disabled children in a clinical and an educational setting. *Journal of Learning Disabilities, 18,* 213–216.

54. Carter, J.L., Lax, B. & Russell, H. (1979). Effects of relaxation and EMG training on academic achievement of educable retarded boys. *Education and Training of the Mentally Retarded, 14,* 39–41.

55. Carter, W.R., Gonder-Frederick, L.A., Cox, D.J. & Clark, W. (1984). Psychological stressor's impact on blood glucose. *Diabetes, 33,* Supplement:1 Abstract #77.

56. Centers for Disease Control (CDC). (1987). Human immunode-

ficiency virus infection in the United States: a review of current knowledge. *Morbidity and Mortality Weekly Report, 36,* Supplement.

57. Cowings, P.S. & Malmstrom, F.V. (1984). What you thought you knew about motion sickness isn't necessarily so. *Flying Safety, 2,* 12–17.

58. Cowings, P.S. & Toscano, W.B. (1982). The relationship of motion sickness susceptibility to learned autonomic control for symptom suppression. *Aviation, Space, and Environmental Medicine, 53,* 570–575.

59. Cowings, P.S., Suter, S., Toscano, W.B., Kamiya, J., & Naifeh, K. (1986). General Autonomic Components of Motion Sickness. *Psychophysiology, 23,* 542–551.

60. Cowings, P.S. (1987). Personal communication and description of NASA Conference Publication #2429.

61. Cox, D.J., Clarke, W., Gonder-Frederick, L., Pohl, S., Hoover, C., Snyder, A. Zimbelman, L., Carter, W., Bobbitt, S., & Pennebaker, J. (1985). Accuracy of perceiving blood glucose in IDDM. *Diabetes Care, 8,* 529–536.

62. Darwin, C. (1859). *The Origin of the Species* (11th printing 1958). New York: New American Library.

63. Darwin, C. (1965). *The Expression of the Emotions in Man and Animals.* Chicago: University of Chicago Press.

64. Denenberg, V.H. & Rosenberg, K.M. (1967). Nongenetic transmission of information. *Nature, 216,* 549–550.

65. Denenberg, V.H. & Whimbey, A.E. (1963). Behavior of adult rats is modified by the experiences their mothers had as infants. *Science, 142,* 1192–1193.

66. Diamond, M. (1987). Mothers' enriched environment alters brains of unborn rats. *Brain Mind Bulletin, 12,* 1&5.

67. Diamond, S., Diamond-Falk, J. & DeVeno, T. (1978). Biofeedback in the treatment of vascular headache. *Biofeedback and Self-Regulation, 3,* 385–408.

68. Druckman, D. & Swets, J.A. (Eds.). (1988). *Enhancing Human Performance: Issues, Theories and Techniques.* National Research Council, Washington, D.C.: National Academy Press.

69. Eaton, R.P. & Schade, D.S. (1978). Modulation and implications of the counterregulatory hormones: glucagon, catecholamines, cortisol, and growth hormone. In H.M. Katzen & R.J. Mahler

(Eds.), *Modern Advances in Nutrition* (pp. 341–370). Washington, D.C.: Hemisphere Publishing Co.

70. Edelberg, R. (1972). Electrical Activity of the Skin. In N.S. Greenfield, & R.A. Sternbach, (Eds.), *Handbook of Psychophysiology* (pp. 367–418). New York: Holt, Rinehart and Winston, Inc.

71. Edwards, M. (1988). Personal communication.

72. Edwards, M. & Mignogna, R. (1988). Personal communication.

73. Edwards, P. (Ed.). (1967). *The Encyclopedia of Philosophy, 5,* New York: The Macmillan Co. & The Free Press.

74. Engel, B. & Melmon, K. (1968). Operant conditioning of rectosphincteric responses in the treatment of fecal incontinence. *Conditional Reflex, 3,* 130.

75. Engelhardt, L.J. (1976). *Here I Am.* Spearfish, S.D.: Healthworks.

76. Engelhardt, L. (1978a). Awareness and relaxation through biofeedback in public schools. *Biofeedback and Self-Regulation, 3,* 195.

77. Engelhardt, L. (1978b). A manuscript prepared to disseminate information regarding: The awareness and relaxation through biofeedback program. Implemented in the elementary and secondary classrooms and at Black Hills State College, South Dakota. (Distributed upon request).

78. Engelhardt, L.J. (1979). *Self-regulation: an Instructors Manual for Implementing Awareness Activities, Relaxation Strategies, Biofeedback Techniques.* Spearfish, S.D.: Healthworks.

79. Erlenmeyer-Kimiling, L., Friedman, D., Comblat, B. & Jacobson, R. (1985). Electrodermal recovery data on children of schizophrenic parents. *Psychiatry Research, 14,* 149.

80. Estrada, N., Kelso, H.G., & Gladman, A.E. (1984). Integrating biofeedback training within a multimodal treatment model for attention deficit disorder. *American Journal of Clinical Biofeedback, 7,* 22–30.

81. Everly, G.S., Jr. & Rosenfeld, R. (1981). *The Nature and Treatment of the Stress Response.* New York: Plenum Press.

82. Farquhar, J.W. (1987). *The American Way of Life Need Not be Hazardous to Your Health.* Reading, MA.: Addison-Wesley.

83. Feinglos, M.N., Hastedt, P., & Surwit, R.S. (1986). The effects of relaxation therapy on patients with type I diabetes mellitus. Duke University Medical School. Submitted for publication.

84. Fehmi, L. (1977). *Open Focus.* (Cassette Training Series, Study

Guide, Basic 1000). Princeton: Biofeedback Computers, Inc.

85. Fehmi, L. (1987). Personal communication.

86. Fehmi, L. & Fritz, G. (1980). Open focus: the attentional foundation of health and well-being. *Somatics, 5,* 24–30.

87. Ferguson, E. (1988). Personal communication.

88. Fernando, C.K. & Basmajian, J.V. (1978). Biofeedback in physical medicine and rehabilitation. *Biofeedback and Self-Regulation, 3,* 435–456.

89. Ferris, C.F., Meenan, D.M., Axelson, J.F., & Albers, H.E. (1986). A vasopressin antagonist can reverse dominant/subordinate behavior in hamsters. *Physiology & Behavior, 38,* 135–138.

90. Fischer-Williams, M., Nigl, A.J., & Sovine, D.L. (1986). *A Textbook of Biological Feedback.* New York: Human Science Press.

91. Fischer-Williams, M. (1988). Personal communication.

92. Fisher, E. & Peper, E. (1985, April). Biofeedback and individualized imagery: enhancing positive self-awareness in children. Paper presented at the Sixteenth Annual Biofeedback Society of America Meeting. Wheat Ridge, CO.: Biofeedback Society of America.

93. Fotopoulos, S.S. & Sunderland, W.P. (1978). Biofeedback in the treatment of psychophysiologic disorders. *Biofeedback and Self-Regulation, 3,* 331–62.

94. Fowler, J.E., Budzynski, T., & Vandenbergh, R. (1976). "Effects of an EMG biofeedback relaxation program on the control of diabetes: a case study." *Biofeedback and Self-Regulation, 1,* 105–112.

95. Francis, D.P. & Chin, J. (1987). The prevention of acquired immunodeficiency syndrome in the United States: an objective strategy for medicine, public health, business, and the community. *Journal of the American Medical Association, 257,* 1357–1366.

96. Friedman, E.H. (1985). *Generation to Generation: Family Process in Church and Synagogue.* New York: The Guilford Press.

97. Friesen, P.J. (1984, October). Function of pain: distance and togetherness. Paper presented at the Twentyfirst Georgetown Symposium on Family Theory and Psychotherapy. Georgetown University Family Center, Washington, D.C.

98. Friesen, P.J. (1987, June). Underlying theoretical assumptions of biofeedback training. Paper presented at the third Physiology in Relationships Meeting, Georgetown University Family Center, Washington, D.C.

99. Furedy, J. (1985). Specific vs. placebo effects in biofeedback: science-based vs. snake-oil-behavioral medicine. *Clinical Biofeedback and Health, 8,* 155-162.

100. Gaarder, K. & Montgomery, P. (1977). *Clinical Biofeedback: A Procedural Manual.* Baltimore: The Williams and Wilkins Co.

101. Gamiel, R. (1988). Personal communication.

102. Gatchel, R.J. & Price, K.P. (1979). *Clinical Applications of Biofeedback: Appraisal and Status.* New York: Pergamon Press.

103. Gellhorn, E. (1967). The tuning of the nervous system: physiological foundations and implications for behavior. *Perspectives in Biology and Medicine, 11,* 557-559.

104. Gilmartin, B. (1986). A review of the role of sympathetic innervation of the ciliary muscle in ocular accommodation. *Ophthalmic & Physiological Optics, 6,* 23-27.

105. Gordon, G. & Fisher, G.L. (Eds.). (1975). *The Diffusion of Medical Technology: Policy and Research Planning Perspectives.* Cambridge, MA.: Ballinger Publishing Co.

106. Gorman, J. (1986, November). Behavioral immunology and Bowen theory. Paper presented at the Georgetown University Symposium on Family Therapy and Psychotherapy. Georgetown University Family Center, Washington, D.C.

107. Green, J.A. (1983). Biofeedback therapy with children. In Rickles, W.H., Sandweiss, J.H., Jacobs, D.W., Grove, R.N., & Criswell, E. (Eds.), *Biofeedback and Family Practice Medicine* (pp. 121-44). New York: Plenum Press.

108. Greene, L. (1986). Letter of October 5 to Dr. L. Fehmi.

109. Greenfield, N.S. & Sternbach, R.A. (Eds.). (1972). *Handbook of Psychophysiology.* New York: Holt, Rinehart and Winston, Inc.

110. Gross, A.M., Levin, R.B., Mulvihill, M., Richardson, P., & Davison, P.C. (1984). Blood glucose discrimination training with insulin-dependent diabetics: a clinical note. *Biofeedback and Self-Regulation, 9,* 49-54.

111. Gruber, B.L., Hall, N., Hersh, S.P., & Dubouis, P. (1986, August). Immune system and psychologic states in metastatic cancer patients: a pilot study. Invited paper presented at the Annual Meeting of the American Psychological Association. Washington, D.C.

112. Gruber, B.L. (1987). Personal communication.

113. Guthrie, D., Moeller, T., & Guthrie, R. (1983). Biofeedback and its application to the stabilization and control of diabetes mellitus. *American Journal of Clinical Biofeedback, 6,* 82–87.

114. Halperin, E. & Yolton, R.L. (1986). Ophthalmic applications of biofeedback. *American Journal of Optometry & Physiological Optics.* 63, 985–998.

115. Harris, D. (1987). The cost of AIDS: we'll all pay. *Money, 16,* 109–134.

116. Harrison, V. (1986, June). The regulation of self in relationships. Paper presented at the Second Physiology and Relationships Conference, Georgetown University Family Center, Washington, D.C.

117. Harrison, V. (1986, April). Biofeedback applications in obstetrics/gynecology. Fourteenth Annual Conference on Psychosomatic Obstetrics and Gynecology. Temple University Conference Center, PA.: Sugar Loaf.

118. Hartje, J.C. & Heyman, S. (1985). The use of thermography as a biofeedback device. *Proceedings of the Biofeedback Society of America Sixteenth Annual Meeting.* Wheat Ridge, CO.: Biofeedback Society of America, 46–47.

119. Hartman, P.E. & Reuter, J.M. (1983, March). The effects of relaxation therapy and cognitive coping skills training on the control of diabetes mellitus. Paper presented at the Fourth Annual Scientific Session of the Society of Behavioral Medicine. Baltimore, Md.

120. Hassett, J. (1978). *A Primer of Psychophysiology.* San Francisco: W.H. Freeman & Co.

121. Hatch, J.P. (1987). Guidelines for controlled clinical trials of biofeedback. In Hatch, J.P., Fisher, J.G., & Rugh, J.D. (Eds.), *Biofeedback* (pp. 323–363). New York: Plenum Publishing Corporation.

122. Hatch, J.P. & Riley, P. (1985). Growth and development of biofeedback: a bibliographic analysis. *Biofeedback and Self-Regulation, 10,* 289–299.

123. Hatch, J.P., Fisher, J.J., & Rugh, J.D. (1987). *Biofeedback Studies in Clinical Efficacy.* New York: Plenum Press.

124. Hersen, M. & Barlow, D.H. (1976). *Single Case Experimental Designs: Strategies for Studying Behavior Change.* New York: Pergamon Press.

125. Hirons, R. & Yolton, R.L. (1978). Biofeedback treatment of strabismus: case studies. *Journal of the American Optometric Association, 49,* 875–882.
126. Howard, K.I., Kopta, S., Krause, M.S., Orlinsky, D.E. (1986). *American Psychologist, 41,* 159–164.
127. Hutchison, M. (1986). *Megabrain.* New York: Ballantine Books.
128. Inouye, D.K. (1986, March). The changing nature of health care delivery in our nation. Keynote address presented at the *Seventeenth Annual Meeting of the Biofeedback Society of America.* Wheat Ridge, CO.: Biofeedback Society of America.
129. Institute of Medicine. (1986). *Confronting AIDS: Directions for Public Health, Health Care, and Research.* Washington, D.C.: National Academy Press.
130. Jacobson, E. (1968). *Progressive Relaxation* (2nd ed.). Chicago: University of Chicago Press.
131. Jemmott III, J.B., & Locke, S.E. (1984). Psychosocial factors, immunologic mediation, and human susceptibility to infectious diseases: how much do we know? *Psychological Bulletin, 95,* 78–108.
132. Johns Hopkins Dateline. (1988). *Johns Hopkins Magazine, 40,* 56.
133. Jones, D.R., Levy, R.A., Gardner, L., Marsh, R.W., & Patterson, J.C. (1985). Self-Control of psychophysiologic response to motion stress: using biofeedback to treat airsickness. *Aviation, Space, and Environmental Medicine, 56,* 1152–1157.
134. Jones, L.D., & Thomas, S.A. (1987, April). Fathers' and infants' blood pressure and heart rate during interaction. Paper presented at the Society for Research in Child Development, Baltimore, MD.
135. Kamiya, J. (1968). Conscious control of brain waves. *Psychology Today, 1,* 55–60.
136. Kamiya, J. (1987). Personal communication.
137. Kanigel, R. (1986). Where mind and body meet. *Mosaic. 17,* 52–60.
138. Kaplan, H.I. (1985). Psychological factors affecting physical conditions (psychosomatic disorders). In H.I. Kaplan and B.J. Sadock (Eds.). *Comprehensive Textbook of Psychiatry, IV,* (pp. 1106–1223). Baltimore: Williams and Wilkins.
139. Kappes, B.M., Chapman, S.J. (1984). The effects of indoor

versus outdoor thermal biofeedback training in cold weather sports. *Journal of Sport Psychology, 6,* 305–311.

140. Kappes, B.M., Chapman, S.J., & Sullivan, W. (1986). Thermal biofeedback training in cold environments: effects on pain and dexterity. *Proceedings of the Biofeedback Society of America Seventeenth Meeting.* Wheat Ridge, CO.: Biofeedback Society of America. 62–65.

141. Kay, M.M., Davis, M., & Fanning, P. (1981). *Thoughts & Feelings: The Art of Cognitive Stress Intervention.* Richmond, California: New Harbinger Publications.

142. Kemmer, F.W., Bisping, R., Steingruber, H.J., Baar, H., Hartmann, F., Schlaghacke, R., & Berger, M. (1986). Psychological stress and metabolic control in patients with Type I diabetes mellitus. *New England Journal of Medicine, 214,* 1078–84.

143. Kerr, M.E. & Bowen, M. (in press). *Family Evaluation: An Approach Based on Bowen Theory.* New York: W.W. Norton.

144. Kerr, M.E. (1980). Emotional factors in physical illness. *The Family, 7,* 59–66.

145. Kerr, M.E. (1981). Family systems theory and therapy. In A.S. Gurman, & D.P. Kniskern, (Eds.), *Handbook of Family Therapy* (pp. 226–264). New York: Brunner/Mazel.

146. Kiecolt-Glaser, J.K. & Glaser, R. (1986). Psychological influences on immunity. *Psychosomatics, 27,* 621–624.

147. Konner, M. (1982). *The Tangled Wing: Biological Constraints on the Human Spirit.* New York: Harper & Row Publishers.

148. Kotses, H., Glaus, K., Crawford, P.L., & Edwards, J.E. (1976). The effect of operant conditioning of the frontalis muscle on peak expiratory flow in asthmatic children. *Proceedings of the Seventh Meeting of the Biofeedback Society of America.* Wheat Ridge, CO.: Biofeedback Society of America, 40.

149. Kulik, J.A. & Mahler, H.I. (1987). Effects of preoperative roommate assignment on preoperative anxiety and recovery from coronary-bypass surgery. *Health Psychology, 6,* 525–544.

150. Kushi, M. & Kushi, A. (1985). *Macrobiotic Diet.* Tokyo: Japan Publications.

151. Lammers, C.A., Naliboff, B.D., & Straatmeyer, A.J. (1984). The effects of progressive relaxation on stress and diabetic control. *Behavior Research and Therapy, 22,* 641–650.

152. Landis, B., et al. (1985). Effect of stress reduction on daily

glucose range in previously stabilized insulin-dependent diabetic patients. (Letter). *Diabetes Care, 8,* 624–626.

153. Lawrence, G.H. & Johnson, L.C. (1977). Biofeedback and performance. In G.E. Schwartz & J. Beatty, (Eds.), *Biofeedback: Theory and Research* (pp. 163–179). New York: Academic Press, Inc.

154. Lawrence, G.H. (1984). Biofeedback and performance: an update. Technical Report 658. Alexandria, VA.: U.S. Army Research Institute for the Behavioral and Social Sciences.

155. Lazarus, A. (1979). *In the Mind's Eye: The Power of Imagery for Personal Enrichment.* New York: The Guilford Press.

156. Levenson, R.W. & Gottman, J.M. (1985). Physiological and affective predictors of change in relationship satisfaction. *Journal of Personality and Social Psychology, 49,* 85–94.

157. Levine, P. (1987). Stress. In M.G.H., Coles, E.D. Donchin, & S.W. Porges, (Eds.), *Psychophysiology, Systems, Processes and Applications* (pp. 331–353). New York: Guilford Press.

158. Levy, R.A., Jones, D.R. & Carlson, E.H. (1981). Biofeedback rehabilitation of airsick aircrew. *Aviation, Space, and Environmental Medicine, 52,* 118–121.

159. Levy, S.M. (1985). *Behavior and Cancer: Life-Style and Psychosocial Factors in the Initiation and Progression of Cancer.* San Francisco: Jossey-Bass Publishers.

160. Locke, S., Ader, R., Besedovsky, H., Hall, N., Solomon, G., & Strom, T. (Eds.). (1985). *Foundations of Psychoneuroimmunology.* New York: Aldine Publishing Co.

161. Locke, S. & Colligan, D. (1986). *The Healer Within: The New Medicine of Mind and Body.* New York: Dutton.

162. Locke, S.E., and Horning-Rohan, M. (1984). *Mind and Immunity: Behavioral Immunology, An Annotated Bibliography 1976–1982.* New York, Institute for the Advancement of Health.

163. Love, W.A. Jr., Hochman, N., Councill, W., Blanton, F. (1976). EMG feedback and relaxation training as an acillary treatment for elevated intraocular pressure. *The Journal of Bio-Feedback, 3,* 3–11.

164. Lubar, J.F., & Deering, W.M. (1981). *Behavioral Approaches to Neurology.* New York: Academic Press.

165. Lubar, J.O. & Lubar, J.F. (1984). Electroencephalographic biofeedback of SMR and beta for treatment of attention deficit disorders in a clinical setting. *Biofeedback and Self-Regulation, 9,* 1–23.

166. Luthe, W. (Ed.). (1969). *Autogenic Therapy: Medical Applications.* New York: Grune and Stratton.

167. MacLean, P.D. (1970). The triune brain, emotion, and scientific bias. In F.O. Schmitt (Ed.), *The Neurosciences: Second Study Program* (pp. 336–349). New York: The Rockefeller University Press.
168. MacLean, P.D. (1972). Cerebral evolution and emotional processes: new findings on the striatal complex. *Annals of the New York Academy of Sciences, 193*, 137–149.
169. MacLean, P.D. (1981). Family feeling and the triune brain. *Psychology Today, 15*, 100.
170. MacLean, P.D. (1982, May). Brain evolution relating to family, play, and the isolation call. Adolf Meyer Lecture presented at the 135th Annual Meeting of the American Psychiatric Association, Toronto, Canada. Printed in 1985 *Archives of General Psychiatry 42*, 405–417.
171. MacLean, P. (1987). Personal communication.
172. Maloney-Schara, A. (1987, October). Towards a Bowen family systems perspective: AIDS in the family. Paper presented at the Biofeedback Society of Washington, D.C. and Maryland. Airlie, Va.
173. Manuso, J.S.J., (1983). *Occupational Clinical Psychology.* New York: Praeger Publishers.
174. Mason, J.W. (1972). Organization of psychoendocrine mechanisms: a reviewed and reconsideration of research. In N.S. Greenfield & R.A. Sternbach (Eds.), *Handbook of Psychophysiology* (pp. 3–91). New York: Holt, Rinehart and Winston, Inc.
175. McLeod, J. (1987). Management of anal incontinence by biofeedback. *Gastroenterology, 97*, 291–294.
176. Meichenbaum, D. (1976). Cognitive factors in biofeedback therapy. *Biofeedback and Self-Regulation, 1*, 201–216.
177. Meichenbaum, D. (1985). *Stress Inoculation Training.* New York: Pergamon Press.
178. Melbye, M. et al. (1986). Long-term seropositivity for human t-lymphotropic virus type II in homosexual men without the acquired immunodeficiency syndrome: development of immunologic and clinical abnormalities. *Annals of Internal Medicine, 104*, 496–500.
179. Metal'nikov, S. & Chorine, V. (1985). The role of conditioned reflexes in immunity. In S. Locke, R. Ader, H. Besedovsky, N. Hall, G. Solomon, & T. Strom, (Eds.), *Foundations of Psychoneuroimmunology* (pp. 263–267). New York: Aldine Publishing Co.
180. Meyer, R.J. & Haggerty, R.J. (1985). Streptococcal infections

in families. In S. Locke, R. Ader, H. Besedovsky, N. Hall, G. Solomon, & T. Strom, (Eds.), *Foundations of Psychoneuroimmunology* (pp. 307-317). New York: Aldine Publishing Co.

181. Middaugh, S.J. & Kee, W.G. (1984). Role of EMG evaluations in the multimodal treatment of chronic pain. *Proceedings of the Fifteenth Annual Meeting of the Biofeedback Society of America*, Wheat Ridge, CO.: Biofeedback Society of America, 136-138.

182. Middaugh, S.J. & Kee, W.G. (1987). Advances: electromyographic monitoring and biofeedback in treatment of chronic cervical and low back pain. In M.G. Eisenberg & R.C. Grzesiak (Eds.), *Advances in Clinical Rehabilitation, Volume I* (pp. 137-172). New York, Springer Publishing Co.

183. Middaugh, S.J. (in press). Biobehavioral techniques. In R. Scully, & M. Barnes, (Eds.), *Physical Therapy*. Philadelphia: J.B. Lippincott Co.

184. Middaugh, S.J. (1987). Personal communication.

185. Miller, N. (1969). Learning of visceral and glandular responses. *Science, 163*, 434-435.

186. Morgan, W.P. & Golston, S.E. (Eds.). (1987). *Exercise and Mental Health*. Washington, D.C.: Hemisphere Press Publishing Corp.

187. National Clearinghouse for Mental Health Information (1970). *Biological Rhythms in Psychiatry and Medicine*. Public Health Service Publication No. 2088). Washington, D.C.: U.S. Government Printing Office.

188. National Dairy Council (1987). An Interpretive Review of Recent Nutrition Research. *National Dairy Council Digest, 58.*

189. NeuroMap Medical Corporation (1988). Boulder, CO.

190. Noer Harold III (1988). Personal communication.

191. Norris, P. (1986). Presidential Address: Biofeedback, Voluntary Control, and Human Potential. *Biofeedback and Self-Regulation, 11*, 1-20.

192. Norris, P.A. (1976). Working With Prisoners or There's Nobody Else Here. Unpublished doctoral dissertation, Union Graduate School, New York.

193. Norris, P.A. (1987). Personal communication.

194. Norris, P. & Porter, G. (1987). *I Choose Life: The Dynamics of Visualization and Biofeedback*. (Originally titled *Why Me?*). N.H., Walpole, Stillpoint Publishing.

195. Olton, D.S. & Noonberg, A.R. (1980). *Biofeedback: Clinical Applications in Behavioral Medicine.* New Jersey: Prentice-Hall.

196. Ornstein, R. & Thompson, R.F. (1984). Illustrated by Macaulay, D. *The Amazing Brain.* Boston: Houghton Mifflin Co.

197. Ornstein, R. & Sobel, D. (1987). *The Healing Brain.* New York: Simon and Schuster.

198. Paskewitz, D. (1983). Computers in biofeedback. In J.V. Basmajian (Ed.), *Biofeedback: Principles and Practice for Clinicians* (pp. 341–347). Baltimore: Williams & Wilkins.

199. Patel, C. (1976). Reduction of serum cholesterol and blood pressure in hypertensive patients by behavior modification. *Journal Royal College of General Practice. 26,* 211–215.

200. Peavey, B.S., Lawlis, G.F., & Goven, A. (1985). Biofeedback-assisted relaxation: effects on phagocytic capacity. *Biofeedback and Self-Regulation, 10,* 33–47.

201. Pelcyger, S.M. & Trachtman, J.N. (1985). Myopia reduction using biofeedback of accommodation: summary data of 100 patients. (Abstract). *American Journal of Optometry and Physiological Optics, 62,* 73P.

202. Peper, E. (1985). Hope for Asthmatics: Biofeedback Systems Teaching. *Somatics, 2,* 56–62.

203. Peper, E. & Schmid, A.B. (1983a). Do your thing when it counts. In L.E. Unestahl, (Ed.), *The Mental Aspects of Gymnastics Performance* (pp. 86–94). Orebro, Sweden: Vate Forlag.

204. Peper, E. & Schmid, A.B. (1983b). Mental preparation for optimal performance in rhythmic gymnastics. *Proceedings of the Fourteenth Annual Meeting of the Biofeedback Society of America.* Wheat Ridge, CO.: Biofeedback Society of America.

205. Peper, E. & Schmid, A.B. (1983c). The use of electrodermal biofeedback for peak performance training. *Somatics, 4,* 16–18.

206. Peper, E. & Schmid, A.B. (1985). Hand temperature of the 1984 Olympic rhythmic gymnasts and gymnasts of the U.S.A. Competitions. *Proceedings of the Sixteenth Annual Meeting of the Biofeedback Society of America.* Wheat Ridge, CO.: Biofeedback Society of America.

207. Pert, C.B., Aposhian, D., & Snyder, S.H. (1974). Phylogenetic distribution of opiate recepter binding. *Brain Research, 75,* 356–361.

208. Pert, C.B., Ruff, M.R., Weber, R.J. & Herkenham, M. (1985).

Neuropeptides & their receptors: a psychosomatic network. *The Journal of Immunology, 135,* 820s–826s.

209. Pert, C.B. (1986a). The wisdom of the receptors: neuropeptides, the emotions, and bodymind. *Advances, 3,* 8–16.

210. Pert, C.B. (1986b). Personal communication.

211. Perry, J.D. (1988). Biotechnologies, Inc., Bryn Mawr, PA.

212. Perry, J.D. & Bollinger, J.R. (1988). *Proceedings of the Nineteenth Annual Meeting of the Biofeedback Society of America.* Wheat Ridge, CO.: Biofeedback Society of America, 147–150.

213. *Physicians Desk Reference* (1987). Oradell, N.J.: Edward R. Barnhart.

214. Prudden, B. (1984). *Myotherapy.* New York: The Dial Press.

215. Public Health Reports Special Section (1985). *Public Health Aspects of Physical Activity and Exercise, 100,* 118–124.

216. Rauseo, E.L. (1981). The physiologic double-blind: speculations and clinical observations on autonomic imbalance and family programming. *Proceedings of the Twelfth Annual Meeting of the Biofeedback Society of America.* Wheat Ridge, CO.: Biofeedback Society of America, 61–63.

217. Rauseo, E.L. (1986, June). Self-regulation and the individuality/togetherness balance. Paper presented at the third Physiology in Relationships. Georgetown University Family Center, Washington, D.C.

218. Rauseo, E.L., Moreland, V., & Rosenbaum, L. (1983). Thermal biofeedback in asthma management. *Proceedings of the Fourteenth Annual Meeting of the Biofeedback Society of America.* Wheat Ridge, CO.: Biofeedback Society of America, (180–183).

219. Ravizza, K.H. (1985). Developing Concentration Skills for Gymnastic Performance. In Lars-Eric Unestahl (Ed.), *The Mental Aspects of Gymnastics Performance* (pp. 113–121). Orebro, Sweden: Vate Forlag.

220. Renold, A.E., Quingley, T.B., Kennard, H.E. & Thorn, G.W. (1951). Reaction of the adrenal cortex to physical and emotional stress in college oarsmen. *New England Journal of Medicine, 244,* 754–757.

221. Restak, R.M. (1979). *The Brain: The Last Frontier.* New York: Doubleday & Company.

223. Rickles, W.H., Sandweiss, J.H., Jacobs, D.W., Grove, R.N., & Criswell, E. (Eds.). (1983). *Biofeedback and Family Practice Medicine.* New York: Plenum Press.

224. Roberts, M. (1988). Special report: be all that you can be. *Psychology Today, 22,* 28-29.

225. Robinson, W.J. & Harris, D.V. (1986). The Effects of Skill Level on EMG Activity During Internal and External Imagery. *Journal of Sport Psychology, 8,* 105-11.

226. Roberts, A. (1985). Biofeedback. *American Psychologist, 40,* 938-950.

227. Rosen, R.C. (1977). Operant control of sexual responses in man. In G. Schwartz & J. Beatty (Eds.), *Biofeedback Theory and Research* (pp. 301-312). New York: Academic Press.

228. Rosenbaum, L. (1980, March). Family systems theory and biofeedback. Organized panel and presented paper at the Eleventh Annual Meeting of the Biofeedback Society of America. Wheat Ridge, CO.: Biofeedback Society of America.

229. Rosenbaum, L. (1981). Biofeedback assisted relaxation in diabetes management. *Proceedings of the Twelfth Annual Meeting of the Biofeedback Society of America.* Wheat Ridge, CO.: Biofeedback Society of America, 64-66.

230. Rosenbaum, L. (1983). Biofeedback-assisted stress management for insulin treated diabetes mellitus. *Biofeedback and Self-Regulation, 8,* 519-32.

231. Rosenbaum, L. (1983, May). Stress management for optimum function. Paper presented at the American Association for the Advancement of Science, Detroit, Michigan.

232. Rosenbaum, L. (1984). Biofeedback in diabetes management. *Diabetes Dateline.* A Bulletin of the National Diabetes Information Clearing House, 5, Washington, D.C.: National Institutes of Health.

233. Rosenbaum, L. (1985). Biofeedback assisted stress management for insulin-treated diabetes mellitus. *Practical Diabetology, 4,* 18-19.

234. Rosenbaum, L. (1986). Biofeedback with family therapy for diabetes mellitus. In J. Humphrey, (Ed.), *Human Stress: Current Selected Research, 1,* 123-132. New York: AMS Press, Inc.

235. Rosenbaum, L. (1987, October). Family therapy and biofeedback with AIDS: theoretical and research considerations. Paper presented at meeting on Theoretical Issues in AIDS Social Research. Minneapolis, Minnesota: Minnesota Institute of Family Dynamics.

236. Rosenbaum, L. (1988, March). Computerized pancreas biofeedback: a window to reactivity. Symposium presented at the Biofeed-

back Society of America. Wheat Ridge, CO.: Biofeedback Society of America.

237. Rosenbaum, L., Barnett, P. & Tannenberg, R.J. (1984). Short-term effect of biofeedback assisted relaxation on blood glucose in IDDM. *Diabetes, 33:* Supplement:1 Abstract #389.

238. Rosenbaum, L., Greco, P., Sternberg, C. & Singleton, G. (1981). Ongoing assessment: experience of a university biofeedback clinic. *Biofeedback and Self-Regulation, 6,* 103–112.

239. Rosenbaum, L. & Tannenberg, R.J. (1983). Biofeedback self-regulation for diabetes mellitus. *Diabetes, 32:* Supplement:1 Abstract #72.

240. Rosenbaum, L. & Tannenberg, R.J. (1985). Differential glucose responses to biofeedback in IDDM. *Diabetes, 34:* Supplement:1 Abstract #794.

241. Rosenbaum, L., Tannenberg, R.J. & Eastman, R.C. (1986). Insulin/dextrose infusion system confirms biofeedback effect: IDDM case study. *Diabetes, 35:* Supplement:1 Abstract #441.

242. Rossi, P.H., Freeman, H.E. & Wright, S.R. (1979). *Evaluation: A Systematic Approach.* Beverly Hills: Sage Publications.

243. Roth, J., LeRoith, D. Collier, E.S., Weaver, N.R., Watkinson, A., Cleland, C.F. & Glick, S.M. (1985). Evolutionary origins of neuropeptides, hormones and receptors: possible applications to immunology. *The Journal of Immunology, 135,* 816s–819s.

244. Ruff, M.R., Wahl, S.M. & Pert, C.B. (1985). Substance P receptor-mediated chemotaxis of human monocytes. *Peptides, 6,* 107–111.

245. Rugh, J., Perlis, D., & Disraeli, R., (Eds.). (1977). *Biofeedback in Dentistry: Research and Clinical Applications.* Phoenix: Semantodontics Publishers.

246. Rugh, J.D. (1980). Biofeedback instrumentation: task force study section report to the Biofeedback Society of America. Wheat Ridge, CO.: Biofeedback Society of America.

247. Rugh, J.D. (1983). Psychological factors in the etiology of masticatory pain and dysfunction. In D. Laskin, W. Greenfield, E. Gale, J. Rugh, P. Neff, C. Alling, & W. Ayer (Eds.), *The President's Conference on the Examination, Diagnosis and Management of Temporomandibular Disorders* (pp. 85–94). Chicago: American Dental Association.

248. Rugh, J.D. & Lemke, R.R. (1984). Significance of oral habits.

In J.D. Matarazzo, S.M. Weiss, J.A. Herd, N.E. Miller, & S.M. Weiss, (Eds.), *Behavioral Health: A Handbook of Health Enhancement and Disease Prevention* (pp. 947-966). New York: John Wiley & Sons.

249. Rugh, J.D. & Solberg, W.K. (1985). Oral health status in the United States: temporomandibular disorders. *Journal of Dental Education, 49*, 398-405.

250. Runck, B. (1980). *Biofeedback: Issues in Treatment Assessment.* Rockville, Md.: U.S. Department of Health and Human Services, Alcohol, Drug Abuse, and Mental Health Administration, National Institute of Mental Health.

251. Runes, D.D. (Ed.). (1962). *Dictionary of Philosophy.* Paterson, New Jersey: Littlefield, Adams & Co.

252. Simpson, G.G., Pittendrigh, C.S., & Tiffany, L.H. (1957). *Life: An Introduction to Biology.* New York: Harcourt, Brace and Company.

253. Sanders, J.D. & Smith, T.W. (1986). Type A behavior, marriage, and the heart: person-by-situation interactions and the risk of coronary disease. *Behavioral Medicine Abstracts, 7*, 59-62.

254. Sandweiss, J. (1980). Athletic applications of biofeedback: task force study section report to the Biofeedback Society of America. Wheat Ridge, CO.: Biofeedback Society of America.

255. Sapolsky, R. (1987). Top baboons have more effective stress response. *Brain Mind Bulletin, 12*, 1.

256. Schmid, A.B. & Peper, E. (1983). Do your thing when it counts. In L.E. Unestahl, (Ed.), *The Mental Aspects of Gymnastics Performance* (pp. 86-94). Orebro, Sweden: Vate Forlag.

257. Schmid, A.B. & Peper, E. (1984). Competition reaction linked with hand temperature: study done with rhythmic gymnasts. *Technique, 4*, 12-14.

258. Schmid, A.B. & Peper, E. (1986). Techniques for training concentration. In J.M. Williams (Ed.), *Applied Sport Psychology* (pp. 271-284). Palo Alto, California: Mayfield Publishing Co.

259. Schneider, C.J. & Wilson, E.S. (1985). *Foundations of Biofeedback Practice.* Wheat Ridge, CO.: Biofeedback Society of America.

260. Schneider, C.J. (1987). Cost-effectiveness of biofeedback and behavioral medicine treatments: a review of the literature. *Biofeedback and Self-Regulation, 12*, 71-92.

261. Schwartz, M.S. & Associates. (1987). *Biofeedback: A Prac-*

tioner's Guide. New York: The Guilford Press.

262. Schwartz, M.S. & Fehmi, L. (1982). *Applications Standards and Guidelines for Providers of Biofeedback Services.* Wheat Ridge, Co.: Biofeedback Society of America.

263. Seeburg, K.N. & DeBoer, K.F. (1980). Effects of EMG biofeedback on diabetes. *Biofeedback and Self-Regulation, 5,* 289–293.

264. Selye, H. (1956). *Stress of Life.* New York: McGraw-Hill.

265. Setterlind, S., Unestahl, L.E., & Kaill, B. (1986). *Relaxation Training for Youth.* Karlstad, Sweden, Stress Management Center.

266. Shapiro, D. & Schwartz, G. (1972). Biofeedback and visceral learning: clinical applications. *Seminars in Psychiatry, 4,* 171–184.

267. Shapiro, D., Tursky;, B. & Schwartz, G. (1970). Differentiation of heart rate and systolic blood pressure in man by operant conditioning. *Psychosomatic Medicine, 32,* 417–423.

268. Sheets, E.D. (1974). *The Fascinating World of the Sea.* New York: Crown Publishers.

269. Shellengerger, R. & Green, J.A. (1986). *From the Ghost in the Box to Successful Biofeedback Training.* Colorado: Health Psychology Publications.

270. Shellenberger, R. & Green, J.A. (1987). Specific effects and biofeedback vs. biofeedback-assisted self-regulation training. *Biofeedback and Self-Regulation, 12,* 185–209.

271. Shily, B.G. (1987). *American Journal of Optometry & Physiological Optics, 64,* 866–970.

272. Shulimson, A.D., Lawrence, P.F., Iacono, C.U. (1986). Diabetic ulcers: the effect of thermal biofeedback-medicated relaxation training on healing. *Biofeedback and Self-Regulation, 11,* 311–319.

273. Silver, P.S., Auerbach, S.M., Vishniavsky, N. & Kaplowitz, L.G. (1986). Psychological factors in recurrent genital herpes infection: stress, coping style, social support, emotional dysfunction, and symptom recurrence. *Journal of Psychosomatic Research, 30,* 163–170.

274. Sime, W.E. (1982). Competitive stress management techniques in perspective. In L. Zaichowosky, & W.E. Sime (Eds.), *Stress Management for Sport* (pp. 117–123). Reston, Virginia: AAPHER Press.

275. Sime, W.E. (1985). Physiological perception: the key to peak performance in athletic competition. In J.H. Sandweiss, & S.L. Wolf. (Eds.), *Biofeedback and Sports Science* (pp. 33–62). New York: Plenum Publishing Corporation.

276. Skeates, T.R. (1988). Personal communication.
277. Skolnick, N.J., Ackerman, S.H., Hofer, M.A. & Weiner, H. (1980). Vertical transmission of acquired ulcer susceptibility in the rat. *Science, 208,* 1161-1163.
278. Snyder, S. (1977). Opiate receptors and internal opiates. *Scientific American, 236,* 44-57.
279. Snyder, S. (1985). The molecular basis of communication between cells. *Scientific American, 253,* 132-141.
280. Solomon, G.F. (1985). The emerging field of psychoneuroimmunology: with a special note on AIDS. *Advances, 2,* 6-19.
281. Solomon, G.F., Levine, S., & Kraft, J.K. (1985). Early experience and immunity. In S. Locke, R. Ader, H. Besedovsky, N. Hall, G. Solomon & T. Strom (Eds.), *Foundations of Psychoneuroimmunology* (pp. 221-225). New York: Aldine Publishing Co.
282. Squires, S. (1987). Biofeedback: even the army is interested, but . . . *Washington Post: Health Magazine,* 12-9-87.
283. *Statistical Abstracts of the United States* (1987). Washington, D.C., U.S. Government Printing Office.
284. *Statistical Abstracts of the United States* (1986). Washington, D.C., U.S. Government Printing Office.
285. Steiner, S.S. & Dince, W.M. (1981). Biofeedback efficacy studies: a critique of critiques. *Biofeedback and Self-Regulation, 6,* 275-288.
286. Steiner, S.S. (1988). Personal communication.
287. Sterling, P. & Eyer, J. (1981). Biological basis of stress-related mortality. *Social Science and Medicine, 15E,* 3-42.
288. Sterman, M. B. et al. (1976). Effects of operant conditioning of central cortical EEG patterns on epilepsy. *Proceedings, Biofeedback Research Society.* Wheat Ridge, CO: Biofeedback Society of America.
289. Stern, R.M. & Ray, W.J. (1980). *Biofeedback Potential and Limits.* Lincoln, NB.: University of Nebraska Press.
290. Sternbach, R.A. (1966). *Principles of Psychophysiology.* New York: Academic Press.
291. Stoyva, J. Barber, T.X., Dicara, L.V., Kamiya, J., Miller, N.E., & Shapiro, D. (Eds.). (1971). *Biofeedback and Self-Control 1971: An Aldine Annual on the Regulation of Bodily Processes and Consciousness.* Chicago: Aldine Publishing Company.
292. Stoyva, J., & Budzynski, T. (1974). Cultivated low arousal: an

antistress response? In L.V. DiCara (Ed.), *Limbic and Autonomic Nervous Systems Research* (pp. 369–394). New York: Plenum Press.
293. Stroebel, C.F. (1975). Chronopsychophysiology. In A. Freedman, H.J. Kaplan, & B. Sadock (Eds.), *Comprehensive Textbook of Psychiatry* (2nd. ed.) (pp. 166–178). Baltimore: Williams & Wilkins.
294. Stroebel, C.F. (1983). *Quieting Reflex.* New York: Berkeley Books.
295. Stroebel, L., Stroebel, C.F., & Holland, M. (1980). Kiddie QR: A Choice for Children. Hartford, Connecticut: QR Institute Audio Cassettes.
296. Strong, D.J. & Wenz, B.J. (1978). A fine tuning model with athletes. Unpublished manuscript.
297. Sullivan, R. (1985). Biofeedback theta training (twilight learning) with subliminal audio suggestions in the treatment of alcoholism. Medford, Oregon: Center for Alcohol Rehabilitation and Educational Services, Dissertation.
298. Suomi, S.J. (1986). Anxiety-like disorders in young nonhuman primates. In R. Gittelmann (Ed.), *Anxiety Disorders of Childhood* (pp. 1–23). New York: The Guilford Press.
299. Suomi, S.J. (1987). Genetic and maternal contributions to individual differences in rhesus monkey biobehavioral development. In N. Krasnegor, E. Blass, M.A. Hofer, W.T. Smotherman (Eds.), *Perinatal Development: A Psychobiological Perspective* (pp. 397–420). New York: Academic Press.
300. Surwit, R.S. & Feinglos, M.N. (1983). The effects of relaxation on glucose tolerance in non-insulin-dependent diabetes. *Diabetes Care, 6,* 176–179.
301. Syer, J. & Conolly, C. (1984). *Body Mind: an Athlete's Guide to Mental Training.* New York: Cambridge University Press.
302. Taub, E. & Stroebel, C.F. (1978). Biofeedback in the treatment of vasoconstrictive syndromes. *Biofeedback and Self-Regulation, 3,* 363–374.
303. Taub, E. (1977). Self-regulation of human tissue temperature. In G.E. Schwartz & J. Beatty (Eds.), *Biofeedback: Theory and Research* (pp. 265–300). New York: Academic Press, Inc.
304. Taub, E. (1980). Somatosensory deafferentation research with monkeys: implications for rehabilitation medicine. In Ince, L.P. (Ed.). *Behavioral Psychology in Rehabilitation Medicine: Clinical*

Applications (pp. 371–401). Baltimore: Williams and Wilkins.
305. Taub, M. (1988). A study of personal evolution through biofeedback. Unpublished manuscript.
306. Templeton, B. (1986). Psychological stress and metabolic control in Type I diabetes mellitus. *New England Journal of Medicine, 315,* 1293.
307. Toman, W. (1969). *Family Constellation.* New York: Springer Publishing Co., Inc.
308. Toomin, H. (1980). Biofeedback Research Institute, L.A., CA.
309. Toomin, M. & Toomin, H. (1975). GSR biofeedback in psychotherapy: some clinical observations. *Psychotherapy, Theory, Research & Practice, 12,* 1–10.
310. Toscano, W.B. & Cowings, P.S. (1982). Reducing motion sickness: a comparison of autogenic-feedback training and alternative cognitive task. *Aviation, Space and Environmental Medicine, 53,* 449–453.
311. Trachtman, J.N. (1987a, November). Biofeedback applications in optometric practice. Presented at the Societe D'Optometrie D'Europe. Brussells, Belgium.
312. Trachtman, J.N. (1987b). Biofeedback of accommodation to reduce myopia: a review. *American Journal of Optometry and Physiological Optics, 64,* 639–643.
313. Trachtman, J.N., Giambalvo, V. & Feldman, J. (1981). Biofeedback accommodation to reduce functional myopia. *Biofeedback and Self-Regulation, 6,* 547–564.
314. Trachtman, J.N. & Pelcyger, S.M. (1986). Biofeedback of accommodation for presbyopia, (Abstract). *American Journal of Optometry and Physiological Optics, 63,* 77P.
315. Turkat, D. (1982). The use of EMG biofeedback with insulin-dependent diabetic patients. *Biofeedback and Self-Regulation, 7,* 301–304.
316. Twenlow, S. & Brown, W. (1976). Subjective responses to brainwave biofeedback training in drug dependent veterans. *Proceedings of the Seventh Annual Meeting of the Biofeedback Society of America.* Wheat Ridge, CO.: Biofeedback Society of America.
317. Valdes, M.R. (1985). Effects of biofeedback-assisted attention training in a college population. *Biofeedback and Self-Regulation, 10,* 315–324.

318. VanderPlate, C. & Kerrick, G. (1985). Stress reduction and treatment of severe recurrent genital herpes virus. *Biofeedback and Self-Regulation, 10,* 181–188.

319. Vessey, S.H., (1985). Effects of grouping on levels of circulating antibodies in mice. In S. Locke, R. Ader, H. Besedovsky, N. Hall, G. Solomon, & T. Strom (Eds.), *Foundations of Psychoneuroimmunology* (pp. 211–214). New York: Aldine Publishing Co.

320. Wald, A. (1981). Biofeedback therapy for fecal incontinence. *Annals of Internal Medicine, 95,* 146–49.

321. Wald, A., & Tunuguntla, A.K. (1984). Anorectal sensorimotor dysfunction in fecal incontinence and diabetes mellitus. *New England Journal of Medicine, 310,* 1282–1287.

322. Weinstock, S. (1976). The re-establishment of intestinal control in functional colitis. *Proceedings of the Seventh Meeting of the Biofeedback Society of America.* Wheat Ridge, CO.: Biofeedback Society of America.

323. Wenz, B.J., & Strong, D.J. (1980). An application of biofeedback and self-regulation procedures with superior athletes: the fine tuning effect. In R.M. Suinn, (Ed.), *Psychology in Sport: Methods and Applications* (pp. 328–333). Minnesota: Burgess.

324. Werner, E.E. & Smith, R.S. (1982). *Vulnerable but Invincible.* New York: McGraw-Hill.

325. Whatmore, G. & Kohli, D. (1974). *The Physiopathology and Treatment of Functional Disorders.* New York: Grune and Stratton.

326. White, L. & Tursky, B. (1982). Clinical Biofeedback: Efficacy and Mechanisms. New York: Guilford Press.

327. Whitehead, W.E. (1978). Biofeedback in the treatment of gastrointestinal disorders. *Biofeedback and Self-Regulation, 3,* 375–384.

328. Whitehead, W.E. (1987). Effectiveness and cost-effectiveness of biofeedback treatment for urinary and fecal incontinence. *Proceedings of the Eighteenth Annual Meeting of the Biofeedback Society of America.* Wheat Ridge, CO.: Biofeedback Society of America, 175–176.

329. Wilson, E.O. (1978). *On Human Nature.* Cambridge, MA.: Harvard University Press.

330. Wilson, E.S. & Schneider, C.J. (1987, unpublished). Human adaptivity – a primer of psychobiology.

331. Wilson, E.S. (Ed.). (in preparation). *My Pain Has No Name – The Challenge of Chronic Muscle Pain.*

332. Winer, L. (now Rosenbaum) (1971). The qualified pronoun count as a measure of change in family psychotherapy. *Family Process, 10,* 243–47.

333. Winer, L.R. (now Rosenbaum) (1976, November). *Biofeedback and family systems theory: work in progress.* Paper presented at the Thirteenth Georgetown University Symposium on Family Theory & Family Psychotherapy, Georgetown University Family Center, Washington, D.C.

334. Winer, L. (now Rosenbaum) (1977a). Biofeedback and family systems theory. (Abstract). *Journal of Altered States of Consciousness, 3,* 91–92.

335. Winer, L. (now Rosenbaum) (1977b). Biofeedback: a guide to the clinical literature. *American Journal of Orthopsychiatry, 47,* 626–38.

336. Wolf, S.L. (1987). The effect of forced use on upper extremity control in stroke and traumatic brain injured patients. Rehabilitation Research and Training Center Annual Report, Grant No. G00080031, National Institute on Disability and Rehabilitation Research. Washington, D.C.: Dept. of Education.

337. Wolpe, J. (1973). *The Practice of Behavior Therapy* (2nd ed.). New York: Pergamon Press.

338. Woodyatt, R.T. & Spetz, M. (1942). Anticipation in the inheritance of diabetes. *Journal of the American Medical Association, 120,* 602–605.

339. Wright, S.R. (1979). *Quantitative Methods and Statistics: A Guide to Social Research.* Beverly Hills: Sage Publications.

340. Yates, A.J. (1980). *Biofeedback and the Modification of Behavior.* New York: Plenum Press.

341. Yeager, J.M. (1988). Personal communication.

342. Yolton, R.L. (1988). Personal communication.

343. Zimmermann, M. (1983). Somatovisceral Sensibility: Processing in the Central Nervous System. In R.F. Schmidt, & G. Thews (Eds.), *Human Physiology* (pp. 193–210). New York: Springer-Verlag.

INDEX

Index

Telemetry, 52
Theoretical orientation, xxvi
Theory, 233
Thermal, 47
TMJ, 5
Togetherness force, 64
Training time, 89–90
Transmission, 73
Triangles, emotional, 75

Triune brain, 34–35
Twilight learning, 181–183
Unlearning, suspending
  response, 37–40
Unwell, 152–200
Vasoconstriction, 46, 47
Vasodilation, 46, 47
Vision, 175–183
Women, xxvi, 22, 229